FRANK WATERS

FRANK

SWALLOW PRESS/Ohio University Press
Athens Ohio • Chicago • London

WATERS

A Retrospective Anthology

Edited by Charles L. Adams

Introduction, bibliography and compilation
copyright © 1985 by Charles L. Adams
All rights reserved
Printed in the United States of America

This work has been made possible in part by a sabbatical leave granted
by the University of Nevada, Las Vegas.

Swallow Press books are published by
Ohio University Press, Athens, Ohio 45701

Library of Congress Cataloging in Publication Data

Waters, Frank, 1902–
  Frank Waters: a retrospective anthology.

  Bibliography: p.
  I. Adams, Charles L.   II. Title.
PS3545.A82A6   1985   818'.5209   84–24065
ISBN 0-8040-0874-4
ISBN 0-8040-0875-2 (pbk.)

To the Frank Waters students
of the past, the present
and the future

...a primary concern of all peoples everywhere is their relationship to their land. This has been the basic source of conflict between the White and Red races on this continent. ... This theme of their conflicting relationships to their earth has provided something of a thematic continuity in all my books, novels and non-fiction.

FRANK WATERS, "The Western Novel: A Symposium," *South Dakota Review*, II (Autumn 1964), 14–15.

CONTENTS

INTRODUCTION

Much of *Frank Waters: A Retrospective Anthology* is the result of my having taught a two-semester course in his works for almost a decade. That is, it reflects the tastes, the enthusiasms, of my students. I acknowledge, gratefully, that I could not have compiled it without them. Not too long ago, I overheard a conversation between a former student of the Frank Waters class and a prospective student. The prospective student asked, "What is Frank Waters all about?" The former student answered, "It takes until the middle of the first semester and then you know. But it's kinda hard to explain." It *is* hard to explain, but this present work is my attempt to illustrate the answer to that question.

Most of Waters' novels, biographies, and ethnological and historical studies deal with the people and the land of the western part of this continent. While it is logical that interest in the American West is concentrated here, British and Canadian sales and translations into Swedish, Dutch, French, German, and Japanese testify to the international interest that has developed both in Waters as a literary figure and also in the Native American people, the ecological problems, and in the moral questions related to both that he has studied and written about for a lifetime. Perhaps, too, this interest is due to the ever-increasing evidence that his work is standing the test of time. (*The Man Who Killed the Deer*, for example, has been in print for over forty years.)

It should be pointed out that this present book is in no way illustrative of all of Waters' work. It has been necessary to omit selections from, or even references to, his beautiful book on the painter Leon Gaspard, to his still-in-print biography of Winfield

Scott Stratton, *Midas of the Rockies*, and to the novels on which he collaborated with Houston Branch. Information on these, as well as on his numerous articles and reviews, can be found in the bibliography at the end of this work.

The selections which have been included were chosen for three reasons: First, to illustrate, through their thematic content, Waters' concern with the people, the land, and the spirit of the American West. Second, to illustrate his artistic development, necessitating, therefore, more selections from his mature work than from his early work. And third, to illustrate selections that have been chosen for their own merit—selections which, in my opinion, *ought* to be read. It is hoped that readers will be encouraged to go from these selections to the works in their entirety. To maintain the focus on Waters' work, I have added what I hope to be a minimum of my own commentary, intended to provide essential explanatory background, continuity, and unity to this anthology of his writing.

Frank Waters was born in Colorado Springs, Colorado, on July 25, 1902. His mother was descended from an aristocratic Southern family; his father was part Indian. A major theme in all his work, the reconciliation of apparently conflicting dualities, resulted, in all probability, from the early necessity of reconciling the opposing forces in his own heritage. The family tradition of mining—the "family folly," he calls it—directed that young Waters enter Colorado College as an engineering student. But before graduation, he left formal education, supporting himself with a series of jobs ranging from ditch-digging in the Wyoming oil fields to working as an engineer for the Southern California Telephone Company.

In recent years, Waters has been awarded Honorary Life Membership in the Western Literature Association, in the Rocky Mountain Modern Language Association, and in The National Honor Society of Phi Kappa Phi. Three of his works have been used as original source material by the C. G. Jung Foundation in Zurich, Switzerland. He has received seven honorary doctoral degrees. He and his wife, Barbara, divide their time between Arroyo Seco, New Mexico, and Tucson, Arizona. Waters continues his writing from both homes.

FRANK WATERS

I

Fever Pitch

In 1925,[1] while working on the Mexican border, Waters wrote his first book, which he subsequently referred to as "a stumbling, bumbling, immature, first attempt."[2] Originally titled The Lizard Woman *and published as* Fever Pitch,[3] *this novel, as Thomas Lyon has pointed out, ". . .foreshadows, in embryo, important preoccupations of the later novels."[4] The primary theme of all Waters' work, the relationship between people and place, is at the heart of* Fever Pitch, *functioning both to determine the story line and to establish the basis for characterizations. Told Conrad-fashion by Eric Dane to a group of men lounging on the porch of a bordertown cabaret, it is the story of the physiological, psychological, and spiritual effect of one of the world's most desolate environments on Lee Marston, a young American engineer. He has been asked by Arvilla, a mestizo bar-girl, to accompany her deep into the desert of Baja California to assay what is hoped to be a huge deposit of gold. Another American, Jim Horne, guards the strike while awaiting their arrival. After terrible hardships, Arvilla and Marston reach the cursed, wasteland heart, a desert valley enclosed by a circular wall of mountains around whose rim lies coiled the semblance of a serpentine body called the Lizard Woman by the local Indians.*

Let us go back to the beginning of the last four days across the desert. At that time all distance had shrunk to a flat ribbon edged with a heat-haze of white flecked with blue. The only tear in that beribboned blue string of heat-mountains, Arvilla had told him, was the wedge-shaped shadow of some prehistoric outpouring of lava which made the only accessible pass. This, then, was the steep ascent they had accomplished during the night. On each side now, in a curling somnolent haze, continued the rope of mountains around him. Like a rope of coral beads, to use his words, flung down in a broken heap because they had changed in color to a lifeless, rusty brown, flaked as the skin of a rock lizard; and each bead a broken splotch of rocky boils, a sandy rash, and pimply lava crust.

Before him—and at the sight Marston felt as though he were squatting in the position of an ancient sun-worshiper, arms outstretched and fingers spread—before him and below him, perhaps two thousand feet, lay a round sea scintillating with untold waves of borax crystals and infinitesimal particles of mica, and sands of aeonage forever unmoved by so much as a hair's breadth. . . . Like a fly-speck on a tea-cup rim he knelt, with the mountains curving round in two outflung sweeps and interlocking with fingers of shimmering heat as indistinguishable as their own outlines. And all inside this great cup of creation was the drifted, crumbled, baked potpourri of nature, whose thick sugary crust lay miles deep. All the shimmering, incandescent softness and sterile whiteness of a sea within a sea, deeper than the level of the desert floor without.

There are times in a few men's lives when the very manifestation of all Nature seeps into their souls and fills the void to completeness. And in its ebb it takes but the inconsequential pride of being, and leaves in its wreckage bits of the very core of a man's birth. Then a man cries out in a very agony of comprehension and prays for relief from his burden. So it was with Lee Marston. He rose to his feet and felt every vestige and semblance of life stripped from him. He felt the knowledge and heritage of all mankind seep and fuse itself into his soul and transmit itself to his understanding.

He could have cried aloud and his words would have followed too closely to be recognized, and their context would have at once defied and admitted all religions. He threw out his arms and felt that should a brush have been placed in his fingers he could have painted the form of that transient heart of all beauty for which men have sought in vain. He was in accord with the music of the Infinite. And with that unlocking of all boundaries, all limitations, all the empty forms of that beauty which is known to man, he saw it as it was, the bare, untouched depth of all humility. And standing there alone in that immensity of creation and alone in the presence of God, he bowed his will to an omnipotent power of nature. He felt that it was as though that spot had never known the presence of a Creator. As though the very mountains seemed like a signet ring of God himself flung on that spot and preserving forever the enclosed space from creation.

It is at such times that a man in an uplift of spirit loses all conception of the present and has removed from him forever that recognition of time and space into which he has been born. Lee Marston, then, was on the very threshold of that realm of thought in which lies stark madness. For when a man has reached that peak at which he is cognizant of nothing but himself and his god, there is no return. Marston was at that point. . . .

II

The Yogi of Cockroach Court

In 1927, while working on the Mexico border, Waters com-
pleted his first draft of The Yogi of Cockroach Court, *perhaps his*
most misunderstood book. Rewritten in 1937 and again in 1945,
it was first published in 1947—and was a total failure. The Brit-
ish agent to whom it was offered refused to present it to "any rep-
utable publisher in England" because of its "salacious" nature.[5]
There was perhaps a legitimate basis for that initial reaction, for
nowhere in his fiction does Waters deal as nakedly with the duali-
ties of human nature as he does in Yogi. *But despite the presence*
of an endnote calling attention to his source for the yogic doc-
trines in the book, most readers, until its successful re-issuance in
1972, seem to have focused on the physical action of the lesser
characters in the novel, missing the point of the title character—
and of the whole book.

In this story, the fascination with place continues. Here, in a
typical Mexican-American border town, Barby, a young half-
breed orphan, is taken in by an old Chinese shopkeeper, Tai Ling,
whose primary effort in life is to achieve liberation through his
yogic practices. Barby falls in love with Guadalupe, a mixed-
breed dancer in one of the local cantinas. The interaction of these
two characters is observed by the philosophical Tai Ling on the
one hand and on the other by Guadalupe's American friend, Sal,
a "percentage girl." The backgrounds of the characters, com-
bined with the bordertown environment which includes open
prostitution, gambling, and the sale of drugs, result in the de-
struction of them all, in one way or another. In spite of their piti-

6

ful hopes and ambitions, life for all of them is a downhill slide.

In later Frank Waters novels, a benevolent spirit of place provides the constant with which the characters can attune themselves, thus not only making possible a harmonious relationship with their environment but also resolving the conflicting dualities of their nature. But here, the bordertown's negative spirit of place prevents such attunement and actually militates against it. The point of the book, however, lies not in the degeneration of Barby, Guadalupe, and Sal, but in Tai Ling's failure, until the very end, to realize the impossibility of separating the principles that guide life from life itself. For while Barby, Guadalupe, and Sal lack the strength and discipline which might have saved them, Tai Ling, who possesses the requisite strength and discipline, fails to see that his personal salvation cannot be effected without recognition of the common humanity which occupies even the negative Cockroach Court—that is, without a relationship with his environment.

In the early part of the story, Tai Ling has been approached by three residents of Cockroach Court, who wish to enlist his aid in a plan to smuggle alien Chinese into the United States. Tai Ling has refused, despite the threats of his visitors; and as they leave, he stands musing about the inhabitants of this border town.

It was past midnight when Tai Ling let his three visitors out of the back door. For a long time he stood staring down the alley. The rain had stopped. The glow of cantina signs had faded. The night was sticky and starless.

Out of this viscous gloom darted two squeaks from a snake-belly fiddle. Again the two weird screeches repeated themselves at odd intervals. As he listened, memories of other songs fluttered to him like moths drawn from the darkness. Songs of the Pear Tree, the Budding of the Lotus, a Chant of Autumn, a Melancholy Emperor's Love—all so short, harsh and squeaky that the same few notes served to express them all. Yet like all familiar songs their different meanings awakened images in his heart. In the lonely fluted notes of the ti-tzu he heard the lapping music of the Whangpoo, smelled saffron and the far flood tide. The tinkle of a three-stringed san-hien echoed the sound of temple bells, reflected the pale sheen of water lilies in moonlight.

Courageously Tai Ling put it all from him for what it was—excessively romantic and unreal, a poetic illusion created by an old man's idle fancy. From across Cockroach Court, so far away that a mechanical piano could hardly carry, a woman's sudden scream rang out. Tai Ling bent his head half an inch but did not stir. He stood staring into the world he knew, knowing that it too was just as unreal and immaterial, created only in the mind of man.

From the railroad tracks to the deep arroyo of Rio Nuevo, from the Border gates to the blue picachos trembling in the desert haze, it was a world apart; a world a stranger has no eyes to see, no pulse to echo. And soon it too would vanish completely; no man would know that it ever existed.

To Tai Ling it was a vast grey brain: its cerebral halves divided by the arroyo; its lobes wrinkled by the convolutions of its winding streets and furtive alleys; clotted with sparse growths of tamarisk and chinaberry; and containing deep in its cerebrum, like a lateral ventricle, the central cavity of Cockroach Court which hid the pineal gland of his tiny shop. Festering in sun and heat and dust, this corrupt grey brain yet lived and pulsed and spumed forth its dreams of faces, its memories of faces, the fabulous and incredible visages of all the thoughts it had known and the sensations it had felt. . . .

There were the faces of all its wandering tribes, its vanished races and enduring breeds. The dark Aztec masks, hard and clean-cut as obsidian. The faces of the few remaining Cocopahs and Mojaves, decadent, pock-marked, eaten by disease and malnutrition; faces hopeless, resigned and yet retaining the unconscious dignity of racial death.

The faces of all the mixed-bloods: those of the mestizo yellow and cunning, with sly eyes and thin lips; those of the cholo broad cheeked and brutal, swinging forward with splendid animal strength and im-measurable vitality; those of the coyotes stained dark red beneath the brown; of the creoles and criollos, sharp featured with purplish lips.

The coarse peon faces swarming into the streets from squalid mud huts across the arroyo; earthy faces of men whose very lives were unde-viating journeys from earthen womb to earthen grave.

Endlessly the yellow faces of China, suave and silent. The big nosed, arrogant faces of brawny, turbaned Hindu cotton pickers. Of giant laughing black children transplanted from the Congo to the Mississippi and drifting hence to this delta of the Colorado.

Streamed also the frank open faces of American Yanquis. The bluff red faces of ranchers. The pallid city faces of merchants, buyers, cotton and melon brokers. The tense pale faces lining the bars and gambling tables.

And all the perpetual animal-faces: of the bloodthirsty tiger man, the lustful swine man, the deceitful fox man, the thieving monkey man, the groveling worm man, the industrious ant man, the stupid and strong ox man.

And the vicious faces of all the petty criminals and poor unfortunates who filled this Border slum: the rateros, the pimps, the human cucarachas, the prostitutes, in their scuffed slippers and sweat-stained shifts, the beggars, the hop-heads and marihuana reefers, all the drunk and the dissolute, the perverted, damned and diseased. . . .

Faces, faces, a thousand faces seen a thousand times, they glided from the convolutions and cavities of this great grey brain like nebulous and disembodied visages of thought. To Tai Ling nothing in their shouts and gestures, nothing of the savage, violent and unfathomed energy of their figures came alive. Only the endless stream of their faces flowing past his door seemed touched by a monstrous enchantment.

Conceived in misery and evil, enslaved by greed and desire, they constantly perpetuated their own untruth, passing and repassing before him silently or with strident tongues to love, to hate, to folly and rapture, power and despair. And forever their efforts were rebuked by the unreality of their existence. In a monstrous enchantment they floated by without real meaning, the strange and fabulous nature of their origin their only truth.

Tai Ling stirred uneasily in the dark doorway. He had reached the core of his real problem. For just as his own past constituted what he called an individual character or karma, so did all these manifested thoughts swarming around him create a karma of locality. A complete objectivity alone would free him. Against this vast grey brain his own was pitted.

Tai Ling was too far down the path of liberation to underestimate his difficulties. It was a dangerous game, as martyrs of many faiths have testified. And he was humorous enough to recognize the paradox. For while most men endeavor to accomplish undetected a bit of evil in a world of good, here he was aspiring to do secret good in a world of evil. This was his only clue to the object of his existence.

The notes of the snake-belly fiddle had died away. The alley was deserted. The vast grey brain slept. There was nothing to remind him of its corrupt fantasies.

He went to his own room, and composing himself for sleep endeavored to remember "The Ten Things to Forget."

III

Easy Meat: A Story

Waters' second publication, and his only published short story, is also set in a border town. "Easy Meat"[6] is the story of a prize fight. It is also the story of a racial encounter. In it, Bolo Boy, an intuitive young Mexican, battles Tendler, a coldly rational American. Thus, it is the story of three battles in one—the conflict between two men of different countries, of different racial make-ups, and of different modes of perception.

From the instant the Bolo Boy espied his opponent in the opposite corner, from that first minute in the ring even before their gloves were laced, he knew he would take the measure of his man.

In the manner of most fighters the Bolo Boy hardly ever took notice of his adversary until the sounding of the bell. Tonight was different. All week the border bars and cantinas had been buzzing about this Gringo Tendler; him and his sporty crowd with their rooms and two baths a day and clean white shirts at supper every night in the swell hotel across the Line; them—a real manager, trainer, seconds, and backers—and their big talk. Still more of it he had heard tonight at the bar as he passed through the Nuevo Mundo Cantina on his way to the Arena. Taking on the Mexican Border just to give their boy the experience of some tough ones that he needed to develop his skill and speed.

Across the ring Tendler stood up for his seconds to remove his robe. The Bolo Boy with casual glances between his own seconds bending over his taped hands watched him to a neutral corner. Carelessly observant, his eyes climbed from the quick-moving feet, crunching rosin into the canvas, to a full and adequate neck, that inescapable index to a man's strength. Tendler was well built in the orthodox gymnasium manner. Tight sinewy knees that well hinged the knotted calves and long

10

muscled thighs. A trim waist with the sharp line of buttocks visible under the white silk trunks held by a narrow band of green. Arms outstretched to the ropes, his shoulders wrinkled and flattened as by a mass of serpents under silk.

Sitting on his stool the Bolo Boy picked at the waist of his own dun canvas trunks, a shade darker than himself.

"All right for you, eh?" Young Fuera, one of his seconds asked.

The Bolo Boy nodded. It was sight of that strand of green through the white silk trunks that made him feel he was going to take Tendler; and the satiny whiteness of that back which made the feeling a certainty. With the instinctive feeling of his peon race for a living field in their parched hills, the royal Aztec green was the Bolo Boy's secret color. All day under the blinding desert sun he worked in the fields. And his toil went to the Gringos to enjoy in the cool fruit of casaba, honey-dew, and cantaloupe. For that matter, till noon that very day he had worked that Tendler might have his melon to eat from a solid silver spoon in his swell hotel. His own supper was what and where it was every other night—beans and beer and pork in the *Lonchería* across the street. And tonight for the first time in all the years he seemed to feel that the fight was something more. As if all those Gringos were washing down across the Line in a big white wave with Tendler on the crest. Well, he knew he was going to take Tendler.

"Watch this baby, Boy. They say he's fast. No playin' now and when yeh hit, soak 'im!" Bud Cross patted his back and handed a bucket down from the ring.

At the referee's beck the Bolo Boy rose and walked to the centre of the ring. He still held a torn sweater over his shoulders and stood listening to the referee's instructions without looking up. One quick glance had shown him Tendler's face under his curly brown hair, unmarked save for a thickened nose and heavy upper lip. Now, with an apparent contemptuous disregard of Tendler, he knew, ring-wise, that the younger fighter was studying him minutely, slightly nettled at the failure to catch his eye. He threw out his hands in a negligent motion, turned cat-like, and slipped back to his corner.

A pleasing deadly calm settled heavily upon the Arena. Everywhere small yellow lights were snapping out until there remained only the white cone overhead and a light at the back door of the bar out in front. The Arena was stuffy, sweaty, still as the bar inside. The fetid hush stilled the Bolo Boy's mind as he lounged with easy grace on his stool. He moved one of his hands resting on his leg. The glove came away slightly damp. He was glad the night was hot, glad that not the slightest breeze was up, and hoped the air would be hot and dry enough to burn your throat before the bout was over. He was used to a night like this— another thing in his favor, and...

The bell; and his stool being jerked from under him.

As Tendler left his corner the Bolo Boy saw a faint nervous smile on his youthful face. Instantly it was replaced with narrowed, watchful eyes, lips firmly closed but not forced; the look of a man intent and engrossed upon his craft. Smoothly the Mexican slipped in. Hands high, he feinted, covered, and shot a straight left to the face. Even as he felt it land—too high—he could feel Tendler's counter and the repeated tap upon his ribs. Tendler had beaten him to the punch. The Gringo was really fast. With the awakening bellow of the crowd in his ears he side-stepped and landed a cross to the neck. The referee behind him, he brought up his right with a backhand slap at the jaw he had missed. Before he could set himself a short body blow put him on his heels. Immediately Tendler was close against him, forearms locking his elbows, a light, even breath on his shoulder.

The house was noisily pleased. The Bolo Boy knew the applause was all his, but was not fooled. Worrying his arms about to give the impression he was still being held, the Bolo Boy admitted to himself that Tendler was better than he had guessed. The lightning lift of that jaw for his own cross was in the order of something he had seldom met. The tough babies of the Border—as he himself was called—stood up and socked until they were dropped, without time for the little things, the subtle little things that go to point a bout. He felt the beginning of a cautious respect for the man against him. As though torn apart from Tendler by the referee, the Bolo Boy sprang back and slipped round lithe and smooth yellow under the brilliant glare.

In the centre of the ring they sparred briefly, each feeling out the other with an exhibition of swift cleverness that deceived all but themselves. As the gong ended the round Tendler threw him a smile of sporting approbation before turning to his corner. A smile that expressed perfectly the self-sufficient attitude of all the Americanos who drifted into the Casinos to win or lose at écarté with the same cheerful insouciance. So the Bolo Boy was all right, eh? Again he knew with that cold mathematical desire that he'd get Tendler.

"You fight thees guy; don' box!" admonished young Fuera, expanding the Bolo Boy's trunks at the waist.

"Yeh. Don't try to box this baby. You just get into him and then Wham!—Savvy?" repeated Bud Cross in his ear.

The Bolo Boy lay back easily in his corner with his slow sleepy eyes staring fixedly across the Arena. The place was packed. All his fellow-workers from the fields; old señoras plentiful on the benches; the Chinos imperturbably cracking watermelon seeds between their stained teeth; and here and there a sprinkling of Hindus under their dirty turbans. Heads and humped shoulders stood out even upon the sky at the top sides of the walls. All there to see how he was going to take the fast Gringo. They were unusually quiet, for that gathering, as though telepathically sensing they were going to see a match. The soldiers at the door and the rurales wouldn't have any trouble with bottle throwing tonight.

The sound of the gong ripped through the heavy air for the second round. And at the signal the Bolo Boy left his stool with an incredibly swift glide that carried his brown crouching body more than halfway across the ring. He was in and out again with a left to the ribs and right to the eyes before Tendler could open with his lead. Again he bored in. A rapid exchange of blows. A stinging sensation on the cheek that snapped his head and gaze toward the dark. He stepped back a foot. Pivoted. Surprised Tendler in his rush with an uppercut to the ribs, solid. Solid. Something caught him in the middle and sent the wind whistling through his lips. Then he was away, graceful, light-footed, smooth as a ripple.

"Thass-a boy, Mex!"

"Go get 'im, Whitey!"

A deep, thunderous applause swept through the crowd. Somewhere the crash of a beer bottle. The Whitey, Tendler, was fast as they said, but when the Mexican moved it was as though they were watching the unconscious but perfect coordination of an animal's muscles. There they were in the centre of the ring again. A flurry of gloves, and the noisy slap, slap, slap, of ineffectual blows. Clinch. The Bolo Boy breaking away and coming in again with the same snap, snap. The round was all his, but the Bolo Boy knew it for a fizzle. Tendler's white girlish skin at the end of the round was spotted with a red that would not have shown on his own swarthy sides, yet the Boy knew that that one body hook would hurt him later in the bout.

He turned his head to spit water and lay back to breathe deeply. Too fast. He'd have to hit, hit hard, damn hard. Hit to drive his man across the Line and back into the Estados Unidos where they all belonged.

Speedy and sporty—that was these Americanos for you. About them nothing slow and sure and inevitable like those of his own race. They did everything as if they were playing at a game. As though they sported in their work. Little did they know of the immense pride of the peon to whom a jest is an insult, an earnestness imbedded upon a greater humility. Or the hate that can be treasured and fondled and hidden—as so it had been for four hundred years—behind inscrutable eyes, too flinty for time to wear.

The Bolo Boy's shapeless lips drew back as he sucked air. Should not get mad in the ring. He wasn't. He just felt a warm surging through his outstretched arms to tear into ribbons the rippling white silk of the torso before him.

The round began slowly with the Bolo Boy trying to maneuver Tendler against the ropes. Doggedly he followed his man across the ring and back. The Boy's ugly brown face was set under his black tousled hair. His obsidian eyes, hard as glazed glass, had the same open fixed stare; never a blink at Tendler's hands flashing in and in again. How fast the Gringo moved. Menancingly fast; around and in and flashing out with an economy of movement that kept him covered tight as a drum. At each flash the Bolo Boy ducked his unwavering eyes behind his raised left and took the blows on his head. Tendler hadn't learned to protect his hands. Well, after tonight he'd have learned you couldn't hit, hit, hit with broken knuckles, strained sinews, and bruises that one by one inexorably shortened the precious life of a fighter's hands. Down here Tendler was finding what fighting meant—the terrific crashing, the steady pound, pound, pound of shifting weight and bone against flesh and nerves.

The Bolo Boy kept boring in, taut and set in the beautiful crouch made familiar by him along six hundred miles of Border: his weight evenly balanced on wide spread legs; left wrist covering jaw and throat; shoulders hunched, right hand down and twitching like a snake's head above its coils. And even Tendler revolved about him raining blows on head, arms, and shoulders, a veritable whirlwind of shimmering white.

Hopelessly outclassed, the Bolo Boy gave ground in two strides backward. Tendler pressed his advantage. His eyes telegraphed the blow and the Bolo Boy saw it coming. A straight left from the shoulder. The Bolo Boy did not wince. But a shaving of a second before it caught him between the eyes, his own short right got home to the belt. He could feel his glove sink deep. Then suddenly the brilliant glare of the light above seemed turned into his eyes so that he could not see. The cords of his neck were violently wrenched. Instinctively he bent and covered.

He felt a bare hand pushing backward against his shoulder. All of a sudden his two senses of sound and sight returned. An immense outpouring of noise burst in upon his ears, and somewhere close he heard a voice: "Two—three"! Tendler was down on his knees, his two arms convulsively wrapped around his sides. His agonized face searched the black open sky for breath.

The Bolo Boy sprang forward and was hurled back by the referee's arm. Like a dog on leash he slunk forth and back before the kneeling Whitey. At five Tendler was on one knee. At six he started to rise, re-strained only by the voices from his corner. At eight he was up and the Bolo Boy was on him forgetful of everything but an insane, frantic de-sire to get at his man before Tendler regained his breath. But Tendler could not be touched. His footwork was almost perfect, weaving him in and out of danger faster than the Bolo Boy could direct his blows which fell harmlessly on arms and shoulders. Then, faster than them both, the bell. *Carape!* The damned bell. The Bolo Boy threw a snarl over his shoulder as he strode in to his corner.

If he could have had a half-minute more! Just another opening to get in before this minute of reviving rest. The applause continued, but above its dying roar the Boy heard the aggravating snap of towels driv-ing air into Tendler's lungs. He inclined his own body eagerly forward to catch the air driven toward him from the towels of his own seconds. Sweat dripped upon his knees. His arms were wet as though they had been immersed in thin oil. Hot? Maria! Yet even as he raised his open mouth for the sponge again, he wished for a thicker, more fuzzy night. So hot it'd stick in Tendler's throat. Anything to stop him just for an instant.

"Keep after him, Boy. And when yeh get him uncovered, sock him."

Tendler gave him half a smile as he came out of his corner, but for two rounds the Bolo Boy could not touch him. The grin burned into him as he followed Tendler around the ring. Why didn't he stand up and slug like all the others? Outpointing him at long range and then gliding away. In-fighting with irritating tricks he did not know. Maneuvering out of distance to make him always the aggressor; inveigling him into a rush and then side-stepping with a parting hook. At the end of each round the Bolo Boy knew that Tendler was the best man he had ever met. A supple white figure untouchable at will as a ghost. And more than at the beginning of the fight, more than ever before, more than anything else, he wanted to take the Gringo—knew that he was going to whip Tendler. In swift phantasmagoria, swift, luminous, pale as a horde of other ghosts, there flashed before him memories of other men whom he had fought and beaten. And none of them, not all of their strength and skill combined would have equalled the Gringo across the ring with the strip of green round his waist. Yet he was going to take Tendler. He knew it. The thought stuck like a pincer in his mind.

Then slowly there seemed revealed to him the reason for Tendler's—for all Gringos'—apparent superiority. Fighting was Tendler's game. It was his business; he had no other. And the Americanos' business was their life. They laughed and joked and talked, talked much and loud.

All business. Summer, winter; wind and sun; night and day. Just business. They didn't live life. They lived business, a routine that sucked in joy and sorrow, the sunshine and rain of men's souls and tears, all hate and hope, and bundled it together like cotton at so much the bale. That was the difference between them and his own people with their slow days in the sun, Saints' Days, innumerable fiesta days, and the days of "*Pues*; but Señor, to work on such a day"...when there was a peso in the pocket and friends in every cantina. The difference between Tendler and himself. And as he thought, in those swift empty seconds in the ring and the minutes between rounds, the Bolo Boy saw himself at a shadowy crossing in his life. Unlike the Gringos, his life had been purposeless, uneventful, without goal. Yet each repeated day had brought him closer to a change. For somehow even he would have to change. Tonight he must cross a line, a line of fate, shadowy and indistinct, looming before him to be crossed. Next week Tendler would be gone and he would be left to hear the talking in the bars. But he'd have to slow up. His lungs, his sides, were bursting with the pace. And that body blow was beginning to take effect, exerting the slightest pull to his every blow.

With a half-minute to go in the sixth round, Tendler suddenly opened up. It was as though he had suddenly stopped short and thrust out a rigid arm. The Bolo Boy was surprised off guard. The left caught him on the side of the jaw and felled him like a log in a neutral corner. Shaken but unhurt, he would have risen but that Young Fuera in his corner caught his eye.

He waited on one knee, both gloves on the canvas, like a starting runner. Wily wisdom came to him while he waited. He ground his gloves into the specks of sand and rosin under him. At the count of nine he was up. He saw that Tendler knew he was rushing for the safety of a clinch. Tendler swung high. Grimly smiling to himself, the Bolo Boy took them on his head and stopped. Purposely he swung short to the body and felt his glove brush across Tendler's ribs. Again before the bell, he pointed a clumsy weak blow to the face and twisted his glove as it landed. Backing across the ring at the bell he saw the angry red rash growing into the skin before him, two splotches not harmful but irritating and as such to be remembered.

Again, when the round opened, Tendler came at him with a jump. It was as though the Bolo Boy was meeting a different man. Tendler no longer weaved in and out, the swift defensive fighter. Shoulders humped, his mouth a rigid line, he met the Bolo Boy's rushes with a counter and straight jabs on toes that never backed an inch. And the Bolo Boy settled down to what he knew were to be the most gruelling rounds he had ever faced. Smack. Smack. Shuffle of feet and the squeak of dried out boards. A continuous multitudinous roar in his ears, for this kind of fighting was what the border money had been paid to see. A quick telepathy told the Bolo Boy the crowd was beginning to change. The knock-down in the last round had done that. By it only, Tendler had won his way into their respect from a mere Gringo outsider to an equally good man in the ring. And that punch meant Tendler was as good as he was fast.

The Bolo Boy was fighting. From bell to bell there was no rest. He was hardly conscious of the scant minutes when he lay on his stool, eyes to the gritty stars, at the base of his brain a wet sponge. He hit Tendler with everything he had. And with despairing surprise he saw Tendler still on his feet after each furious exchange. Again, with a cold dread forming a clot on the certainty of his licking the Gringo, he went in for Tendler.

Then once more, from the same straight left that had caught him earlier in the bout, he seemed to fall headlong into thick darkness. An unconsciousness that passed like a swift-moving curtain before his eyes, but that could not have lasted a full second. Young Fuera saw his knees buckle as he fell into a clinch, and the Bolo Boy could feel the referee and Tendler furiously fighting to free the Gringo from his weight. The next second the black curtain passed and the Bolo Boy was gazing down at an old Señora on the floor outside the ring. Stolid, unmoved of face as brown wood, she sat with open breast nursing a child and watching him back. The blow cleared the Bolo Boy's mind. For the first time in his life he felt like a beaten man. If only the old woman, his own crowd, weren't so...But that was their way. Like him, they knew what the Gringos were doing. Yet they sat just waiting and watching and taking it on the chin.

The round over, he knew that he had shot his best. The night, the thick black night that had sunk of its own torpid weight down upon the low floor of the ring, the blur of massed faces, the water that was hardly wet, oppressed him with an unconscious futility. He felt old; so shaken that he wondered why his loose body did not fall apart whenever Tendler got home to his middle. Yet it was impossible to think of losing to the Gringo. They'd swarm over him like white ants. He'd have to give Tendler the works.

The works. The sly, dirty tricks banned to the ring, not so dirty or underhanded to the Bolo Boy because he was accustomed to using them and protecting himself against them. A tacit agreement always springing between him and his opponent to use every one whenever the referee could not see. Against Tendler he used every one. Each time he went into a clinch he went in low with a heave of his shoulder against

Tendler's ribs. He pushed and tried the rabbit punch. He remembered to grit his gloves stealthily on the canvas between rounds. And he made them all count.

Already Tendler was marked from eye to belt. He came out of every round with great red splotches that stuck to his white body like painted pinks. One cheek bore red scratches suspiciously like the marks of a cat's claws. Still the Bolo Boy kept playing for the ear, knowing that Tendler would remember him even as he remembered his own disfigured ear. Time and time again his hands crashed home to Tendler's head. And each time he could have winced, feeling his knuckles give, also knowing that it would be a week before he could use his hands in the fields. Yet, for all the cauliflower ear, he felt that Tendler bore him no ill-will. At the end of a round when they both fought on, the bell unheard, Tendler extended both his hands in apology when parted by the referee. He was only fighting his Gringo way and the Bolo Boy his.

The Bolo Boy became aware that the fastening of one glove was loose. In the second clinch he was successful. With the cord between his wrist and Tendler's temple he managed to cut Tendler's face as he pushed himself out. Seconds later he had opened the cut over Tendler's eye. The sight of blood filled his veins, his mind, his hopes with the illusion of winning. With terrific expenditure of his waning strength he got Tendler against the ropes. But for every blow he took three. Blood spattered his forearms, his own breast, the canvas. The crowd was on its feet. This was what they knew and wanted. The soldiers in the aisles quieted before the sound.

The Bolo Boy forgot caution. Two smashing rights to the sweaty pink body. To draw down that protecting left he took a hard right over the heart and then another. Anything to get his chance. He got it. Blinded in one eye, Tendler misjudged and lurched forward as his left went past the Boy's head. The Bolo Boy hooked with his right for the unprotected jaw. Even as he struck he knew he had suffered defeat. A minute cramping pain from those repeated body blows took the accurately timed snap from his blow. If he'd just got this chance two rounds ago! Yet those at ringside saw his glove flash home (to them) squarely on the point of the jaw.

Tendler dropped as though the floor had given way under him. He bent to rise and then straightened on the floor. Three! Four! He regained one knee and the look from his one visible eye went blankly past the Bolo Boy. Six! Would his legs have strength? What was the matter with the referee's arm that it moved so slowly! Only eight and the Gringo's rigid legs were waiting for nine. Would his own knees hold out, he wondered. Nine, and his chance, his last and only chance was gone.

With all his strength the Bolo Boy beat at the limp body that clung to his shoulders and tried to drag him to the floor. He cursed the referee who himself could not tear Tendler away. As the seconds passed the Bolo Boy seemed to feel the strength flowing from his own weakening arms into the Gringo. That was just like the Gringos, sucking strength from defeat, never knowing when they were down, making everyone else pay for their mistakes. With every moment Tendler grew lighter on his feet. He became animated with lazy life. Left arm crossed over jaw and dripping eye, right arm covering heart and solar plexus, he played for time until the saving bell, retreating to his corner. And at its sound he sat down on the stool that had been waiting outside the ropes to receive him. The Bolo Boy slouched back to his corner.

"Three more for you, Boy. You get him sure, now."

The Bolo Boy did not even shake his head. His body wouldn't obey. For twenty-seven minutes he had bent it to his will. Now he couldn't drive it. His heart seemed ready to burst his breast. Ammonia and smelling salts no longer cleared his mind. His knees trembled. It took the ropes to hold his heavy outstretched arms. If only a breeze would come up! The damn night was too heavy and black to breathe. The heat burnt his throat raw as though he sucked in fire at every breath. If his body had only done what he had willed. In like a flash to the jaw, a half inch over, with a quick snap, the weight of his shoulder behind it. But all it did was push, push Tendler over. And now over there his seconds were putting life back into him. More driving, smashing life that every Gringo miraculously seemed to have; more power; more snap with every punch.

They were in the ring again. Washed clean, his cut well closed, revived by the minute's rest, Tendler looked fresh as ever. And at every counter the Bolo Boy felt the Gringo's strength coming back again into him. He just couldn't be stopped. His body smarting pink, his eye torn, ear puffed, his lips swelling, the Gringo was good as a new man. He had taken all that the Bolo Boy had and was willing to take more. But the Boy knew he had no more in him to give. He had reached the turning of his luck. Like crossing a summit to go downhill. Tendler was going on; the Gringo had passed him a round ago, whether by chance he won or lost the bout. A great lassitude swept over the Bolo Boy. The melancholy futility of his race ate into his thoughts. He saw himself going out of the ring like others he had watched before. Stopping at the bar behind a row of backs, for him faces only in the mirror. The shaking of hands, back-slapping the Gringos for their free drinks, even his own workers joining in. Not one of the girls to shout at him "Beeg Boy!" who had shouted so many times before. Out the cantina as he had never gone before; a last look behind. Was that he, the Bolo Boy, alone, going down the dirty darkened street into the arroyo?...A flash of green. All because of the Gringo. The thud, thud, thud of gloves. Would the round never end?

Tendler fought warily. He dared not take a single chance or the Bolo Boy was on him like that! The Mexican was a revelation at every round, swift as a cat, a natural fighter, with whip in every punch. If he'd only had the science, the coaching, what a champion he might have been! Fighting to the last step. Yet at every step the Bolo Boy could feel himself slowing up. He could feel it in his legs, the first to give way. The dreary lassitude thickened about him, a smother of light and heat. Then that flash of white and he would be mixing it with savage fury. Just like horses before a sunstroke in the summer fields. Plodding, sleepy-like, then snap! heads up, hard on the traces for a dozen steps before they fell over dead. He oughtn't to have worked that morning, wouldn't have if he'd only known the Gringo was like this. The Gringos. Nothing ever seemed to stop them. The flash of green again and a slap on the face he could hardly feel but which turned him on his heels. Green...miles of blinding desert brown, the hazy, far smoke-blue hills against the sky, and against them his own bit of secret green. A peasant, peon passion for his land. He took a hard right to the middle and doubled up in an arrested crouch. They didn't give draws in the Arena, but for the bout he didn't care. Yet he didn't know how he was going to take Tendler. Only two more rounds and he didn't, he did not know. . . .

As he straightened, another straight left caught him in the ribs. A right cross to the side of the head spun him half around.

Against the background of dark and yellow faces he remembered the Señora on the bench. Nursing, unmoved of face, whether he or the Gringo won. Before the faces had stopped sliding in a mass something hit him on the jaw and darkness rushed in upon his sight.

He could not see. There was nothing before him but a scanty sprinkle of lights that seemed like stars. In his ears a yelling that beat like the roar of surf down where the fishing boats come in.

"Four!—Five!" Mother of God! He was on the floor.

He crawled to his knees. Got to his feet. And still could not see clearly in the light that dazzled so. He was only sure of the Gringo poised before him as on a crest of a moving wave.

And as he willed, tried to raise his arms, something struck him between the eyes, and in a whir of rushing blackness he dropped heavily to the floor.

IV

Colorado Mining Trilogy

Between 1935 and 1940, Waters published his Colorado mining trilogy, The Wild Earth's Nobility, Below Grass Roots, *and* The Dust Within the Rock. *Rewritten in 1971 as the one-volume* Pike's Peak, *the story becomes more sharply a fictionalized account of Waters' grandfather Joseph Rogier, who came to Colorado in 1872, made a fortune in contracting and building, and lost it through a series of mining ventures. More significantly, however, it is the story of his psychic search for his inner Self, symbolized by Pike's Peak.*

It is worth noting that in this novel, place has not yet become beneficent: in Fever Pitch *place is aggressively hostile; in* Yogi *it is negative; and in the trilogy it becomes the focus of Joseph Rogier's psychic search. This latter work tells of a first-comer to a strange and alien land and of his inability to come to terms with it. It focuses on Rogier's search for psychic wholeness outside of himself. It is the story of a man alien to the land, fighting the land—"perhaps epitomic for the whole white experience in North America."[7]*

We are fortunate to have Waters' own condensation of this theme from the seven-hundred-page Pike's Peak. *In 1980 when he was the featured speaker at the annual meeting of the Rocky Mountain Modern Language Association, held in Denver, Colorado, he was asked to read from the novel. The following selection is based upon that reading.*

The reading here of excerpts from my novel *Pike's Peak* does seem appropriate. Pike's Peak itself has loomed high in history for many centuries. It was a sacred mountain and mecca for many Indian tribes. It

21

became a beacon for the "Pike's Peak or Bust" wagon caravans and White gold seekers, the site of Cripple Creek, the greatest gold camp in the world. And it is now the location of the Air Force Academy at its foot. Such high mountains are regarded throughout the world as repositories of psychic energy, places of access to higher consciousness. And it's this psychical aspect with which this novel is concerned.

It is the story of two main characters, Pike's Peak itself and Joseph Rogier, its human protagonist. Their confrontation takes place on two levels: Rogier's practical mining ventures to reach the gold deposits in its heart, and his projection of his own unconscious self upon the physical Peak.

Rogier, soon after the Civil War, was traveling west in a wagon train on the Santa Fe Trail, to prepare a home for his family. But far out on the buffalo plains he saw to the north the snowy peak which Zebulon Pike had first mistaken for a cloud in the sky.

It appeared to him "...like something risen from the depth of a dreamless sleep to the horizon of wakeful consciousness, without clear outline yet embodying the substance of a hope and meaning that seemed strangely familiar as it was vague." This is the first sentence in the long novel. Clearly, Rogier's first glimpse of the Peak triggered in his unconscious an intimation of his inner self. He couldn't resist its call. He turned off the caravan trail and in his lone wagon crawled up Fontaine Creek to a new settlement at the foot of Pike's Peak.

A carpenter by trade, he secured work, sent for his wife and daughters, raised a large family, and became a successful builder and contractor in growing Colorado Springs. He was rich enough, eventually, to support a stable of harness horses, trotters and pacers. He made fun of all the fools following the silver strike at Leadville and the gold discoveries in the San Juans. Then in 1890 gold was discovered on the south slope of Pike's Peak along the stream called Cripple Creek. The discovery shook him to the roots of his being. He, too, finally succumbed to gold fever.

His approach, like his character, was pragmatic and methodical. He trudged for days over the Cripple Creek district, studying it thoroughly. The district, 11,000 feet high, lay on the south slope of Pike's Peak. Its main producing area of only six square miles contained a hundred and seventy-five shipping mines, eleven reduction mills. Three railroads were entering the district. Its production began exceeding that of the Mother Lode in California, the Klondike in Alaska, the Comstock lode in Nevada. It was beginning to lead the world in gold production, with an eventual total of 450,000,000 dollars, based on twenty-one dollars an ounce.

Returning home, Rogier was asked by one of his daughters, "Did you

find a gold mine, Daddy?" "No," he growled, "I'm not a dumb fool al-
falfa miner!" Rogier was in no hurry to join the hoards of tenderfeet
staking out mere surface lodes.

Late every night, he sat at his drafting board studying geological records and topographical maps. The district, he had learned, was the
core of an extinct volcano, of which remained only Pike's Peak. During
the eruptions, volcanic material had burst through the granite and
cooled in fissures. Through these, hot water ascended, was changed by
chemical action, and gold ore was finally precipitated. Hence most
mines were surface workings, and Cripple Creek was commonly regarded as a grass-roots mining district. But gold had been found in the
granite walls at some depth.

Now, hunched over his midnight lamp, Rogier traced on his map the
trends of all the important veins. They formed a pattern of a great
heart-shaped granite cup, converging on the north, beneath the very
summit of Pike's Peak. Standing before the window, gazing at the Peak
touched gold with the sunrise, he knew that here was the key that
would unlock the secret of its hold upon him. He knew now where to
search for the bloodstream of its living flesh, where to sink a shaft to tap
that great arterial fountain, whose viscous veins ran through pulsing
stone.

So Rogier began developing successive unproductive mines, each one
closer to the summit of Pike's Peak. He refused to list them on the mining stock exchange to be controlled by stockholders. He used his own
money, selling his business properties one by one, even his stable of race
horses. All the time he kept two old hard-rock miners, Abe and Jake,
working with the exhorbitant promise of the riches they'd find. Assay-
ers' reports showed no gold content. Abe said, "It ain't you, Colonel.
You're a smart man, like I always said. And it ain't us either. What I
think, it's this workin'. We ought to give her up."

Rogier's fist came down on the table with a bang. "No, by Jove!
Never! You boys are stickin' to me till Hell freezes over! There'll be no
more such talk." He changed his tactics now, by reiterating his prophecy that here some day would be found treasures greater than Croesus
ever took from the sands of Pactolus or Solomon from the mines of
Ophir. Right here!

"Ain't never heard of them fellers or mines either," grumbled the
sulky Jake.

"Exceeding the amount of gold Cecil Rhodes took from the mountains of South Africa, then," continued Rogier. "Deposits that will make
the fortunes of Tom Walsh, Tabor, and Stratton look like a poor man's
bread tax. You've heard of them, hey? Not gold *ore*, you fool, that has to
be shipped to the mill in car loads. You remember what I told you about

breaking into a stope floored with grains of gold sand you can scrape up in sacks, whose walls and ceilings are hung with gold crystals glistening, glittering, like an Aladdin's Cave! It's right here under our feet, boys, somewhere. No, I won't let you leave me now. You've been too faithful and suffered too many disappointments for that. You've got to stay and get your share!"

* * *

During all this time, the Peak began to emerge as a living symbol of his inner self. Calendar pages kept turning. Events outcropped above the sensory horizon and sank back down. Buildings were going up; bills were being paid. But time stayed still. The flowing linear stream of time—what an illusion it really was! Time was a great still pool, an element as basic as earth and air, water and fire, in which life developed at its own immeasurable pace to its own degree of fulfillment. Time! What did it mean to him now? In that invisible, immeasurable, impalpable pool both he and the Peak had been rooted for aeons to confront at last the meaning of their inner selves. In geologic time it had stood there, a monstrous volcano belching fire and smoke upon a world that had sunk beneath forgotten seas. It had stood there in orogenic time, a lofty snow-crowned peak looking down upon a virgin continent yet unraped by greedy man. Through the quick gasp of a century it had remained inviolable while lesser prophets, robed in silver, had been gutted of their riches. And now it had come to its moment of revelation. Gold, in all its shades and tints! And what was that? Let other greedy fools scratch the grass roots of its rocky epidermis for a modicum of pay dirt to make them rich and famous! Not he! For he also was a growth within that immovable, immeasurable, deep still pool of time, as old as the Peak itself. And now at last in their moment of truth they faced each other like two adversaries bound together in a common selfhood. Over them both a common golden sun rose and set. Through both their flesh ran the veins of liquid golden life, pulsating to the same diastolic and systolic beat. And in each of them glowed the reflections of the one great sun, the golden sun that was the heart of all. Gold! A great gold heart embodied in the depths of that extinct volcano whose remnant was the puny Peak. Of course he would reach it, if he had to blast the whole damn top off the Peak and dig down by hand to the convergence of its golden veins in the heart that lay beneath!

* * *

Things weren't going too well. He was pretty well broke by now and a little discouraged, and he stayed in town trying to raise a little more money somewhere. It'd been three months since he'd been to Cripple Creek and seen Abe and Jake. Then one afternoon they came in to see him.

"You ain't taken up with business, are you, Colonel?" Jake asked.

"No. You boys give an account of yourselves. I ain't seen you for three months."

"Aw, we was running short of money so we worked in the Mary Mc-Kinney and saved part of our wages." Abe nudged his brother. "We ain't forgot you, Colonel. We got something for you." Again he poked Jake, who hauled a specimen out of his pocket. Another came out of a second pocket. Two pieces of grayish ore the size of both fists, which he laid in Rogier's lap. "Not a hundred yards from the old tunnel! It was there all the time, covered by a slide. A defined vein, Colonel. We followed it. The assays say it's shipping ore. What you were lookin' for." What could be more natural? "Look at this stuff! Look at it man! We got somethin', sure as Moses."

Rogier sat, a specimen in each hand, listening with an inscrutable face to the rising voices of Abe and Jake driving like iron into the granite recesses of his being. He spun around on the stool, swept papers aside, and laid the specimens on the board. With a glass he examined minutely the silver-clear crystals imbedded in the rock. "Crystals, huh? Hum," he muttered softly.

"One piece ran thirty-two dollars," said Jake. "I told you we'd find out if it was a mine or not. It won't be all this good. But I figure there's enough to go down on if you got a mind to, Colonel. It'll take a piece of money to sink a shaft. Do you reckon you want to?"

"Want to!" Rogier tried to control his voice. For an instant his impassioned intensity of purpose illumined in awful splendor the depths within him.

"It's just a mine, Colonel," cautioned Abe quietly, "and we can only go as far as shipping ore holds out."

"A mine!" Rogier shouted irritably. "God almighty! There's your mine!" He pointed out the window to the lofty face of the Peak. "We're going down to her rock bottom if we have to blow off her whole top! There's your mine. I won't be stopped again. Not by God or granite or human flesh. We're going way down."

Shaken by the discovery, he sat all night, bending over the two pieces of sylvanite ore. The sun was rising, but a few stars still shone brightly in the sky. Once again, it loomed before him as it had the first time he glimpsed it a quarter of a century ago; like something risen from the depths of a dreamless sleep to the horizon of wakeful consciousness, without clear outline yet embodying the substance of a hope and meaning that seemed vaguely familiar as it was ineffable. The clouds lifted.

Shadows, seams, and wrinkles smoothed out. And under the rising sun
it lifted a face, serene, majestic, and suffused a glowing pink, yet wearing a look benign, compassionate, and divine that he had never recognized before. Oh, great mother of mountains, womb of all creation, Self
of all selves, how he had misjudged her! She was not an adversary but
an ally in his quest. Men had lived and died, never knowing what they
sought while she had waited to clasp them to her granite breast, to take
them to the porphyric womb from which they had been born, and to
welcome them home again to the one vast golden heart of which they
had been a single beat. Time! He could feel the ages born within him
hardening his bones as they had hardened the sharks' teeth embedded in
the limestone cliffs, running through his veins with their ebbs and tides,
evolving the brain cells that had envisioned the image of the goal now
clear before him. Time! Eternity would give him all the time he needed
to achieve it.

Mrs. Rogier pushed open the door. "Daddy, you haven't been to bed
all night! You wanted to catch the first train to Cripple Creek, so I came
down." He patted her clumsily on the back. "It's going to snow up there
in Cripple Creek. I've laid out your winter coat and packed your bag.
You better get ready."

"I'm ready, Martha! Been ready a long time," he answered cheerfully.

So he opened his last mine, the Sylvanite, named after the sylvanite
ore sample which Abe and Jake had found. It lay far up a rocky canyon
in the side of the Peak. The working was simply a vertical shaft down
which the men had to go in a tin ore bucket, suspended on a steel cable
unwound by a gasoline operated motor. Jake and Abe worked underground with hand drills; and to operate the motor above, Rogier now
persuaded his son-in-law to come up and work for him. His son-in-law
caught pneumonia and died. But Rogier, still indomitable, persuaded
his daughter to give him the life insurance, leaving her two children and
herself penniless. This did not worry him. He went down into the
depths of the mine.

Getting into his boots and overalls, he crawled into the rusty iron
bucket with his sputtering carbide lamp. As he began to descend, his
troubles and worries flitted upward like the faint splotches of daylight
on the cribbing. Now, dropping swiftly down, he gathered to himself
the consoling mystery of the deep velvety blackness rushing up to engulf
him. At the first level Rogier got out and walked the length of the drift,
exulting like a man returning to his native haunts. Quick, sharp, and
hollow the sound of his steps echoed along the abandoned passages.
Then he walked back to the level station and impatiently rang the bell,

went down to the second level and still to the third, prowling alone through abandoned drifts, stopes, and cross-cuts. The deeper he descended the more secure he felt. Often he hooked his lamp to the wall and stood staring into the unfathomable gloom of a cavernous stope.

And then, for an instant, he lost his sense of balance, when his lamp went out. It was as if he were metamorphosed into a creature who, like a fly, could walk and stand head down. Dizzy with the vision that suddenly possessed him, he sank down on his haunches, bent over, and held his head in his hands. It was as if he were on the verge of a vast abyss, at the perimeter of the aura of an undiscovered sun in the center of his planet, fixed and immutable within a universe duplicating the one outside. The vision, with all the force of indisputable truth, vehemently refuted the unsubstantiated theories that the interior of his planet was solid, molten, or gaseous. What need had his earth of another sun millions of miles away in outer space? Here it had its own. Was there not a living world constricted within a drop of water, a grain of sand, a microscopic cell invisible to the naked eye? Let men stand alone then, self-reliant and serene in their own completeness, admitting the universality within their own earth as within themselves. Here beneath their feet was the one disregarded mystery of all times: a vast subterranean universe upon whose surface they trod without a thought for what lay below. Where, oh where, were the intrepid explorers of modern scientific thought? Diving like frogs into the shallow seas, ballooning aloft into the air; thoughtless fools to whom the subterranean core of their own earth was so mysteriously unknown that they ignored it to conquer others! Thousands of years behind the intuitive ancients, they did not yet know that at the center of their own earth lay the golden sun of life, surrounded by its galaxies and constellations.

* * *

Well, it just couldn't keep up forever, decided Abe and Jake. They had to quit; they hadn't been paid for a long time. So they trudged down to the little railroad station in Cripple Creek, to meet Rogier when he came back from Colorado Springs. But first they had something to show him. "Damn me!" said Rogier. "What's going on up here? You both look like the cat that swallowed the canary. Have you hit another streak of shipping ore?"

"No, Colonel, it ain't the Sylvanite. It's the Cresson."

"Why that ol' workin'?" What had got into these two old fools, Rogier kept wondering as they walked toward the Cresson Mine. Why should they be so excited about it? The Cresson had been a marginal working ever since its discovery in 1894; the government report on the district in 1906 didn't even list it. But somehow the mine had been foisted on a couple of real estate agents in Chicago who sold a few shares of stock and leased its working levels to different operators, who could never make its low grade ore pay. The shaft was down 600 feet and the mine was $80,000 in the red. They reached the surface plant; what a wonderful plant it was. It looked tidy enough: a great smooth-rolling drum, clear indicators, a commodious new cage that would have graced a hotel in Denver. A man stepped out with a gun.

"We come like you said we could, Luke. Only for a look, just a peek, understand?" said Abe. They stepped into the cage and dropped swiftly to the twelfth level. A man with a sawed-off shotgun met them when they stepped out. "Hold the cage," ordered Luke. "It's only us. We're just gonna take a quick look."

He struck off into a drift, and turned into a lateral, another drift, and another cross-cut. The four men brought up short against a huge bank-vault, steel door. Luke sounded a signal, and it was opened by three guards with drawn revolvers. "It's me," said Luke, "I'm just giving these boys a quick look." The guards stepped aside to reveal a large hole in the back about the size of a doorway. "Go on in!" directed Jake. Rogier, pushed ahead, climbed up the platform, followed by Abe and Jake. Luke behind them raised over their heads his magnesium flare.

Rogier uttered one gasp—a gasp that seemed to empty his lungs and bowels—and then was silent. What he saw was a geode, a vug, a "poop hole"—an immense hollow chamber in solid rock nearly forty feet high, twenty feet long, and fifteen feet wide. A cave of sparkling splendor that almost blinded him, on whose walls and ceiling hung crystals of sylvanite and calaverite, and flakes of pure gold as big as thumbnails glowing in the light. A cave floored with gold particles thick as sand and glittering like a mass of jewels. Everywhere he looked were gold tellurium, sparkling gold crystals, glittering gold sands. Here it was as he had envisioned: an Aladdin's Cave transported from an Arabian Night to the twentieth century, a treasure greater than Croesus ever took from the sands of the Pactolus, or Solomon from the mines of Ophir.

A hand on his collar jerked him back. In a daze, he was taken by Abe and Jake to their own mine, the Sylvanite. Rogier knelt on the floor, ran his hands over the rock walls. "Abe, keep out all trespassers! Lock off this vug!"

"Colonel! There's nothin' here! That was the Cresson vug we saw, remember? Not here!"

"The Cresson! Not here!" Rogier clawed at the bare rock walls.

Abe picked him up, carried him to the station, and rang the bell. Once up, he carried Rogier to the cabin and laid him on his bunk. "He's havin' a spell," he told Jake. They found some whiskey, poured it down his throat. He stopped mumbling, the old body stiffened, then relaxed in sleep.

Day after day Rogier sat on his bunk or at the table, reading the newspapers brought him. Fourteen hundred sacks of crystals and flakes had been scraped from the walls of the vug and sold for $378,000. A thousand more sacks had been gathered from the gold-littered floor, bringing $90,000. Eight four-horse wagons with armed guards had transported a shipment of ore from the collar of the shaft to five broad-gauge cars sealed and marked for the Globe Smelter of Denver, which brought more than $686,000. And in the window of the bank was a cancelled check showing the amount of $468,637 more for a shipment of 150 tons. All the world was astounded by these richest shipments of ore ever made. They raised the yearly mean ore value of the Cresson to $33 a ton and raised the annual production of Cripple Creek, yielding an extra dividend to the stockholders of more than a million dollars.

Rogier kept lying on his bunk, refusing to get up and eat. A hammering began on the inside of his head, sounding like a jack hammer down in the mine. When the lights went out and Abe and Jake went to their bunks, he turned over. The men were asleep, and he waited for the flames to die down in the fire. For an instant he debated whether to scribble a note. Deciding that the flicker of the candle or the scratch of a pencil might waken them, he got up, put his coat over his shoulders. Now he tiptoed across the plank floor, opened the door carefully, and stepped outside. He turned to the shaft of the mine. Gathering his coat about him, Rogier knelt on the shaft collar. Before and above him, looking down with passionate serenity, stared the enigmatic face of the Peak. Ever and always since his first glimpse of it from far down on the Fontaine-qui-Bouille, its white seamed face had drawn him step by step without compassion, merciless and compelling, to this insignificant aperture into its unsounded depths. All his vain conjectures, the deceptive glitter of success, and his countless failures he saw now as milestones of a monstrous folly which could have no end but this. He bent his head, leaned over to stare into the velvety blackness of the open shaft. A single movement and to the secret of that mighty Peak he would consign himself forever.

Crack! Crack! The blows keep sounding in his head. At that moment the last blow came, shattering his skull and driving into his brain. There was a terrific explosion of sound and light, of a golden radiance, into which both he and the Peak dissolved with a final shriek torn from his bowels. He felt Abe's brawny arms gathering him to his breast like a woman with a child. "I know, Colonel. I know."

* * *

Just what had happened to him, none of the family in Colorado Springs could quite understand from Abe and Jake's confused account. He hadn't fallen down the shaft or been crushed by a rock; nor had he suffered a stroke of paralysis. The doctor murmured indecisively something about a seizure, epilepsy, a mental breakdown. Abe and Jake, of course, had to leave. Mrs. Rogier gave them the mine: "The mine will never be worked again. If there is anything you can sell, do it before you leave. The cable, the reel, the hoist engine, somebody may want. The old boiler we'll have to let rust away. But there's some boxes of powder and hand-drills and all that stuff."

Meanwhile, Rogier slowly pulled out of it. The family had to keep the old man out in the backyard where he could get some fresh air, so they suggested that he use some spare material and build a little greenhouse. This he did, going out every day to work in it. The peculiar thing about this greenhouse was it had glass sides on three sides but on the fourth it was flanked with a windowless plank room like a toolhouse. In here Rogier would close the door after him, lock it with a padlock. He worked out the great plan to burrow into the Peak. Up in Cripple Creek at the Sylvanite mine, he had begun work at an elevation of eleven thousand feet. But here in Little London, in Colorado Springs, he was at an elevation of only six thousand feet, a mile below the collar of the Sylvanite. What a head start! He had only to dig a lateral tunnel to the base of the Peak to achieve his objective.

Oh, there were difficulties, of course, because the base of the Peak was six miles away, a long distance for one man to dig. Also, he would have to bore underneath the downtown district with water mains, sewage pipes, and underground conduits to avoid. And last, he must preserve utmost secrecy. So to this great new project he devoted himself. As he dug his tunnel, another problem came up. The declination of the tunnel of a degree or two would bring his tunnel under Ute Pass, or a few degrees to the south under Cheyenne Mountain. So he'd have to hit it square. To achieve this accuracy of aim, he mounted on a board an old mariner's compass bought at a pawnshop. Taking a reading on this as he would sight the Peak from outside, he'd carry it inside. Also he had to know whether he was driving at a level instead of inclining or declining his tunnel, so he strung a plumbline and he'd take a reading on it with a carpenter's level. Now he got really into it. He walked in and resumed digging. His pick was dull. He seemed short-winded; his legs trembled. He was getting old. But there was no time to rest.

Suddenly the earth caved in. He retreated, but only to confront another avalanche. A serious miscalculation, no doubt. Then a rush of falling dirt blew out his candle. A clump of dirt dropping on his head knocked out his wind. Staggering forward, he dropped into a pool of water. Cussing, he clawed his way up, dislodging another ton of black dirt.

Simultaneously the alarm clock in his head went off. In explosive darkness he lurched forward, grabbed at a support, and fell backward. A few faintly colored, fish-shaped petals began to whirl around before his eyes, trying to arrange themselves in a pattern he had never seen but which he seemed to know would be that of a great golden flower. He did not see it take shape. There was a tremendous crash as the timbers came down, followed by the shattering of glass. Then he was flooded with darkness and silence.

* * *

Rogier was brought home from the hospital. Coincident with his seizure he had suffered a serious blow on the head and a deep cut over his left eye, whose scar gave him a sly and sinister look, and a rupture which necessitated his wearing a tin truss—injuries enough to have killed a dray horse. But it was miraculous that he had pulled through. He limped around the yard. His powerful body had shrunk to a bag of sticks draped in a coat and pants that hung on him in folds. He looked like a scarecrow. He had lost most of his teeth and lived on mush, French toast, and sweet potatoes. Rogier did not mind that he looked like a scarecrow, his injuries, nor the ridicule of the neighbors. For after a lifetime of work and worry, success and abysmal failure, he had discovered at last the greatest treasure a man can find.

Sitting in the afternoon sun he stared at the Peak. Like something risen from the depths of dreamless sleep to the horizon of wakeful consciousness, without clear outline yet embodying the substance of a hope and meaning as strangely familiar as it was vague—thus had he first glimpsed it years before, believing it was that high snowy Peak which had drawn and held him like a lodestone he could not escape. Into its granite depths he had drilled and blasted toward its glowing heart, the luminescent sun, the golden flower of life. But now he stared at it without seeming to see it. It was where it had always been—inside him; a symbol of his own secret inner self. After a lifetime of search and failure, old, broken, and destitute, he finally had discovered the greatest treasure a man can find.

V

The Earp Brothers of Tombstone

Between 1934 and 1938, Waters wrote the first drafts of Tombstone Travesty, *finally published in 1960 as* The Earp Brothers of Tombstone. *While this work is significant as exposé, history, and biography, another value lies in the development of a theme to be fully expressed several years later in* The Colorado: *the failure of all of the conquering European-Americans to make a satisfactory adjustment to the land itself, to the spirit of the land.* The Earp Brothers of Tombstone *is not just an exposé of a band of itinerant card sharks, gunmen, saloon-keepers, and con men, but an indictment of a whole culture based on exploitation, materialism, and violence. Waters suggests convincingly that the psychic insecurities caused by the conquerors' inability to come to grips with the physical and psychical heartland of the new continent were projected outward in huge acts of destruction against the animals, the native peoples, and even the land itself.*

Against this background, Waters shows us, through the reminiscences of "Aunt Allie," Virgil Earp's widow, a true portrait of the Western Gunman. And, Waters suggests, it is our own unconscious understanding of such a man that has caused us to make him a cultural hero.

He tells the story of the book's genesis and final publication in his Introduction, aptly entitled "The Anatomy of a Western Legend."

This book is not only the recollections of Mrs. Virgil Earp and a narrative of the early settlement of Arizona. It is an exposé of the Tombstone travesty, laying bare under the scalpel of her merciless truth the anatomy of one of the legends contributing to the creation of a unique and wholly indigenous myth of the American West.

Who knows yet what this American Myth will be when it finally flowers? A myth vaguely outlined by mysterious snow-capped mountains rearing abruptly above barren, sun-struck deserts. Threaded by slow red rivers timelessly unwinding through illimitable space. Splotched with immeasurable herds of buffalo moving slowly and darkly as shadows of clouds in the sunshine. In its mystic unreality little ghost towns nameless in space and lost in time, figures and faces somber in flamelight, will take on a new reality. Tribal chiefs regal in paint and war bonnets, buffalo hunters in broad hats and buckskins, the Mountain Men, solitary prospectors, settlers in trains of covered wagons, the bad-men and those who brought them to dust—all these will assume a little of the operatic in the resplendent American myth of westward expansion that culminated in the Winning of the West within less than a single century.

But within the confines of this triumphant saga of conquest we are beginning to discern today the subjective and tragical history of a people who failed to comprehend the forces that drove them. Pioneers fleeing the comforts and lusts of civilization, fleeing home, companionship; a people still Puritans fleeing from themselves. That was the nemesis that pursued them. To get away, anywhere, under any conditions... only to confront suddenly the shattering forces of that great entity, psychical as well as physical, that was the heartland of a new continent.

The towering mountain ranges bulked up inside them. The mysterious rivers ran in their blood. The empty deserts ate into them. And finally loneliness engulfed them, more vacuous than the spaces between the stars above. And as the fear and tension kept mounting within them, they struck out at everything, the land and its people, with a blind compulsion to dominate and destroy.

The outward transference of their fear and pain was naturally directed against the only people indigenous to the land: the Indians who embodied all its invisible and inimical forces. So mile by mile, and year by year throughout America's Century of Dishonor, we watch the extermination of tribe after tribe, nearly a whole race. A cold and ruthless decimation sanctified by church and state that has few parallels in all history. "The only good Indian is a dead Indian." The motto of our conquest of good over evil. If this concept is today the basis for America's only true Morality Play—the Cowboy-and-Indian movie thriller, an indigenous art form as formal and fundamental to America as the symphony or ballet to Europe—it is also the basis of our tragic national psychosis, a fixation against all dark-skinned races, beginning with the Red, which was killed off, and carrying through to the Black, which was enslaved, the Brown legally discriminated against, and the Yellow excluded by legislation.

With the Indian was exterminated that other species of living creatures uniquely indigenous to the land—the buffalo. Not solely for food or hides, nor sport or profit. But an insane wanton slaughter estimated to have amounted to 31,000,000 animals and left a single pile of bones twelve feet high and a mile and a half long. It is not surprising that out of this orgy of mad killing there rises today one of the notable characters in the great American Myth. A largely fictitious character conceived by a theatrical entrepreneur in New York, and played by a talented exhibitionist whose biography was rewritten by a press agent expressly to fit his role—the illustrious Buffalo Bill.

The Indian and the buffalo: the two prime symbols of the American Myth, engraven for a time on the opposite faces of the buffalo nickel, which has itself vanished in the march of progress.

There were beaver and gold too in the most remote fastnesses. But the bales of beaver and the fabulous lucky strikes the solitary trappers and prospectors sold for a song or squandered as quickly as possible so they could hit the lonely trails again. For to these lonely and solitary outcasts beaver and gold were empty symbols too. They were not searching for riches and ease. They too were driven by the same nemesis on an endless quest that had no name or goal.

And behind them all, with ever-increasing violence and momentum, rolled the juggernaut of conquest. Leveling forests, uprooting plain and prairie, gutting mountains. Creating a materialistic ideology utterly opposed to the indigenously American and original Indian concept that all matter has a spiritual essence as well as a material composition; that even a mountain has a spirit form as well as a physical shape.

To what end? To prove the ever-transient victory of the flesh over the spirit? It is inevitable that the great American Myth, when it does flower, must contain both the historical fact and the psychological.

What in it, we may now ask, is the role of the Western bad-man?

* * *

The Two-Gun, the Six-Gun Man, the Killer, the Outlaw, the Bad-Man, as he is variously called, has beat us to the draw all right, all right. There he stands, frozen in a stiff crouch; hands open and dangling loosely before him; his cool gray eyes narrowed to slits in his handsome, somber face. The immemorial portrait constantly painted by pulps, slicks and paperbacks, one-reel Westerns, super-colossals, and the TV.

Just who was he? The young New York Bowery tough now glorified as Billy the Kid was one. Some were gamblers, cattle rustlers, and holdup men. Others were merely down-at-the-heels ranchers, cowpokes, barflies, and young adventurers who loved liquor and noise on Saturday night. But when it happened, the one was set distinctly apart. A few drinks in a crowded saloon, a quarrel, a drawn gun; thereafter he was a marked man. Hiding in the hills, he rode into town knowing that he would last just so long as he could live up to his sudden reputation for being quick on the draw.

Everything about him betrayed his fear and inferiority. Without real strength, he had no gentleness. Lacking all but the physical courage of desperation, he gave no odds and shot on sight. Even his face grew into an unemotional mask to match his taciturnity. Appearance and action, both added up to the fear of his fellowmen. The fear of the immeasurable, inimical landscape dwarfing him to an infinitesimal speck, and its haunting timelessness, which overemphasized the brief and dangerous span of his own life. And the fear of his own fears. A man forever self-conscious, tense and inhibited, he epitomizes more than any other the compulsions of his time and place.

Of all the characters in the American Myth he is the most to be pitied, for he suffered most. We understand this suffering. It is what makes him our favorite hero. So of course we sanctified his role. A few realistic citizens prevailed upon him to become sheriff, or his town confederates managed to secure for him an appointment as a deputy marshal. The now confirmed gunman was free to shoot his enemies without taking chances and without having to run for it afterward. With a tin star he might wear the halo of righteousness instead of a hangman's noose. An American happy ending that sanctified a career of senseless murder.

The legend of Wyatt and the "Fighting Earps" of Tombstone conforms in every essential to this prototypal pattern. It is not enough to read in Walter Noble Burns's childishly melodramatic *Tombstone* that they were Knights of the Golden West appointed by manifest destiny to sweep the forces of evil from Arizona with their six-shooters. Nor to learn from a legitimate history like Paul I. Wellman's *Glory, God and Gold* that they were indeed peace officers who saved Tombstone from a malign horde of desperados. We have only to refer to Stuart N. Lake's allegedly authentic biography, *Wyatt Earp, Frontier Marshal*, long considered the authority, to recognize in Wyatt Earp the greatest frontiersman of the entire American West. Out of this veritable Wild West textbook have been built dozens of other books, pulp-paper yarns, movie thrillers galore, radio serials, a national TV series, Wyatt Earp hats, vests, toy pistols, tin badges—a fictitious legend of preposterous proportions. It is the cream of the jest that in Tombstone itself is now re-enacted yearly the unjustified three-man murder outside the O.K. Corral on which the Earps' claim to fame largely rests today.

It is pertinent—if not impertinent—to ask before they are memorialized by Congress and canonized by the Church, just who were these men, what was the manner of their lives, and what did they leave to posterity?

Jim was a saloonkeeper and professional gambler. He entered Tombstone quietly, lived obscurely, and left Tombstone to vanish into oblivion.

Warren was a youth in his twenties when in Tombstone. He later became a stage driver, and was shot and killed during a drunken quarrel in a saloon.

Morgan was a laborer, professional gambler, and gunman. He was killed in a Tombstone saloon by a shot in the back while playing pool.

Virgil was a wandering stage driver, ranch hand, prospector, and town marshal. In Tombstone he was ambushed at night outside a saloon, shot and maimed. Throughout the rest of his life he roamed the West, prospecting vainly for gold, and died unknown.

Wyatt was an itinerant saloonkeeper, cardsharp, gunman, bigamist, church deacon, policeman, bunco artist, and a supreme confidence man. A lifelong exhibitionist ridiculed alike by members of his own family, neighbors, contemporaries, and the public press, he lived his last years in poverty, still vainly trying to find someone to publicize his life, and died two years before his fictitious biography recast him in the role of America's most famous frontier marshal.

Yet out of their aimless, awry, and tragic lives emerges a deeper truth. They were human. They were loved by women to whom they were faithful or whom they betrayed, each according to his nature. With the limited visions of uneducated and uninspired men, they still sought at a rainbow's end their heart's desire—a simple little ranch, a steady job, a measure of fame and fortune. They killed and were killed for it. They were men of their time, and all they were and did is a measure of the forces that made them. It is this deeper truth, rather than the fictitious legend grown up around them, that belongs eventually to the great American Myth. A truth that could have been told only by one who knew and loved them best, the subject-author of this book.

I first met her twenty-five years ago, sitting on my mother's sofa in Los Angeles. A wizened little old lady, some eighty years old and eighty pounds little, with a nut-brown face, sharp blue eyes, and white hair cut short and combed straight like a schoolboy's. Each afternoon she made the round of the neighborhood in gray gingham, white stockings and high button shoes, accompanied by her dog Twinkle and carrying little bunches of artificial flowers for sale. We learned that she lived with relations nearby and that she was familiarly known as "Aunt Allie."

It didn't take long to discover that Aunt Allie was a character. At any provocation she would draw from the hip and fire a tall tale in a Western vernacular that was all Americana and a yard wide. She was hard and sentimental, with old-fashioned customs but startlingly original in thought, and always jovial. This jutting humor marked all her tales. In it was the eternal freshness and unvarying zest for life of those who in turmoil and tragedy remained young in a time when their world too was young.

I finally agreed to write down her "true life story"; she desperately needed the few dollars it might bring. We began. A little short-breathed, quick to tire, she invariably ended the afternoon hour with, "Now boy, you put some Fleischmann's Yeast in this and raise it up. You're just gettin' the facts now."

They were astounding. I discovered that Aunt Allie was the widow of Virgil Earp and that she was giving me an authentic biography of the famous "Fighting Earps" of Tombstone. It differed completely from that given by Stuart N. Lake in his *Wyatt Earp, Frontier Marshal*, which annoyed her to no end. "A pack and passel of lies! It's just that Josephine Sarah Marcus, Wyatt's third wife, what put him up to all that gingerbread. Now this is how it really happened..."

In order to substantiate her account with adequate historical research, I went to Arizona. When I came back, I learned that Mrs. Josephine Sarah Marcus Earp had called on my mother and sister, threatening to bring court action against me if I published Aunt Allie's story, which had grown to book length. I then confronted Aunt Allie with the demand that she explain why Wyatt's third wife, whom he had married after he had been run out of Arizona, should be so strangely fearful about the book's possible appearance; almost as if she had heard the rattling of a skeleton in the closet.

Aunt Allie refused point-blank. "I know all about that Marcus woman and I won't tell! It'll besmirk the good name of Wyatt's second wife, Mattie, the one who went to Tombstone with us. We went through thick and thin together, me and Mattie did! And I know about Wyatt's fancy doin's and talkin's too. But I ain't goin' to have that black shadow fallin' over my Virge's grave neither! I won't tell! Not till hell freezes over and the ice'll have to be pretty durn thick then!"

Her refusal endeared her to us forever. It was a baling-wire testimonial to the magnificent loyalty and integrity that built Arizona and the whole West, and that today refutes Wyatt Earp's grandiloquent boasts.

What did a family skeleton and a few obscure points matter? They were already clearly indicated in the book. Despite the threatened suit, I sent out the book but no one was then interested in the lurid happenings of more than fifty years ago. A few years later both Mrs. Josephine Sarah Marcus Earp and Aunt Allie died, and I presented the manuscript to the Arizona Pioneers' Historical Society in Tucson merely as a valuable record for its files.

However, in my book *The Colorado* I summarized these facts in a subchapter on "Outlaws." Shortly thereafter I was confronted by another possible lawsuit, this time by Stuart N. Lake, author of *Wyatt Earp, Frontier Marshal*, threatening legal action in the California civil court against the publishers of *The Colorado*, its editors, and myself if public retraction were not made.

This I refused on the grounds that Aunt Allie's dictated narrative was substantiated by my own documented research based upon public records, and that the Arizona Pioneers' Historical Society concurred in the manuscript's views as against Lake's. I also pointed out that while most of Lake's book consisted of allegedly verbatim quotations from Wyatt, Lake in his letter to my publishers affirmed that Wyatt never dictated a word to him, never saw a word of his writing, and died two years before the book was published. Lake thus denied the purported authenticity of his own book and admitted sole responsibility for its wholly romantic, untrue, and fictitious contents. One of Lake's attorneys then went to the Arizona Pioneers' Historical Society in Tucson, consulted my manuscript, and promptly dropped the threatened suit.

I was still content to let the subject stand as an old controversy immured in historical records, but it became a bear's tail no one could let go. "Posses" of "The Westerners" in a dozen cities began to debate the issue. Letters applauding and condemning my remarks poured in. More and more books and movies on Tombstone and the Earps came out. Even a ship plowing through antarctic ice to the Bay of Whales was christened the *Wyatt Earp*. All this was followed by radio programs; the current national TV series on Wyatt Earp; the appearance of a Virgil W. Earp on the recent TV $64,000 Question show; the renaming of a street in Dodge City after Wyatt Earp; and the rejuvenation of Tombstone itself. Within another few years, then, this eighty-year-old Tombstone travesty had become again, not only Arizona's biggest story, but a phenomenon of national interest. Daniel Boone, Kit Carson, even the Davy Crockett craze were old hat. Their roles in the American Myth had been superseded by the preposterous new legend of Wyatt Earp.

Yet something about his unbelievable heroism and psychopathic exhibitionism has aroused an almost equally fanatic resentment against him. For eighty years his neighbors, contemporaries, and the public press, writers, researchers, and historians have increasingly succumbed to the compulsion to search out the truth about him. Requests for my own book manuscript at the Arizona Pioneers' Historical Society became so numerous that the secretary removed it from the open files for safekeeping, and suggested to me that it finally be published.

So at last, twenty-five years after it was written, this book has itself become a chapter in the history of the fabulous legend it reveals. More hidden records and suppressed information have come to light. The family skeleton has finally walked out of the closet. Now is the time to let Aunt Allie have her say. Hers is a small voice, but a true one. She speaks against the current fiction, but for the great American Myth, which will be a composite of all such legends, containing not only the historical fact but the psychological, which is assuredly manifested in our almost psychopathic interest today in a fiction that has no parallel in Western history. It will be a healthy sign if we can heed her.

VI

People of the Valley

Soon after completing the third volume of the mining trilogy, Waters began People of the Valley, in which he achieved for the first time a story of a character in total harmony with her environment. It is the story of a woman whose inner growth and closeness to her land elevate her above her people and, more significantly, continuously above her own past selves.

People of the Valley *is the story of Maria, who lives for over ninety years in New Mexico's isolated Mora Valley. She is the orphaned daughter of an Indian mother and a presumably Spanish-American "stranger"; she has been raised by two old goatherds, who are themselves drowned in a flood when she is still a child. Maria grows up wild and free, surviving by instinct and her wits. She bears a succession of children to a succession of men, raising them with the same survivalist techniques. She is simply a natural product of the land. Her reputation as a* curandera *and seer grows; the people consult her for both her knowledge of folk medicine and her mystical insights. Near the end of her life, the people are faced with the erection of a flood-control dam, which will require them to give up their land. They come to Maria.*

At first she opposes the dam: "This is the meaning of any dam, that it would obstruct the free flow of faith which renews and refreshes life and gives it its only meaning."[8] *But she grows to realize that ages, like all life—people, plants, animals, and mountains—grow, mature, then give way to new life. She sees that to oppose the dam would be equivalent to building one—to obstruct the inevitable flow. She is able to say,*

No man can belong to a time until it has also a faith he can belong to. That is what people do not like about this dam. It has no faith behind it to

40

give it meaning. And so you must accept your own time which has a faith until the new time also gives rise to a faith, and you are ready for it.[9]

She finds a temporary solution by securing for her people new land in a higher, more remote valley. The story is thus one of the corrupting advance of Anglo technology and also of Maria's spiritual growth.

In this work we see some of Waters' most serious and mature thought. It is significant that this book was originally entitled The Dam. *John Farrar (Farrar and Rinehart) firmly rejected the title, perhaps seeing that Waters had achieved here more than he had attempted; for the story does rise above the portrait of Maria and the somewhat abstract concept of dams to become a revelation both of the plight of people everywhere when one age begins to supersede another and also of all peoples' need for a maturation of consciousness. We are told "Maria believed in fulfillment instead of progress" and that "fulfillment is individual evolution."[10] And we come to understand that Maria saves her people not so much by securing them land (as important as that is) as by securing them time—time to learn to live in the inevitable new age. More importantly, we understand that their salvation is the result of Maria's own personal growth, her evolution of consciousness. We see here the first appearance of a major theme that comes to full fruition many years later in* Mexico Mystique, *the concept of the evolution of human consciousness and the need for that evolution within each individual.[11] Maria herself accomplishes that evolution and illustrates both the necessity and the possibility of such growth in all people.*

In the following two selections, we see Maria, first, as the self-reliant young mother of Teodosio and Nina on a stormy day in early spring. In the second selection, she is nearing the end of her long life.

Like buffalo, the black-humped clouds stampeded over the ramparts of the valley. The thunder of their hoofs shook the sky-plain. From their locking horns leapt zigzags of fire.

Suddenly rain fell. Great warm drops hissed on the dry, dusty earth. Then slanting silver threads unraveled abruptly the whole texture of the shower. Within two hours the storm was spent.

A rainbow brilliantly colored as a Chihuahua serape hung over the shoulder of the sky. Pines and piñons glistened with water. The sharp smell of sage cut with a whetted edge. The black plowed fields began to steam. The whole earth seemed quickened, in heat, and straining at invisible bonds.

Maria with arms crossed stood at her window. She was holding her full and strangely aching breasts. Maturity had filled the hollows of her face. The sun, coming out again, enlivened the dull red underneath her brown cheeks. Her black eyes were no longer dead and empty; they were alive and restless. Her firm body had reached the softness of a ripe peach that waits to be plucked, to rot with decay or wither.

The devil take it! She whirled around and put on her shoes. She grabbed down her rebozo and hurried out of the house. Three o'clock in the afternoon. Quitting her work, her house, and going to town for no reason whatever. Mother of God! What gets into a woman?

What comes over the whole earth at times like this? Maria stopped and plunged her hands into the black steaming loam, crumpled the wet clods under her nose. In the pasture beyond, a roan stallion raced blindly and alone, tearing up the turf. The crows applauded insanely.

At the edge of town Maria stopped in the road. A bedraggled gray hen squawked past her and cowered against the fence. After her flapped a rusty rooster. He flew at her, screaming, drove her out of the weeds with beak and spurs. Before she could break away, he leapt upon her.

Maria stood watching. The gray hen squatted in a puddle without struggling, her wings half outspread, her head bent meekly forward. On her, his talons dug in her wet feathers, titillated the rusty rooster with his powerful, rocking tread. In a moment he stepped off daintily, shaking his feathers. He glared around haughtily, but with the fierceness gone out of him, and stalked away.

The little gray hen remained the victor. She chuckled over his betrayal, smoothing her ruffled wings and lifting her langorous yellow claws, one at a time, to shake free of mud. She looked smug and self-sufficient, as if the road had encircled the world to meet in her plump, bedraggled ball of feathers.

Maria went hot with anger. She stooped and threw handfuls of mud at the hen who only walked away disdainfully. "Cochina! Pig! Sorda hija de tal!" The hen threw a look and a cackle back over her shoulder, and ducked through the hedge. Maria, still steaming, walked angrily into town.

At Pierre Fortier's she banged back the door and stalked inside. Pierre left the men grouped at the stove and clumped to her on his wooden leg. "Ah, it is Maria! Whom I have not seen for these many weeks. You are well? And the children? And doubtless needing new supplies. . . . What a shower! I feel spring in my bones. It makes me hungry for life and meat. Fresh meat. Look! Behind, there in the corral, they are butchering. I have bought two steers. Look. A bit of fresh meat to take home for a change. Fresh beef from the mountaintop pastures. Maria—"

Maria spit on the floor. "Beef! Santísima! You are talking to a poor old woman? An old woman who praises God when she can season the pot with a piece of goat flesh? Pagh! You and your talk!" She glared at the men crowding the stove. "Well, come and talk here at your desk, over your papers, about how much I owe you. Why you have cheated me, on paper, thinking my memory weak. Talk! Sí! It will take much talk."

It was as good as anything to vent the nervous excitement that had filled her veins—this long harangue over salt, sugar, thread, lime. Pierre, with spectacles on, sat his stool quarreling. Maria squinted at the flyspecked paper as if she could read. Neither was angry, neither misjudged the accuracy and shrewdness of the other.

At the end Pierre Fortier slapped his leg. "What a magnificent memory! The like I have never seen!"

"So that is what I owe?" mumbled Maria. "Well, it is good for both of us to know that when I have the money I shall pay. Certainly. But not now. Does silver grow on trees?"

Pierre reached behind him and took down a red cotton kerchief—the most faded and fly-specked of the dozen that hung on a rope. This he flung around Maria's neck and knotted. "A present. For my best customer. This most beautiful of all my fine scarfs. Madre! It makes you look like a girl! What beautiful red cheeks!"

Maria stamped her foot. "Fool! You think to shame me before all these men?" But she stole a look into a mirror, and swiftly reckoned the amount he would somewhere squeeze into her bill.

"Now. That fresh beef," Pierre reminded. "You will walk by the corral? You will see the fresh, firm red meat? Then you will return tomorrow for the piece I shall save?"

"I shall walk by," promised Maria at the door. "But no more. Am I a wealthy woman that I can eat beef like the rich and yet keep my friend waiting for his money?"

Pierre sighed. "It shall go on the paper. Do I not know my people?"

It was as he had said: in the corral just off the plaza the men had waited to slaughter until the shower was over. Maria leaned over the fence.

Two steers had already been killed. Dripping blood, they were hung up to be skinned. Two others waited their turn in a small corner enclosure. Their hoarse, frantic bellowing, the stark fear in their rolling eyes, roused no pity in Maria.

The puddles in the corral seemed to reflect the sun lowering on the

Sangre de Cristo. The mud itself was red and slimy. It seemed to give off a heat that crawled under her clothes. It smelled. The smell was aphrodisiacal. Maria's black eyes glittered. She loosed the red kerchief about her throat, and panted quick pale breaths into the cold afternoon. Crowding close against the fence, she kept rubbing her breasts back and forth over the top aspen rail.

Two men had come out of the log enclosure. One was a bearded old man in a leather coat who carried an axe. The other was a tall lean man naked to the waist, and carrying a long knife. His strong smooth back revealed long ropey muscles writhing under the skin. Maria sucked in her breath and shuddered as the hard tips of her breasts drew back over the rough bark. Then she pressed forward again upon the fence, the pink end of her tongue showing between her lips.

The bearded old man threw open the gate, stepped back and lifted his axe. As the frightened steer came out plunging, he swung once, twice. The blunt end of the axe thudded on the steer's forehead. He dropped to his knees.

Before he could roll over, the tall lean man stepped forward and drove up from his thigh the naked blade. He gave it a twist. From the steer's throat gushed a warm flow. It covered his knife, hand and wrist as he stepped back.

"Santána! What a steer!" he laughed, turning around and shaking his arm. "As full of juice as a ripe peach!"

Through a film of dizziness Maria could see the cold pink peaks, the corral filling with blood and its hot sweetish smell. She could see the man's chest now, hairless and sharply outlined as if carved out of wood, his flat muscular belly, the strong sharp lines of his jaw and cheekbones. He was laughing. His teeth gleamed white, like a wolf's.

Then, just as he turned around, he saw her. His look was dark and quick, sharp as a knife. It cut through the film over her eyes which dropped away like a curtain. It twisted; she opened to receive it, and something deep inside her gushed forth to meet his knifelike gaze.

A moment did it. Maria straightened, adjusted her new red kerchief, and moved a few paces along the fence. The man had stopped laughing. He was tense, impatient.

"Carajo!" he called to his companion as the steer was dragged away. "Why do you wait? The sun sinks. Let us have the other." But he kept glancing obliquely at Maria sauntering along the fence.

The last steer plunged out to meet axe and knife, to roll over sideways in blood and mud. The man stepped aside, drawing the blade between his bloody fingers. Maria had reached the end of the corral fence, and was walking demurely into the road.

"There!" he called loudly. "It is the last. I have bargained for no more. There is just time to return to the mountains before dark." He walked to a hollowed log trough and began to wash.

"But compadre," complained his bearded companion, "how is it you do not wait? A good drink to finish a nasty job. Has it not always been so?"

"Carajo!" sputtered the answer through the cold rain water. "Am I a butcher, a meat carver, a shopkeeper? From the hills I delivered my beef. I killed them as was agreed. I go. Adiós. Adiós, compadre." He threw on shirt and jacket, saddled and rode out of the corral.

Maria was not a kilómetro up the road when he drew rein beside her.

"Cómo está, Señora?" he spoke in a voice soft as the dusk.

"Bien. Y usted?" she answered quietly.

But again the sharp dark look passed between them.

They walked along without speaking, Maria trudging along the side of the road, and the man jogging slowly beside her on his horse. He had put on his hat, and rode head down. His boot and trouser leg was stained with blood. The horse smelled it, threw up his head and twisted from side to side. The leather squeaked. The bit jangled faintly.

When the tall cliffs jutted out, Maria turned aside without speaking. The man followed her up the lane on his mount. They stopped before the house.

"It is where I live," Maria said simply.

"You are the woman with the strange power," he answered in a deep, quiet voice. "Perhaps to this one you will bring luck?" And he stared down quietly from his saddle.

"Quien sabe?" she smiled. "Come."

He dismounted and followed her into the long back room. The dusk was thicker inside the hut. He could hardly see the rows of pale skulls, but the smell of drying herbs wrapped around him. He rolled a cigarette with fingers that trembled a little in the light of the narrow window. Then he sat down before her on a stack of sheepskins.

His breath was coming quicker now. His shirt front was open at the collar, and at each breath his smooth powerful chest swelled toward her.

Maria reached out and took his hands. She turned them palm up, squinting at the few lines etched into the firm calloused flesh. Their heads lowered, almost touched. Their breaths made one heat. Now Maria laid his hands in her lap. Her finger tips began to trace the lines up his corded wrist. From the touch little zigzags of fire leapt up his arms. Others leapt up her legs as he rubbed the backs of his hands over her knees. The room was darkening as with a storm. Its clouds flushed the cheeks of their bent heads. Abruptly he grabbed her by the wrists.

Maria stiffened, raised her head. From outside came the sound of wagon wheels and voices. The man drew back, wary, remote. Maria rose. She laid her hand on his warm throat, pulled his ear, then stalked to the door. Teodosio with Niña had just driven up in the buggy.

Shrieked Maria, "Sick pig of a litter! And you, lazy one! Can you not see there is one here to consult me? Are you blind to his horse tied there, that you would interrupt? Go! Stay as you have stayed away all this day. Go to the tienda and there obtain the bit of fresh meat Pierre is saving me. Ungrateful children! Shameless ones! Go!"

When the wagon turned down the lane into the dark, Maria closed and latched the kitchen door. Then she walked swiftly into the long back room, taking off her new red kerchief.

Thus it was. A quick look from a man's eyes, the chance touch of a hand in the plaza, a meeting in the dark. They came unbidden, unlooked for, but with the imperative gestures of destiny to punctuate the monotone of Maria's life.

* * *

Maria tottered toward ninety.

She resembled an ancient Santo on one of Pierre Fortier's shelves except that her robes were threadbare and tattered black cotton instead of dusty motheaten silk. Under them her body had shrunk like seasoned wood. It was knotted and cramped from rheumatism. Her flesh was a dark, lifeless brown that had long lost its gelatinous sizing of boiled cow's horns and gypsum yeso, its paint of oxide and ochre mixed with egg yolk, its sheen of polished mutton tallow. Her white hair was thin and brittle as straw. Bent over, when erect, she posed a question mark supported by a cedar stick.

The fingers which clutched it were the prehensile talons of a hawk. But in her face still lived all the sorrow and fecundity, the passion and wild violence of the span of life measured by that human receptacle recognized by men as Doña Maria of the Valley. Its powerful and primitive features faceted them all. Her promontory beak of nose, high cheekbones and solid, cleft jaw jutted out from her dark wormwood face a savage, sad visage battered by time but still inviolable, a look that only an old Indian can encompass.

Her eyes refuted it all. They had gone dead. Their bright blackness was dulling to a smoky gray which only a brief flicker of the spirit behind could light up like milky opals. Perhaps they had been in-turned too long and deeply to focus readily on the surface life outside.

So when walking she began to poke ahead with her stick. It was a habit few observed. She received visitors while seated in front of her fire.

Maria, then, gave to all simply the aspect of a citadel beleaguered but still impregnable. She so regarded herself.

Yet, because the families of Gertrudes, Niña and Antonio anticipated her weakening blows with an axe, she was persuaded to accept the companionship of a granddaughter.

"This Piedad of ours and yours," they lied, "is a good girl but a little wild through ignorance. She needs counseling. We wish you to take her, Doña Maria."

"I will accept her for the winter. To instruct her," Maria lied in turn.

Piedad's exercise book was a jag of frosty piñon and a rusty axe, her schoolmates a few shivering goatewes whose teats were torn by briars, her reward a bowl of porridge and a few leathery tortillas. She was small, sixteen, quick as a squirrel and more inquisitive. She was simpática. Maria liked her.

At night they crouched together before the fire. A white-bearded storm shook the hut and blew his frosty breath down the chimney. Piedad shivered, drew closer to Maria.

"Mi abuela, my grandmother Doña Maria," she asked, "why is it that children call that frightening boogie man whom none have ever seen 'El Abuelo'—a grandfather? Surely you frighten me not at all."

"My child," replied Maria. "To youth, age is incomprehensible. To ignorance, wisdom is frightening. So that El Abuelo having age represents the learning which the ignorant child fears. Now this is wrong. But even grownups have it. They possess learning and knowledge, and still fear the wisdom which they have not attained. We must all learn to be unafraid of the dark: the child of learning, the man of wisdom. Hence we shall all reach the true maturity which is eternal youth."

The fire writhed into a heap. Piedad threw on another stick. The flames uncoiled, rose up and shook like snakes. The resin rattled. The glare outlined pinkly the rows of goat and ram skulls on the rafters.

"Doña Maria," spoke the girl again, "it is said by all that by skulls and herbs you could read stars and weather, foretell good crops and misfortune, the future of man. Why is it you use them no more?"

Maria sighed. "Ay de mi, child! For many years I have ceased to read them. They were helpful in those days of my youth when like you I mistrusted the unseen trail ahead. It is true I had a knowledge of the signs and the events they portend. But not wisdom—the wisdom to perceive the future in each moment, in each stone and blade of grass. The past also.

"It is like this. A child looks at life as a wolf at the trail of his quarry. He has no sense of the past, only a hunger to devour the future. Thus, to pursue it with success, he soon stops and raises his head. He sniffs the wind. He observes the signs—even those on goat skulls. He listens to all the world around him.

"Now, you understand, he is at middle age. Having memory, he can see part of the trail behind him as well as the present he treads. But still the future winds unseen before him, up toward the cliff top shrouded in mist. He reaches it. Pues! That dreaded and hungered for future is no more than the present which resembles the past. They are all one. His fears were nought, his predictions useless.

"Entiende, muchacha? I will say it again for your simple ears.

"Life is a great white stone. You, a child, stare at it and see only one side. You walk slowly around it. You see other sides, each different in shape and pattern, rough or smooth. You are confused; you forget that it is the same great white stone. But finally you have walked around it, stared at all of it at once from the hillside above. Verdad! Then you see it: how it has many different sides and shapes and patterns, some smooth, some rough, but still the one great white stone: how all these sides merge into one another, indistinguishable: the past into the present, the present into the future, the future again into the past.

"Hola! They are all the same. With wisdom who knows one from the other? There is no time, which is but an illusion for imperfect eyes. There is only the complete, rounded moment, which contains all."

And Maria, with gray filmed eyes which saw more, clouded, than when they had been bright, reached blindly for her little sack of tobacco. "Ay de mi! Often I hear steps outside. I look up to see a man in the doorway. It might be Onesimo as he was called, a certain gringo soldado, Don Fulgencio himself, dead these many years. No! It would not surprise me if he were any of these. There are shapes of men less alive than shadows of men. So do even I confuse what has been and will be again with what is."

Thus in her wisdom she taught that winter the lessons which must be learned by each alone, and did not see the incomprehension in the girl's sleepy eyes.

But everyone else throughout the valley paid her homage with extravagant praise as they plowed and sowed their fields again.

"Well, well, primo. We will have our land, thanks to Doña Maria. In our ignorance we voted for a dam. Then, with the Señora's wise advice, we refused land for it. Now there will be no dam. Ah, how black this loam is. How it smells!"

Maria had reached the peak of their regard: they almost called her

Santa Maria. Yet she had no ears for their praise. She heard only the gaping silence behind it—the lull before a storm. And far off, the faint rustle of that paper which was to build the dam.

To the families of Gertrudes, Niña and Antonio she said, "This Piedad of ours. She has learned the old ways. Let her leave me now. To go down into the valley and observe the new ways. Thus will her faith be strengthened."

To Piedad, alone, she said, "You have helped me well here, child. You can help me more, away. So leave this hut. Go down to the village. It is said that a criada is needed in the old inn. I would that you do the work."

Piedad was shocked. "A servant in a public inn? To strangers and gringos? It is not our way. We have always remained on our land, for better or worse, having no other master. What will happen to my modesty, my dignity, my pride?"

"As you know," went on Maria quietly, "that old inn has been empty for years, save on court days. Now it is full of gringos who are no doubt talking about this dam. Make their beds, serve their food and wash their dishes as instructed. But keep your ears open: you understand their tongue. Here!" She passed the girl an old square gold piece. "Buy yourself a horse. An old one but well breathed. From one of Antonio's neighbors. Ride up here to me weekly with news of what you hear. Teodosio is sick again. Besides, it will save his old buggy from falling apart and breaking your neck. Sabe? Listen to all, tell only me."

And Maria again drew back into the loneliness of her mountainside. She never left it.

VII

The Man Who Killed the Deer

It is in The Man Who Killed the Deer, *written in the early 1940s, that Waters fully combines his two major themes of people–land relationship and resolution of conflicting dualities with his ability to handle historical detail. Maria, constantly in tune with her land, had few, if any, internal conflicts. But the central character of* Deer, *Martiniano, is a young Indian boy who has been forced to leave his pueblo to attend the government "away school." There he has been taught a trade, carpentry. He has also been taught White values and thought processes. He is returned to the pueblo, where he finds himself in constant trouble with the tribal leaders. At the pueblo and in the nearby town, there is little demand for his carpentry skills, and it becomes necessary for him to farm the land previously alloted by the Pueblo elders to his deceased father. Thus, while he is economically dependent upon the land and upon the Indian way of life, he is psychologically estranged from them both. Needing meat for himself and his wife, he shoots a deer. Because he has killed the deer out of season, he has broken the White Man's law; because he has failed to ask the deer's permission and to perform the requisite ritual after killing it, he has broken the Indians' law. As his troubles increase, Martiniano finds in the deer a kind of psychological scapegoat, onto which he can project all of his problems.*

Combined with this story of Martiniano's internal conflicts is the historically accurate but fictionalized account of the Taos Pueblo's attempt to secure the return of their sacred Blue Lake, which had been "confiscated" by the government. For over seven centuries, the Indians had been making pilgrimages to this lake, which they believe to be the point of origin of their people. Their right to the land had been confirmed in 1551 by King Charles of Spain; in 1687 by the Royal Council of the Indies; in 1821 by Mexico, upon gaining her independence from Spain; and in 1848 by the United States, after acquiring the New Mexico area. In 1906, a presidential proclamation had converted Blue Lake and the surrounding area into a National Forest.

The trial of Martiniano by the White authorities becomes the springboard for the tribe's renewed demands for settlement of their land claims. A more significant point of contact of the two stories lies in Martiniano's failure to understand the Indians' closeness to the land, their attunement to total environment. At the heart of his difficulties with the tribal elders is his sense of individuality, which the elders see as his insistence on the illusion of separateness.

Thus, Martiniano inadvertently becomes the mechanism for the eventual return of the sacred lake, and at the same time he learns to understand "the inseparableness and mutuality of all seemingly discrete matters."[12] The process of this growth is slow and painful. Yet the story is simply and beautifully told as Waters leads both his character and his reader to an understanding of Martiniano's complex problems and to an understanding of what is needed for their resolution. In this work Waters successfully combines a mystical approach with the historical accuracy of real people, real time, and real place.

The first of the following selections occurs shortly after Martiniano has killed the deer. A meeting of the Pueblo Council has been called to consider his action and its ramifications. In the second selection, we see Martiniano's ever-increasing conflicts beginning to affect his relationship with his wife, Flowers Playing, and Martiniano turning to his friend Palemon.

As evening dusk began to blur the two pale splotches on the highest house-tops, a third appeared. For minutes his deep, clear voice sang out sonorously to all below. It was like a summons, like a muezzin's call at twilight. Each man stopped to listen, then continued to his task.

Wood and water were brought. Horses were shut up in their corrals. Burros were herded into their communal log inclosure. The people shut themselves up in the pueblo like a race self-entombed in a pyramid.

Strips of ribs were cut from carcasses hanging from the rafters, cooked and eaten with chile and tortillas. Cheap fresh coffee was added to the morning's grounds, boiled and drunk. Corn-husk cigarettes were rolled and puffed. And now in warm, smoky households, the people sat resting in flamelight.

Children rolled up in serapes and blankets, stretching out along the seating ledges. Women prepared beds and floor mats. But the old men still sat nodding before the coals.

Who knew what o'clock it was? There were no battered clocks, no dollar Ingersolls that kept time. The people likely couldn't read them anyway. They had no sense of time, these people. To them time was no moving flow to be measured, ticked out and struck at funny intervals. Time was all one, ever-present and indestructible. It was they who moved through it. There was only the consciousness of the moment for right action. No one knew how it came. But when it came they obeyed.

So suddenly, all at once, doors began to open. And the old men; drawing their blankets closer over head and shoulders, stepped out into the dark. They walked in their aloneness, slow and silent, across the two squared timbers over the stream. Toward the end of the pueblo where a door stayed open. A trickle of light flowed out upon two men, swathed in blankets, standing against the wall. They would stand here in cold and darkness all night on guard.

A meeting of the Council had been called.

The old men walked in slowly and sat down silently on the ledge running around three walls. Palemon wore a new red blanket and a proud, dark face. Martiniano a white bandage around his head, and a sallow face. Being young men, not members of the Council, they seated themselves close to the door. Beside two, younger still, already there.

It was a big room. Scattered on the plank floor were little wooden boxes filled with clean sand. The whitewashed walls were clean and bare except for the silver-headed canes of authority of the Governor and the Lieutenant-Governor hanging below a picture of Abraham Lincoln, their donor. The vigas supporting the roof gleamed dark yellow as honey. A man dipped into the flame a branch of cedar. As it burned in his hand he walked about the room so that its sharp, clean odor filled the air.

In the middle of the room sat a deal table holding one candle stuck in a shiny black stick of Santa Clara ware. The only two chairs in the room were drawn up before it. In one sat an intelligent-looking, middle-aged man in "American" clothes save that the heels of his shoes had been removed and a blanket was wrapped round his middle. He would probably not open his mouth all evening, for while most of those present spoke Spanish and understood English, they would speak tonight only in their own tongue. But this was his usual post.

The occupant of the other chair drew it back closer to the fire. He was a seamed crag that still jutted out, unbroken, into the waves of life. There was snow in his straggly hair, moss on his face. His eyes were like those of a sun-hawk, of a mystic, of an old, old man who really couldn't focus very well on near objects. They were the most compelling things in the room. For while those of the Governor who sat behind him saw through all the passions of weather and men to the calm heart of all storms, these eyes saw farther. They saw the stormy soul of creation within the calm. They were the eyes that watched the sunsets from the highest house-top to make solar observations as the sun left its house mountain between the two peaks on the western horizon, that determined for his people the solstices and the times for ceremonial dances. He was the Cacique, holding hereditary office for life.

On the ledge behind him, on each side of the Governor, sat the Lieutenant-Governor, the War Captain, the Fiscal, and their assistants, and all the Kiva Chiefs. And about them sat the old men with faces sharp as hawks', and old and wrinkled as cedar bark, with blankets drawn up around their shoulders. Nearly forty men, all old, but of whom it was more respectfully said, "Councillors sing, they do not dance."

The door was closed. And still they sat unspeaking, hunching blankets closer. It was a terrible tension, the deathless silence, the dim light, the dark somber faces now shrouded so that only the eyes stared out black and bright as beads. It was as if they had gathered to read from symbols those meanings which were themselves symbols of a life whose substance they felt but could not see, whose edges they touched, like the shape of a door, but could not open.

The Governor broke it. He grinned a little toothlessly, and picked up a brown paper bag from the floor to slide across the table. The interpreter walked with it around the room, pausing before each man. In it was a roll of huge black tobacco leaves folded when damp and now dry and hard. Punche from the mountains of Mexico. Strong as the kick of a horse. A gift from the strange white man, Rodolfo Byers, their favorite trader for over thirty years. So each man chuckled and made a little joke as he broke off a pinch, crushed it between calloused palms, and rolled a cigarette. They sat and smoked and spit into the little wooden boxes filled with sand on the floor before them.

Now the silence, impregnated with smoke, seemed thicker, heavier. And the tension held again. As each man threw away his stub, he leaned back against the wall and drew the blanket up around his head. They might all have been settling for a sleep. Then suddenly the talk. Slow, measured, polite and wary. The Governor began it.

"Martiniano here, and these two boys. They have got themselves into trouble. They have caused trouble in the air. There will be more. There is much to consider. Is not this true? Or has my tongue betrayed me?"

Ai,ai,ai.

"Well then. Let us consider it fully and calmly. Like men. Not old women or chattering magpies. Let us move evenly together. Martiniano here and these two boys. They went into the mountains. A deer was killed. They were arrested. Now let the young men speak. Filadelphio, are you ready to empty your heart? God knows, will help us, will give us medicine."

Filadelphio spoke. Like his companion he was just twenty. With short hair, and better known by his Spanish name.

"This is what I say. It makes two days I started with Jesús here, and Martiniano whom you see also. We went up the low trail, the high trail. We crossed the stream. We entered the cañon that is long and steep and narrow. We went past the Saltillo, past the beaver dams. We came to the small mountain pastures among the aspens. We cooked our meat and our tortillas. And then it was dark. We slept."

Low and measureless his voice went on. "We got up. It was gray and cold. We had nothing left to eat. We thought, We will go back now. The cooking pots are on, the ovens full of bread. But Martiniano saw the fresh spoor of a deer. He said, 'I will just put a shell in my gun. I will just kill this deer. My wife will like fresh meat.' We started forth. Up the cañon, over the ridge. Myself on one side, behind. Jesús on one side, behind. Martiniano in the middle, ahead.

"What man does not know how a deer bounds up the slope when startled in the brush? We saw it. Martiniano shot it. It fell dead. Down to the vega we carried it. The sun was high. It was past dinner time. Two men rode up on horses. White men, Government men. They were angry. They said, 'It is past the Government time for killing deer on Government land. We arrest you. Come now and pay heavy fines.' And one man on his horse led away Jesús and me on foot.

"But Martiniano did not look up. He was busy taking out the deer's insides. He said, 'I am Indian. I am hungry. Why should I hurry for Government men?' We heard no more. We saw no more. We went to the jail. The Jéfe took our names, he looked into our faces. He said, 'There may be heavy fines. There may be none. I would have your fathers come see me.' And we came back as we were bid. And now my heart is empty. This I say."

It had taken him nearly a half-hour; and it took Jesús almost as long to confirm it. But these were the mere details of action. What was the substance of this action? Why did two young men go with Martiniano into the mountains, without food, to stay all night away from their beds? Are we not all in one nest?

Jesús tried not to look surprised. Why did one go to the mountains? What man did not go to the mountains, and if it was dark did not sleep quietly before his fire? There were the stars, the moon, the shimmer of brittle leaves. There was, if the truth be emptied from the heart, the sweet smelling sachet growing so high and which the young girls treasure. Moreover, there was this about the fresh spoor of a deer. One minute a man has no thought. The next minute he has but one thought. Has it not always been so with our people?

Jesús was very modest about these things; his voice was very low. No man reproached him with word or look. But still his heart told him that he had been too confident in his assertions and assumptions, too bold in speaking thus. And he sat down, a little too haughtily to mask his shame, and wondering what his father would say to him tomorrow.

Now Palemon spoke forth. He too was a young man and would so be regarded till he was fifty. But he had wife and children. He worked his land. He obeyed the customs. He did his ceremonial duties. And so he was old enough to empty his heart in proud humility.

"My wife was in bed. My children were in bed. I was in bed. They were asleep. But I was not asleep. So I lay awake and wondered why. I looked this way and that way, into my body, my mind, my heart. You know how it is when there is something in the air. You cannot touch it, you cannot think it, you cannot feel it. But it is there.

"I listened to the heart of my body. I listened to the heart of the mountain. And I knew that something was wrong. So I waited.

"I heard Grandfather Coyote cry. I heard him cry four times. Each time he was more angry because I would not listen to his message, because I would not answer. I went out and saddled my mare. And I listened to the heart of my body, and I listened to the heart of the mountains. And I knew I had done well.

"Grandfather Coyote no longer cried; he was no longer angry. But Grandfather Crow and his brothers were calling; they were calling, 'Pa-le-mon! Pa-le-mon!' And so I rode up to the mountain, and they stopped calling because I had come.

"I rode up the cañon, past the beaver dams, into the tall pale aspens. Above me the Night People came out clear. Morning Star Older Brother showed me the way. So I came to where the trail winds up to cross the crest of the mountains and dip down to the lake. The little blue eye of faith. The deep turquoise lake of life. I could hear the great heart of the mountain. I could hear my own heart. And they were one. So I went no farther. And there I found him. Martiniano. With his broken head. So I brought him down.

"This I say. You know how it is. The things that no words speak, but which live in all our hearts. And now my heart is empty too."

No man applauded him by word or look. They sat faces bowed, eyes downward, wrapped in blankets, swathed in silence. But this silence was pregnant with the ever-living mystery; and the tentacles of mind and heart groped through it to feel its shape and form and substance. And Palemon knew he had spoken well. He slumped modestly on his bench no longer conscious of his new red blanket.

A Council meeting is a strange thing. The fire crackles. The candle gutters. And the old men sit stolidly on their benches round the walls. When a man speaks they do not interrupt. They lower their swathed heads or half close their eyes so as not to encourage or embarrass him with a look. And when the guttural Indian voice finally stops there is silence. A silence so heavy and profound that it squashes the kernel of truth out of his words, and leaves the meaningless husks mercilessly exposed. And still no man speaks. Each waits courteously for another. And the silence grows round the walls, handed from one to another, until all the silence is one silence, and that silence has the meaning of all. So the individuals vanish. It is all one heart. It is the soul of the tribe. A soul that is linked by that other silence with all the souls of all the tribal councils which have sat here in the memory of man.

A Council meeting is one-half talk and one-half silence. The silence has more weight, more meanings, more intonations than the talk. It is angry, impatient, cheerful, but masked by calmness, patience, dignity. Thus the members move evenly together. Now it suddenly thickened. It boiled. It was the taut silence of a hunter the moment before striking.

For it was true what had happened. They had looked at this thing one way, another, before, behind. Now let them look at its center, at its heart.

Ai. Now let Martiniano put out his face and his belly before us, and so speak as to empty his heart. God knows, will help us, will give us medicine.

Martiniano began to speak. He had a cinnamon-sallow, pain-racked face, and a bloody white bandage round his head. He was not as young as Filadelphio and Jesús, or as old as Palemon. He had been to the government away-school and wore old store clothes and shoes like the former, but hair braids and a blanket like the latter. His face and demeanor showed that he was at once of the old and the new, and that it was not the first time he had been caught between them. His voice was sullen but respectful.

"I went to the mountains and I took my rifle. I wanted to kill a deer," he stated defiantly, but with lowered face. "The Council does not give me the privileges of others since I have come back from away-school. It would not give me my turn at the thresher for my oats, my wheat. So I had to thresh them the old way, with my animals' hoofs. It took me a long, long time—what should have taken but a day. Then my friend, the good white trader, loaned me his machine—for one sack out of ten. Yet it was two days after hunting season that I finished. Should my wife be without fresh meat, a skin for boots and moccasins? Should I go without my rights for two days of white man's law? The white man's Government that took me away to school, for which you now do not give me the privileges of others? What is the difference between killing a deer on Tuesday or Thursday? Would I not have killed it anyway?"

He paused to twang at the Council the arrow of accusing silence. It missed the mark. Or perhaps the mute impenetrability of those rows of covered faces was too sturdy a shield to pierce. And completing its arc, like an arrow shot into the sky and which must fall again to earth, it turned home.

Martiniano resumed. "This I told the Government man who remained with me as you have heard. I did not have to look up to hear his angry voice, to feel the hate steaming from his body. 'You dirty Indian, who kills deer out of season in the Government's National Forest!' he cried. 'I am going to ride up to that old mine for rope to tie you up. Try to run away and I will shoot you like a dog!'

"As he went away I laid back the flap of the skin, I cut off a piece of my deer. I had no fear; I had hunger. I had not eaten since the day before. While it cooked over the coals I hid my deer in the bushes. But before I could eat it, he came back. The rope was on his saddle horn, the rifle raised to my breast. He smelled the meat. His face was red with anger.

"I turned over the meat. What Indian makes a foolish move before an angry white man's gun? I but raised my hands to wipe off my fingers on my hair.

"At that moment he struck. With the iron of his gun. Across my head. I woke up. My head was cracked open. Blood ran down my face. He had taken my knife. My hands were tied behind my back. When he kicked me, I tried to stand up. He lifted me like a sack of meal to the rump of his horse. We started off. I could not sit up, but fell upon his back. Blood ran down his shirt. This made him very angry. He put me in front. Still I bled and kept falling, save for his hand upon my collar.

"Now my thoughts returned. I said, 'There is a thing I must do, which every man does, behind a bush. You understand it is this hurt which makes my kidneys weak.'

"He stopped the horse. I fell off and stood up. 'Pardon,' I said, 'but my hands are tied behind my back.'

"'Oh no you don't!' he said, and with his rifle butt he swept open the front of my trousers. See? How he tore off the buttons?"

His eyes hard as black obsidian, Martiniano stated quietly, one leg forward, showing the gaping flap of his blood-stained trousers. No one looked. They saw it in his voice.

"If he had done more than this," Martiniano stated quietly, "there would be more for this venerated Council to consider. I would have killed him.

"But now"—a shade on the apologetic side to balance his unseemly show of passion—"I went noisily into the bushes. Then I quietly waded upstream against the noise of the falls. I hid in water, deep between the logs of a beaver dam. I heard him call. I saw him plunging through the bushes to find me. Suddenly he rode off. Quickly. In a gallop. Fear pursued him. He had forgotten me, my rifle, my deer.

"For a long time I cut at my rope on the sharp rocks. I was too weak to walk when my hands were free. I crawled back up the trail. I was weak, but the thought of the strength of my deer meat made me vomit. I knew I was sick. Too sick to make a fire. So I lay down beside the stream.

"I slept sleep, and I slept a sleep that was not a sleep. I thought many thoughts, but there are no words for my thoughts. And strangely, when Morning Star rose, though I was cold and weak and ill, I felt good. I felt good because I knew help would come. It came. It was Palemon.

"This I say, with my face and my belly put out before you. And now my heart is empty."

Had they all fallen asleep—these rows of old men slumped against the walls, the whitewash rubbing off on their blankets, head down or arm upraised to shut out the last sputtering pulgado of candle? If so, they continued dozing. Only the Cacique sat upright in his chair, a rock jutting into the waves of sleep. Somebody threw another piñon knot on the fire. Somebody spat noisily into one of the little sand boxes. One of the sentinels opened the door and stood inside to get warm. When he went out, the two boys, Filadelphio and Jesús, followed him.

Well, here were the facts thrust down the maw of silence. You could hear them being digested. They fitted into the responsibilities of the Governor and Lieutenant-Governor of the pueblo, the "Outside Chief"—the War Captain, the Chiefs of the Kivas, all the officers, all the Council. And so one after another, with proper pause, the guttural Indian voices began to speak.

Let us move evenly together, brothers.

A young man went into the mountains. He killed a deer out of season. He got arrested, and a knock on the head to boot. He will have to pay a fine, doubtless, for disobeying those Government laws we have sworn to uphold with our canes of office. A simple matter.

But wait. Was it so simple?

This young man was an Indian, born in our pueblo, belonging to our tribe. Or was he, properly speaking? There was the definition of an Indian by the Government—so much Indian blood, land ownership, all that. But there was the definition of an Indian by the Council according to his conformance to custom, tradition, his participation in ceremonials. Now this young man has been lax, very lax; we have warned him. He has disobeyed us; we have punished him. And now he has disobeyed the laws of the Government outside, likewise. What have we to do with this, that we should interfere?

Now there is this. There are good Indians among us, and there are those who look under their eyes. But we are all in one nest. No Indian is an individual. He is a piece of the pueblo, the tribe. Is it proper to consider that we have done wrong against the Government, our white father, betrayed our canes of office?

Yet there was this to consider. All this land was ours—the mountain, the valleys, the desert. Indian land. We have the papers to it from the Spanish King. The Mexicans came, the white people—the gringos. They built themselves a town on our land, Indian land. We got nothing for it. Now when the Spanish King opened his hand, Our Father at Washington closed his own hand upon the land. He told us, "You will be paid for it. The day will come with compensation." What did we want with money? We wanted land, our land, Indian land. But mostly we wanted the mountains. We wanted the mountains, our mother, between whose breasts lies the little blue eye of faith. The deep turquoise lake of life. Our lake, our church. Where we make our pilgrimages, hold our ceremonials...Now what is this? We have waited. The day of compensation has not come. The mountains are Government forests. Not ours. The Mexicans pasture their sheep and goats upon the slopes. Turistas scatter paper bags unseemly upon the ground. They throw old fish bait into our sacred lake. Government men, these rangers, ride through it at will. Is any man safe? Look at this one's broken head. Will our ceremonials long be inviolate from foreign eyes? Now then, is it we who are injured and must seek reparation, demand our rights, our mountains? This is what I say. God knows, will help us, will give us strength.

The voices kept creeping around the room...

In the Government office two hundred miles away there is that Indian lawyer, our mouth in many matters. There is the judge in town, a short walk. Are we to turn this young man alone over to a judge? Or are we to call this Indian lawyer? And what are we to tell him? We must move evenly together. We must be one mind, one heart, one body.

Silence spoke, and it spoke the loudest of all.

There is no such thing as a simple thing. One drops a pebble into a pool, but the ripples travel far. One picks up a little stone in the mountains, one of the little stones called Lagrimas de Cristo—and look! It is shaped like a star; the sloping mountain is full of stars as the sloping sky. Or take a kernel of corn. Plant it in Our Mother Earth with the sweat of your body, with what you know of the times and seasons, with your proper prayers. And with your strength and manhood Our Father sun multiplies and gives it back into your flesh. What then is this kernel of corn? It is not a simple thing.

Nothing is simple and alone. We are not separate and alone. The breathing mountains, the living stones, each blade of grass, the clouds, the rain, each star, the beasts, the birds and the invisible spirits of the air—we are all one, indivisible. Nothing that any of us does but affects us all.

So I would have you look upon this thing not as a separate simple thing, but as a stone which is a star in the firmament of earth, as a ripple in a pool, as a kernel of corn. I would have you consider how it fits into the pattern of the whole. How far its influence may spread. What it may grow into . . .

So there is something else to consider. The deer. It is dead. In the old days we all remember, we did not go out on a hunt lightly. We said to the deer we were going to kill, "We know your life is as precious as ours. We know that we are both children of the same Great True Ones. We know that we are all one life on the same Mother Earth, beneath the same plains of the sky. But we also know that one life must sometimes give way to another so that the one great life of all may continue unbroken. So we ask your permission, we obtain your consent to this killing."

Ceremonially we said this, and we sprinkled meal and corn pollen to Our Father Sun. And when we killed the deer we laid his head toward the East, and sprinkled him with meal and pollen. And we dropped drops of his blood and bits of his flesh on the ground for Our Mother Earth. It was proper so. For then when we too built its flesh into our flesh, when we walked in the moccasins of its skin, when we danced in its robe and antlers, we knew that the life of the deer was continued in our life, as it in turn was continued in the one life all around us, below us and above us.

We knew the deer knew this and was satisfied.

But this deer's permission was not obtained. What have we done to this deer, our brother? What have we done to ourselves? For we are all bound together, and our touch upon one travels through all to return to us again. Let us not forget the deer.

The old Cacique spoke. It was true that the young men nowadays did not observe such proper steps. And it was true that the game was becoming scarce because of it. Was it true that next the water would fail them, the air become dull and tasteless, the life go out of the land?

"So I would have you consider whether it is not time to be more strict with our young men so corrupted with evil modern ways, lest we ourselves dwindle and vanish entirely. This I say," he ended. "Dios knows, will help us, will give us medicine."

Here they were then, all these things and shadows of things ensnared like flies in the web of silence. They fluttered their wings. They shook and distorted the whole vast web. But they did not break free. For it was the web which binds us each to the other, and all to the life of which we are an inseparable part—binds us to the invisible shapes that have gone and those to come, in the solidarity of one flowing whole.

So the night grew thin as the thinnest gray blanket around the walls. The embers heaped upon growing gray ashes. The little wooden sand boxes filled with cigarette stubs. The two sentinels came in a last time for warmth. In with them stalked daylight.

And now the old men rose and stretched their stiff, bent limbs. They gathered their blankets about their dark faces and bent shoulders. They hobbled out across the plaza in the dawn-dusk.

The meeting of the Council was over. They were one body, one mind, one heart. They moved evenly together.

* * *

Flowers Playing was already dozing in bed; she would be up at dawn. He quietly put up his tools and walked outside for a last look at his animals. The night was frosty, the peak shone white in the clear air. Returning, Martiniano undressed and got into bed beside her.

He lay staring into the coals across the room. Turning over, he stared up through the little square window high up under the vigas. The Night People smiled. Wind Old Woman brushed her skirts along the walls. Life was good. With her beside him, Martiniano was content.

But suddenly, just as he flung his arm around his wife, a few brittle leaves pattered on the portal. They sounded like the light hoofs of a scampering deer, a frightened, an angry deer, a spirit deer. Martiniano straightened out stiffly, and removed the arm flung around his wife.

Resolutely he tried to put sound and thought from him. He could not. He lay sleepless.

So a coldness grew up between them. Flowers Playing no longer lounged beside him of an evening in front of the fire while he caressed her. As if ashamed of her body which had failed their desire, she went to bed and huddled close against the wall, back to him, knees up, staring openeyed into the darkness. Martiniano crawled in late beside her. His hand no longer gently stroked her long thigh or drew her against him for warmth. His breath did not bathe her cheek and throat in sleep. He lay apart. And between them always lay this new strange coldness that was like a pain for which neither had a remedy.

Martiniano felt betrayed. He remembered how barren a waste had been his life before she had come, an oasis of love and faith in a desert of unbelief. It was nothing but a mirage! And the bitterness, the corrosive loneliness, filled him as before.

The chokecherries had been gathered. Wagon loads of wild plums had been spread out to dry upon the flat roof tops. The corn had come in. Great heaps everywhere, holding women like hens in their nests, shucking and laying aside the brightest colored and most perfect ears to be braided together and kept for ceremonial, seed and ornament. Scarlet necklaces of chile from the lowlands hung along the walls turning blood-red, black. Between the walls, like long lines of flags and pennants, hung drying pelts and intestines of butchered sheep. The corrals had been lined with branches of pine and spruce to keep out the wind. Hundreds of burros staggered down the trails with loads of piñon and cedar.

Then slowly a warm hush ate into the cold afternoon like a bad spot in a sound apple. Out of the low gray sky fluttered a speck of white. It looked like a loose feather dropped from the breast of a solitary wild goose. It twisted and turned buoyantly against the blue mountain wall, fluttered down lazily past the brown adobe wall, settled lightly on the hard reddish earth. Another. Others. They came! They came! The mystery, the miracle, the beauty of the first snow.

By morning it was all gone. The sun was bright, the air warm. But the message of a new mystery, new miracle and new beauty remained. A sonorous voice proclaimed it from the high house-tops. It was time when all must move in from their summer houses out in the fields, from their little huts in the cañon. It was time when all must move into the pueblo, into one nest together.

Martiniano went to the Governor for the assignment of a vacant room or two. The price was too high, and he walked back to his little adobe outside the walls with his stubbornness and pride unspent.

Flowers Playing assumed a consoling cheerfulness. "We have a home. In that old trunk of mine I found it. This pretty cloth which makes us curtains for our windows. When the snow flies past we shall just reach out our hands and pick these red raspberries!"

Martiniano's sullen look rent the curtain of her smiling consolation. He had seen that cloth printed with red raspberries in her old trunk; it was one of her old school dresses. Scowling at her foolish attempt to obscure the tawdry truth between them, he strode in to sit gloomily in front of the fire.

A quick fright leapt into Flowers Playing's eyes. Her lips trembled. She went on with her work.

So the coldness grew between them.

Martiniano began to ignore her. She was merely a woman, a wife. He began to go to Palemon.

There was a great difference between them as they sat together, so much alike in appearance. One was vivid, sharp-witted, personal. The other sat with drooping head, relaxed, impersonal, silent. Martiniano felt the gulf between them. But because he also felt the dark, upwelling stream of compassion, he gave way to the repressed pain and bitterness within him.

"They fined me because I did not cut off the heels of my shoes and cut out the seat of my pants. They whipped me because I did not dance. My use of the thresher they forbade. They ignore me, they shame my wife. We are outcasts. They will not let us move within the walls. No! All winter we must plod through snow to our little adobe. We must break the trail to the road for our wagon. . . . What have we done to deserve all this? What is good about these old ways of yours which you uphold—this cruelty, this injustice to a blood-brother?"

The older man sucked slowly on his cigarette. He was not unaware of certain superficial injustices which had caused the younger one's sufferings, but he was amazed at the persistent, stubborn individuality which prevented him from seeing the real trouble. Perhaps it reflected the one's away-time in school, when he had lost the precious instruction at home. Palemon did his best to reveal his understanding. "There are no words for talk, for all my feelings, friend. Heart, mind, body. They are all together. All is one, everything. You are separate, alone. It must not be, my friend."

You see, it is like this. I am mortal body and I am immortal spirit; they are one. Now on this earth I am imprisoned for a little while in my mortal body. This gives me no discomfort; I have learned its needs and limitations and how to supersede them.

Now I, in this mortal body, am imprisoned also in a form of life—

that of my tribe, my pueblo, my people. Nor does this give me discomfort; I have learned its needs and limitations also and how to supersede them. For as my body blends into my tribe, my pueblo, so this greater form blends into the world without—the earth, the skies, the sun, moon, stars, and the spirits of all.

I have faith in my body. I have faith also in the form of life which is my greater body. How then can I object to its demands also? So I feed it with faith; I am obedient to its coarser needs; I lighten its burden by prayer-dance and ceremonial.

Now if I quarreled with my body, my spirit would not be free. Now if I quarreled with my greater body, my spirit would not be free. But by existing harmoniously in each, I am free to escape them for my greatest need—to become one, formless and without bounds, inseparable from the one flowing stream of all life.

Palemon rolled another corn-husk cigarette.

Now you, my friend, have your mortal body also, and are at peace with it. You too have a greater body, your form of life. It is not mine, for our old ways you reject; nor is it the Government's, the white man's, for you reject it also; but one you must have. Who knows which is best? They are all the same. All are merely shells of life. But they must be lived within harmoniously to be free. For only when there is no sense of imprisonment in form is the substance of spirit able to overflow and become one with the flowing stream of all life, everlasting, formless and without bounds.

Forgive me, my friend. Do you see what you lack? Not a form of life, for there are three for you to choose from: our old ways, the white man's new ways, or your own which may be part of both or newer still. You lack only a faith in one of them. The faith that will set you free from bitterness and envy and worry. That will free your spirit into a formless life without bounds, which will overflow and taste of all life.

Palemon's feelings continued to gush out from him in waves of silent compassion. Martiniano's conscience illuminated his terse words quickly enough. He broke out into another tirade.

"Faith! What can a man have faith in nowadays? The Government betrayed me. My own people reject me. You remember how empty I was until my wife came. Then I was a new man. She was my faith. And now? That has gone too. Perhaps I should not have married her—not yet. She is as miserable as I. Why?

"Why?" he repeated stubbornly. "That deer!" he exclaimed suddenly. "That's what they are holding against me most of all. That cursed deer which I killed! That is what has destroyed my wife's love and faith!"

"Perhaps that is so," agreed Palemon calmly. "Perhaps there is something else about that deer you killed which you have forgotten. *I re-member how clearly your spirit called. It was as if it left your mortal, wounded body, as if it broke the boundaries of this form of life of yours. It seemed that it stood beside me, whispered in my ear, pulled at my heart until I answered. That is how it seemed. I have not mentioned it to you. I do not know how you awakened this sleeping power. I do not ask. There is something about this thing that lies beyond words. We do wrong to question it.* But I would think about this thing when I think about faith. Listen not only to your body. Listen not only to your mind. Listen to your heart which holds the feelings of all."

Martiniano went away comforted. Always afterward he felt enriched by Palemon's silent awareness. But in his presence he was also tortured by this same silence, as if in front of him he was no longer Indian but a talkative white.

VIII

The Colorado

Later in 1941, Waters began The Colorado. *Originally part of the* Rivers of America *series, it is an examination of the history and the people of the great Colorado Pyramid. In this major work, Waters develops his examination of the relationship between the land and its inhabitants on a grand scale. Here a basic tenet is that the life in the total environment of Western America cannot be fully perceived by the usual Western-European rationalistic outlook. Rather, a mystical outlook—perception through intuitive awareness—permits a person to experience an attunement that results in personal psychological adjustment. Waters then applies this concept to the American people: to the Native Americans, who, he suggests, had this "apperception" (which Lyon calls "perception squared"[13]), and to the waves of White settlers, who did not. The Indian, psychologically in tune with his perceived environment, is patient, intuitive, introvertive, and respectful of the land. The White is quick, eager, extravertive, rationalistic, and power-oriented. Waters depicts the conflict between the two as something far deeper than military-political. Rather, it is a psychological conflict deep within the character of both. While the conquering Whites are depicted as just that— conquerors of people, rivers, land itself—Waters is careful not to depict the Indian as Noble Savage. Rather, linking these ideas with his belief in the evolution of consciousness, he suggests that over-emphasis on either point of view is ultimately destructive, and that what is needed—what is possible—is a synthesis of the apparently opposing points of view into a wholeness in both individual and mankind.[14]*

The following essay is the final chapter of The Colorado.

GRAND CAÑON

No writer of worth has ever seriously attempted to describe Grand Cañon; no artist has ever adequately portrayed it. None ever will. For while it is the most compelling single area on the earth's surface, it is not a landscape.

The regal ermine-cloaked Rockies; the somber moss hung swamps and bayous of Florida and Louisiana; the romantic orange groves of California; the sweet clean meadows of the Ohio; the majestic bluffs along the Hudson; the poignantly beautiful prairies of Kansas; the dreamy plantations of the Deep South; the rugged grasslands of the Far West—all these and a hundred others offer true landscapes. Each has a distinctive tone, key, spirit and character which hold true and unique despite their infinite variations. They can be known, loved and partially expressed.

The Grand Cañon is beyond comprehension. No one could possibly love it. It is not distinguished by any one dominant quality. It is not unique in the individual sense. It is universal.

One cannot define humanity. One can only define the terms of humanity expressed by its many components: beauty, cruelty, tenderness, strength, awe, horror, serenity, sadness, joy. But to define life—the blended summation of all its infinite aspects—is impossible.

The Grand Cañon in nature is like the humanity of man. It is the sum total of all the aspects of nature combined in one integrated whole. It is at once the smile and the frown upon the face of nature. In its heart is the savage, uncontrollable fury of all the inanimate universe, and at the same time the immeasurable serenity that succeeds it. It is creation.

Never static, never still, inconstant as the passing moment and yet endurable as time itself, it is the one great drama of evolutionary change perpetually recapitulated. Yet the cañon refutes even this geological reality. In its depths whole mountains contract and expand with the changing shadows. Clouds ebb in and out of gorges like frothy tides. Peaks and buttes change shape and color constantly in the shifting light. None of this seems real. It is a realm of the fantastic unreal.

If I were forced to describe so sublime an immensity, I would define it with only one word: the ancient Sanskrit word for the nonexistent material world of the senses: *Maya*, or Illusion. It embodies all that man has ever achieved of the knowledge of reality: that all matter, as our own science now suspects, is but a manifestation of that primordial energy constituting the electron, whose ultimate source is mind, and hence illusory and insubstantial. Grand Cañon seems such a world. A world whose very mountains are but the shifting, dissolving, recreated thoughts of the One Omnipotent Mind. It is beyond sensory perception. It lies in the realm of metaphysics—the world of illusion, *Maya*.

No one is ever prepared for the cañon as one is for the gradually rising Rockies as he approaches across the plains. One simply crosses a flat plateau hirsute with cedar and great pines, and there at his feet it suddenly yawns.

The Rocky Mountains upside down; an immense intaglio instead of a cameo. A mountain chain, as it were, nearly 300 miles long, up to 18 miles wide, but a mile deep instead of a mile high.

Say this and there is no more to be said. See it in one look and there is nothing more to see.

A competent writer, justly noted in his generation for his appreciation of western America, once described the first impact of the cañon by relating that he had seen strong men break down and weep. Sentimental bosh! I think more of the curt remark of that old Westerner who at his first sight is reported to have shrugged and said, "Now, by Jesus, I know where we can throw our old safety razor blades!"

Like all great things, the cañon takes time to appreciate. So be wary of your companion's instant rhapsody of applause. Be more wary of that sacred hush affected by others. Simply take your look, turn on your heel and leave. The cañon will be there if you ever return. And if you are drawn back, you will know then that it is a great experience not to be taken lightly, and not before you are ready for it.

El Tovar on the south rim, Fred Harvey's luxurious oasis at the terminus of the Santa Fe railroad spur and the highway from Williams, Arizona, has long been the stranger's starting point. From here convenient government roads lead to several other points of vantage: Hopi Point, 2 miles northwest; Yavapai Point, 1½ miles northeast; Grand View Point, 11 miles southeast; Desert View, 20 miles east; and Lipan Point, just off the road between these latter. At their tidy observation lookouts provided with telescopes, you can briefly encompass a faint idea of the main cañon's length of 217 miles, and its average width of 12 miles.

For the first time the absurdity of a letter to M. R. Tillotson, superintendent of the Grand Cañon National Park, will strike you as funny. He relates that a Hollywood movie director once wrote him, requesting aid in selecting a convenient, scenic spot where his cinematic hero could be filmed in the act of jumping a horse across the cañon. Actually the chasm is so long and wide that it has prevented the migration of animals to and from the forests on each side. Only on the Kaibab Plateau to the north are found the Kaibab white-tailed squirrels, the only species with ear tufts in the world. Parachutists have been dropped on certain buttes to search for prehistoric forms of animal life possibly isolated in the cañon. In this largest virgin forest in the United States roam queer dwarf burros which have strayed here, gone wild, inbred and become stunted. The north rim abounds in deer. A government trapper killed five hundred mountain lions in four years.

Winding down to the bottom are two easy horseback trails, Hermit Trail and Bright Angel. Descend one of these and the third dimension of the cañon begins to be apparent—its appalling depth. A sheer drop of one mile from the south rim, and 1,300 feet more from the north rim. Remembering that one mile in altitude is comparable to 800 miles of latitude, you can travel here the equivalent distance from central Mexico to northern Canada. It is a trail that drops from a snowstorm at the rim into semitropical weather at the river below. And one which leads through all the zones of plant life from the mesquite of the Lower Sonora Zone, through the Upper Sonora and Transition, to the quaking aspen of the Canadian Zone.

In length, breadth and depth the cañon grows. Its mere immensity takes hold. Yet these dimensions are but its frame. Like a drug, the more of it you take in, the more you want. Often riding through the forests along its rim I have come across lone wanderers held there a month, a year, a lifetime, by nothing more than its strange and indefinable quality of compelling fascination. Ostensibly they are vacationists and invalids, photographers and artists, mere sheepherders, old hunters and trappers—even a crackpot religious waiting for the world to come to an end. But it is the cañon that holds them. It is the most powerful mesmer I know.

What is there in it that exerts so universal an appeal? For one thing, it contains every shape known to man. Lofty peaks, whole mountains rise out of its depths. There are vast plateaus, flat-topped mesas, high buttes and monoliths. And all these are carved in the semblance of pyramids, temples, castles; of pinnacles, spires, fluted columns and towers; porticoes and abutments, bridges and arches, terraces, balconies, balustrades. They are solid and fragile, bare and covered with latticework and delicate carving. It is a stage that seems expressly built to contain in perpetuity appropriate sets for every dynasty, every religion, every legend and myth-drama that man has known—a vast universal depository, as it were, of mankind's structural and architectural heritage.

Cardenas and his men, the first we know to look into the cañon, saw in it shapes resembling the towers of their beloved Seville. Cardenas Butte is named for him; another for Coronado, who headed the first land expedition into the region; and Alarcon Terrace for the first ship captain to ascend the river.

Named for the pre-Columbian race of Mexico, which they conquered, is Aztec Amphitheater, and for the race that preceded it, Toltec

Point. There is a point for ancient Centeotl, and one for Quetzal, which gave a name to the vanished, mysterious quetzal bird and the legendary, feathered serpent-god Quetzalcoatl.

For the Greeks there are temples named for Apollo, Castor and Pollux; for the Romans, the temples of Jupiter, Juno and Diana.

The Christian Bible is not forgotten. There is a temple here for Solomon more enduring than one made of Lebanon cedars, and another for Sheba that will last as long as the fable of her beauty.

Here, far from Egypt's land, is Cheops' Pyramid, a Tower of Ra, and the temples of Horus, Isis and Osiris.

There is a Persian temple for Zoroaster, Chinese temples for Mencius and Confucius.

The immortal Hindu philosophers, saviors and deities—perhaps the oldest known to man—have here as everywhere their proper shrines. There are temples for Buddha, Brahma and Devi; a Krishna shrine; and a temple for Manu, who throughout the destruction and rebirth of all continents, all worlds, watches over the progressive evolution of all life including that of man, its latest form.

Here as nowhere else are background and settings spacious and majestic enough for the great Germanic myth-drama. Across the titanic cañon to the Valhalla Plateau could race the winged steeds of the Valkyries carrying heroes killed in battle. There is Wotan's Throne; castles for Gunther and Freya; a lofty promontory named for Thor, with room to swing the mighty hammer whose blows echo back and forth from the cañon walls; and Siegfried's Pyre forever flaming in fiery rock.

So too are the English myth-dramas of the Arthurian legend and the Quest of the Holy Grail recapitulated in enduring stone. Here stands King Arthur's Castle with that of Guinevere. There is another for Sir Galahad; and one for the tragic maid Elaine to stand in, grieving at its casements for the peerless knight's return. There rises Lancelot's Point, there yawns Gawain Abyss. Holy Grail Temple still holds at dawn and sunset the light no man saw on its tragic quest. Here is a mighty stone named for the magic sword Excalibur—itself first drawn from stone. Still others are named for the magician Merlin, the traitor Modred.

Point after point emerges to mark all these, simply named for the people who have always known this as their traditional homeland: Apache Point for the mother tribe and others for its subtribes, the Jicarillo, Mescalero, and Mimbres Apaches; still others for the Hopi, Navajo, Walapai, Pima, Yavapai, Papago, Cocopah and Comanche.

So they loom out of time and space, a named minimum out of the vast anonymous multitude. . . . What shape or form has man ever conceived of mind and built by hand that the cañon does not hold? Is that its secret which holds a watcher at its brim—to see foretold in it the yet unborn form of his wildest imagining, the shape of his secret longing?

Why, many a man has hardly noticed shapes in it at all. They are merely blobs of color. Color so rich and rampant that it floods the whole chasm; so powerful that it dissolves like acid all the shapes within it. Here, if you will, is a drama whose characters are colors: the royal purples, the angry reds, the mellow russets and monkish browns, soothing blues, shrieking yellows, tragic blacks and mystic whites, cool greens, pale lavenders and anemic grays.

A lifetime is too short to watch their infinite variations in key and tone. They change with every season, every hour, and with every change in light and weather.

In the blinding glare of a summer's noon its tints are so muted that the cañon seems a delicate pastel. But watch it at sunset. The yellows slowly deepen to orange; the salmon pinks to reds; the greens and blue-grays to damson blue; the lilacs to purple. Sunrise reverses the process. The whole chasm lifts bodily, inch by inch, toward light. The paint pot tips and spills over. The colors run and seep down the walls, collecting in pools below.

If it is a picture, winter frames it best. Preferably after a heavy snowfall when the plateaus are solid white, and better yet when every twig and needle is still sheathed in ice. Deeply inset in such a frame the cañon has all the warmth and color of a child's stereopticon slide held up to the table lamp. Into it snow never descends. A summer rainstorm is more potent. Then mists and clouds are formed below. Like tiny puffs from father's pipe they spurt out of the warm cañons and swelling like balloons gradually float to surface.

But the cold, clear, cloudless days of October—that is its time. Its colors stand out flat and positive. They relate it, not to the universal, but to the earth in which it is set. Red Supai sandstone, the rich red rock with the Indian name, the bright red Indian earth that stains land and river alike and gives both their name. Green Tonto shale, green as pine and sage, bright as turquoise, clear as the turquoise sky above. Red and green on limestone white. These are its distinctive colors as they are the colors of the old Hopi ceremonial sashes, the masks of the giant Zuñi Shalako, the Navajo blankets, the fine old blankets of Chimayo so faded with their lost and unduplicated colors.

In this, of course, I must own to a sentimental but helpless preference. This is my land and to it I belong with all it expresses and with all by which it is expressed. It is merely a matter of vibration. We are each keyed to that band of the spectrum which determines our own characteristic tone.

Little wonder then that the cañon is universal in appeal. It is the complete spectrum, and in its vast range there is no one who does not find his own harmonic key. Color is a mysterious thing. Within the written memory of man, as we know, there was a time when he could not distinguish between the blue of the sky and the green of the forest. Still today there are colors not all of us can perceive. But they are there in the cañon—a thousand gradations invisible and unnamed, yet each vibrating upon our consciousness. Is this the "music of the spheres" that fills us so with wonder, a celestial symphony of color that drives us to still another terminology to express the inexpressible feeling it evokes?

In an instant the whole thing is forgotten when suddenly after midnight a slash of lightning rips through the dark. One hears the bolt strike. It is as if it has cracked the hinge of a cañon wall. A cliff caves in. It tears down another, and it another, like the collapse of a pack of stacked cards. A tremendous and prolonged shattering, accompanied by a thunderous concatenation traveling down the whole cañon.

Before it is over you have thrown off your blankets and raced half naked to the rim. This is the end of the world as predicted by the crackpot religious. Bolt after bolt strikes into the gorge. In the hot dry air sheets of flame light up the crumbling buttes and peaks. A second later they have vanished, swallowed by a vacuous immensity of flame red and pitch black. It grows greater and greater to the echo of thunderclaps thrown back and forth from the remaining walls—an inferno bathed in fire, a chaotic underworld. This is the apocalypse, the most awful and most sublime sight you can experience. Before it you cling to a piñon, insensible to self, the shrieking wind and the lash of rain.

As suddenly, it is over. The last reverberation dies away. Overpowering silence breaks louder upon the eardrums. In this monstrous, unearthly calm the first light of day breaks over the clifftops. They are still standing. And in the clarity of rain-washed dawn you see a world reborn in the semblance of the old. But new, enthrallingly new!

Such a storm articulates that quality which subtly and powerfully impenetrates every other quality and every dimension of Grand Cañon. Time is its palpable fourth dimension. Yet its effect is indescribable. One can only stand mute and prosaically view its geologic record.

Grand Cañon is the world's largest and oldest book. It is over 15,000 feet thick and it contains the history of 2,000 million years. Though its pages are wrinkled, creased and worn, they are brilliantly colored and beautifully engraved. A few chapters are missing. But so clearly are the others written that their meaning is revealed without break in continuity.

Thumb down through its rock pages.

The forest-covered plateaus on each side terminate at the rims of the cañon in cliffs of light-gray limestone, almost white in sunlight, and filled with fossil shells, chert, agates and carnelians. This is Kaibab limestone, a layer 800 feet thick and named after the Kaibab Plateau on the north. Kaibab itself is a Paiute name meaning "Mountain Lying Down."

Under this is a stratum of Coconino sandstone darker gray in color and 300 feet thick. Its name comes from the Coconino Plateau to the south, whose rim is more than a thousand feet lower than that of the Kaibab.

Intruding below are massive bodies of red shales and ledges of red sandstone, 1,100 feet thick. This Supai Formation forms the wall of Cataract Cañon in which the Supais live, hence its name.

Below it stands a 500-foot wall of limestone called simply Redwall. It is almost pure calcium carbonate. Not only in texture does it differ from the shales and sandstone above, but in its shade of red. Originally blue-gray and still so when freshly broken, the wall has gradually been stained a dark red by wash and drippage from the overhead beds.

These four chapters, consisting of 2,700 feet of rock pages, form the upper part of Grand Cañon.

Below lies another part composed of two chapters called the Tonto group. The first of these is a layer of green Tonto shale 800 feet thick, and under it a thin 150-foot layer of basal Tonto limestone, much, much older than the Redwall above.

Below this opens the most complex and thickest formation in the whole book. It is aptly called the Grand Cañon Series, and it is 12,000 feet thick. The Unkar group comprises the first chapters. It is composed of brown Dox sandstone, dark Bass limestone, Hotauta basal conglomerate and Shinumo quartzite enlivened with bright red Hakatai shale. Such a mixed mass is well named in part at least; Shinumo was the name applied to the old Hopi confederacy. The Chuar group is somewhat similar. Its pages are torn, twisted and crumpled. For unlike the horizontal Tonto group, these formations are warped, folded and tilted, sloping to the north.

And now we see the last pages in Grand Cañon. The oldest rock system in the world, part of the original earth's crust. Great vertical layers of gneiss that formed before the earth had cooled, and huge blocks of granite forced into them in a molten state by heat and enormous pressure.

Such is Grand Cañon—15,650 feet and more of rock pages; pages of light gray, white, dark red, vivid green, blue-gray, bright red, brown; pages of coarse sandstones, fine-textured limestones, shales, rough conglomerates, quartzite, sturdy gneiss and granite. Never smooth, neatly pressed. But in horizontal layers, in vertical walls, in great folds. Warped, twisted, broken. Laid slantwise to encompass three miles of thickness within a vertical depth of one mile. And finally gouged out and eroded into a geological maze.

What is the story it tells? Gradually we read back up the meaning of the pages.

For man time goes back no farther than the beginning of this geological record when the earth was still molten, but cooling to form its sturdy crust of gneiss and granite. This first Archeozoic era leaves no record of any primordial life for over a billion years, not even a single fossil. But gradually the earth cooled, atmosphere formed, water vapor condensed into rain, and the surface was eroded down into a plain.

The first chapter suddenly ends. This immense, immeasurable plain sank under the sea. Upon it were deposited the thick beds of sediment composing the Unkar and Chuar groups. First the limestone laid down upon the granite on the floor of the sea. Then the sandstone on its beaches. Finally the shale in its estuaries. For now something else was happening. The earth was rising again. Uplifted, it shook mightily, with vast distortioning shrugs, tilting and faulting the new layer on its crust.

So begins the next great era, the Proterozoic, which left in its seaweeds and crustaceans a record of the first life beginning on earth. But now again the persistent forces of destruction began—the solution of limestone by rain water, heat and cold, which expanded and contracted the rock, frost that cracked it, erosion by wind-blown sand. And again the surface was a rolling plain.

For a second time the earth sank under the sea. Again deposition of sedimentary beds took place—green muds of Tonto shale and limestone that buried even the small, hardcapped Unkar and Chuar islands.

But when it rose in Cambrian times, the third great era had begun: the Paleozoic, the era of ancient life. Algae and seaweeds were abundant, trilobites, brachiopods and crustaceans.

There is a gap in the rock record here. Two whole chapters—the Ordovician and Silurian—are missing, during which shell-forming sea animals and reef-building corals developed. We know they exist; their formations have been found elsewhere throughout the earth. Of a third period there remain but a few isolated buttes; the Devonian, the "Age of Fishes," when amphibians and land plants began to form. Yet so clear is the pattern before and after this gap that there is little doubt that there were more submergences whose deposits here were washed away without trace.

The story resumes with another deep submergence during which the

Redwall deposit was laid down. As the uplift slowly followed, the red Supai muds were deposited in the shallow water and then the Coconino sandstone on the beaches by strong currents. Each sand is distinctly formed and polished. This leaves little doubt that the uplift was exceedingly slow.

Still remains another submergence, deposit and uplift, showing the top layer of Kaibab limestone, which forms the present surface of the high northern plateau.

With this ends one of the great periods in geological history, the Carboniferous, in which all the oldest coal deposits throughout the world were accumulated and laid down under great pressure. It was the "Age of Amphibians," of sharks and sea monsters. Primitive flowering plants and the earliest cone-bearing trees began to form. Backboned animals came into being for the first time.

It ends too the third great geological era, the Paleozoic, 340 million years long. The end of all "ancient life" forms, as the Proterozoic was of all primordial life. And yet these last four formations—the Redwall, Supai, Coconino and Kaibab—took shape in its last period, the Carboniferous, and end the story of Grand Cañon.

What about the two following eras? The Mesozoic, era of medieval life, 140 million years long, the "Age of Reptiles"—of the great land monsters, the dinosaurs, and the flying reptiles. The Cenozoic, era of modern life, the age of man, of modern animals and plants. Already it is 60 million years in extent.

All around Grand Cañon remnants of its formations rise on the horizon—Vermilion Cliffs to the north, Cedar Mountain to the east, Red Butte to the south. All the rest has been swept away. Swept away by the great red river as it cut Grand Cañon. They were, in fact, the river's tools—every grain of sand, every frost-shattered boulder, every mountain peak. The teeth by which time has cut a visible gash through eternity.

This, then, is the story of Grand Cañon. The geological record of an earth at least 2,000 million years old, nearly three-quarters of which had transpired before the first record of life, and all but a million years before man came into existence. Over three miles thick it is, yet the whole of man's evolution is not represented by so much as the thickness of one sheet of paper.

We know so little and we are so contemptuous of each other's knowledge. The oldest man here, the red man, has spoken in the science we call "myth." The white man speaks in the myth we call "science." Yet their identical story of these million missing years could be written on this paper in a few paragraphs.

In the Beginning, it would read, God created the world and the waters subsided and the earth rose. But in the eternal palingenesis, which proves an evolutionary scheme for living earths as well as for living plant and beast and man, this continent has had many such beginnings. Seven times, as we have seen, America has been submerged in the darkness of the deeps. And each time it has risen to stand in the light of a day millions of years long.

This day has hardly yet dawned.

In its first dim light only the summits of the highest peaks stood out. The little islands that are today the peaks and ridges of the Colorado Rockies, the oldest dry land on the American continent.

A moment more and the whole vast land rose shudderingly, streaming water from its flanks like an old buffalo from his wallow. It was a land whose size and shape and texture are hidden in the memory of an indigenous mythology not yet deciphered, and in a science not yet infallible to reasonable guess.

For suddenly it was changed. There began one of the greatest dramas America has ever known or will know until it disappears again from sight. The earth shook in a last convulsive tremor. Mountains split asunder. Peaks burst into flame. Whole upper halves of 30,000-foot volcanoes blew off, leaving only the stumps long afterward named peaks by men like Long and Pike.

And now the molten earth cooled, solidified. The last of the waters receded, hissing, leaving seashells and sharks' teeth imprisoned in rock. Whole forests lay level, petrified into stone. Mountains of debris washed down, packed solid; and still retaining their latent fire, became vast beds of coal. Wind and water gnawed at the rough-edged portrait of the land, changing it into the face we know now. Green life began, and that which fed upon it. But above all this stood out the ranges, shining with pristine smoothness, glitteringly white. The Shining Mountains, as they were first known and are still called by man.

And then the rivers began to form in their snowbanks and their glaciers. The hundreds of little rivers that drew into one. The great red river which cut its way down peak and mountain, through mesa and plateau, across the desert to the sea below. The river that has written these last few moments of earth-history.

Thus near dawn it stands, fresh, serene and virginal, yet old and worn and warped by the tortuous pain of rebirth—this vast river basin of a continent newly risen from the depths of time. The high, rugged Colorado Pyramid, which is at once the newest and the oldest dry earth of America.

And now breaks the first light of this, its new day. It strikes a few dark figures born of the earth itself who are watching a sail far off on the horizon. In a moment the ship enters the mouth of the river. A few strange figures step off—white. The two groups, white and dark, meet and intermingle for a moment on its shores. The shores of the river that expresses for both the common mystery of their lives and the earth they tread—the strange red river that flows and ever flows between them.

And still it is not yet dawn.

This is all we know of the Colorado's history. It is all that these paragraphs have been about.

IX

Masked Gods

The underlying themes of The Colorado *are developed further in* Masked Gods: Navaho* and Pueblo Ceremonialism *(1947), in which Waters further suggests that the problem is not simply within White orientation or Indian orientation but that the conflicting dualities are present in each individual, in any time or place. The dichotomies are part of human nature, and are part of outer Nature as well. Waters suggests that the Pueblo and Navaho Indians have long recognized these conflicting forces which make up the universe and human nature; and recognizing as well the need for internal harmony and harmony with one's environment, they have, for centuries, used ritual to portray the cosmic dualities and to dramatize their equilibrium. Thus the focus of these ceremonies is on universal harmony and on psychic wholeness. In the closing sections of* Masked Gods, *"The Crucible of Conflict," Waters postulates that the Indians have intuitively perceived through their necessary closeness to the forces of Nature a universe greatly similar to that being discovered by modern science. He cites the evidence of contemporary atomic physics, biology, and astronomy that describes a universe of inter-dependence, of mutuality—a "process reality." This is the universe that has been dramatized in dance by the Navahos and Pueblos for centuries. That the Indian view is being approached by modern science Waters sees as hopeful evidence of mankind's achieving the synthesis*

Two spellings for this word—Anglicized with an "h" or Hispanicized with a "j"— appear throughout Waters' works and reflect usage then current among writers, publishers, and the Navajos themselves. I have made no attempt to standardize the spellings, retaining instead the spelling that appeared in the original work.

necessary for its survival and of an evolution of human conscious-
ness already begun.

The first selection below deals with the Pueblo and Navaho
myth of the creation of our present world. The second selection is
"The Crucible of Conflict."

In the Beginning the people lived in several worlds below. Successively they emerged from them to a new world above. In the middle of
this new world stood a great rock. Extending through all the previous
underworlds and protruding above this one, it was the core of the universe, rooted in time and space. It was oriented to the four directions,
and its sides glowed with their corresponding colors—white on the east,
blue on the south, yellow-red on the west, black on the north.

Emerging from the world below, the people gathered at its foot. And
when they planted seeds to make the earth spread out, and when they
called to the Holy People to help them plant the Holy Mountains, it was
around this great natal rock. Hence they called it simply the Mountain
Around Which Moving Was Done, the Mountain Surrounded by Mountains, or the Encircled Mountain.

To the east of it they planted the Holy Mountain of the East, made of
sand and white shell. To the south they planted the Mountain of the
South, made of sand and blue-green turquoise. To the west, the Mountain of the West, of yellow-red sand and abalone. And to the north, the
Mountain of the North, of black sand and jet. In each they placed a
Holy Person, a Talking God to guard the mountain and to listen to the
prayers and songs offered it. Extra mountains they transplanted, and
seeds of the four sacred plants. They made a fire with four kinds of
wood and a hogan with four logs. Everything—the stars, the winds, the
seasons—they put in order and named, and they became. For "when
you put a thing in order, give it a name, and you are all in accord: it becomes."

Thus the pattern of the Navaho world at the Emergence. The great
central Encircled Mountain. The four directional Holy Mountains. The
lesser transplanted mountains, the plants, the trees, with the winds, the
seasons, and the sun and moon and stars above. A world spread out like
a four-petalled flower as seen from above. This today in a Navaho sand-
painting is the symbol of the great axial rock, the Encircled Mountain: a
four-petalled flower, like a four-leafed clover, like a lotus.

The four sacred mountains still bounding the ancient Navaho homeland are physical mountains: the Mountain of the East variously identified as Mount Blanca, in Colorado; Wheeler Peak, above Taos in the

Sangre de Cristo range; or Pelado Peak, near the pueblo of Jemez; Mount Taylor, of the San Mateo range, as the Mountain of the South; the San Francisco peaks, in Arizona, as the Mountain of the West; and a peak in the La Plata or San Juan range as the Mountain of the North.

The Encircled Mountain is something else. It has been identified as Huerfano Peak, above Chaco Cañon, which bears its name. But by its very nature it cannot be so constricted. Being the core of the whole cosmos, it existed when the First People were still in the lower worlds; and spanning a time and space beyond our earth-dimensional comprehension, it is too great and too powerful to be visible. This is its metaphysical reality. El Huerfano is merely its material image, its physical counterpart.

The meaning of this is amplified by reference to the cosmography of Tibetan Buddhism, in which is found the most striking parallel to the Encircled Mountain.

The core of the cosmos is Mt. Meru. It is shaped like a truncated pyramid, three of its four sides glowing with the same directional colors of the Navaho world-axis: white on the east, blue on the south, red on the west, and yellow on the north. It is eighty thousand miles high and eighty thousand miles deep. Within it are several underworlds and several heavens. Around this mighty cosmic core are seven concentric circles of mountains separated by seven encircling oceans. Each of these fresh-water oceans and its corresponding wall of mountains is a separate universe with its own sun and moon and planets.

Outside these seven universes, and floating in the outer salt-water ocean of space, are four main continents or land masses spreading out in the four main directions. The eastern continent is crescent in shape, white in color, as are the faces of its inhabitants. It is nine thousand miles in diameter. The western continent is round in shape, red in color, as are the faces of its inhabitants; its diameter is eight thousand miles. The northern continent is the largest of all, being ten thousand miles in diameter. It is of square shape and yellow color, and its inhabitants have corresponding faces. The southern continent is our planet Earth. It is the smallest of the four, being seven thousand miles in diameter as now verified by our modern scientific measurements. It is pearshaped—and we agree that rather than being round it is flattened at both ends and bulges in the middle. Blue is the color assigned to it; and the faces of its inhabitants are oval shaped and greyish blue.

Below this mighty Mt. Meru the cosmos thus spreads out like a great four-petalled flower, a lotus. Each of the world-petals is protected by a Lokapala, or World Guardian, as each of the four Holy Mountains of the Navahos is guarded by its Talking God. And just as the Navaho world and the Encircled Mountain is symbolized by a four-petalled flower, so is the Buddhistic cosmos represented as a lotus.

These are striking pictorial and mythological parallels. But their full significance would be lost without their metaphysical meaning. The whole cosmos is represented as a lotus; but this cosmos is also identical with the goddess-mother called "The Lotus"; and our earthly universe is located within her "at about the level of her waist." In its duality, then, it is both that which was created and that which created it. And each living being, himself created in the image of the Goddess Mother of creation, also duplicates within his own psyche the complete cosmos.

Only by this can we understand the cryptic opening sentence of the legend of the Navaho ceremonial *Where The Two Came to their Father:* "When they put the extra mountains around, they took Mountain Around Which Moving Was Done out of First Woman's belt."

This too explains the Zuñi references to the Sacred Middle which their ancestors found at Zuñi after their emergence from the underworld, and the location of their corresponding Mountain of Generation as being just below the navel of the Earth Mother. Above all is their striking conception of the Earth Mother as the goddess-mother of creation, through whose successive womb-worlds they emerged to this one.

The conception of this four-cornered world structure is not confined to them alone in America. In the sacred *Popol Vuh*, recording the creation myth of the Quiché Maya, the world is described as "four-pointed, four-sided, four-bordered." In the *Chilan Balam of Mani* this cubical world-block is further alluded to as the altar of the gods. The truncated pyramid temples of the Toltecs, Zapotecs, and Aztecs themselves suggest such world axes.

Hence we understand now, at the outset, that in Pueblo and Navaho mythology we are dealing not with easily comprehended, childish legends, but with a cosmographic concept as abstract, imaginatively vast and old as that of any people on earth. It is strangely consistent that the area today still contains this mythological meaning in its name of the Four Corners. Its original prototype, its greatest physical image, may well have been, not El Huerfano, but the Colorado Pyramid, the high hinterland heart of America. Its central section, the Colorado plateau region, is still the sacred middle, their traditional homeland. The Pueblos and Navahos have always regarded life as dual: the physical and psychical. And it is both of these realities of the Rock to which they have clung against the assault of erosion and materialism alike.

THE CRUCIBLE OF CONFLICT

From our back pasture, a meadow among the pines on the high slopes of the Sangre de Cristos, we stare down upon a corner of one of the most beautiful, paradoxical and significant panoramas in the world today. In its entirety we know it as the four Corners, the immemorial domain of the Rock and the Canyon, the center of gravity of the continental Colorado Pyramid, the wilderness heartland of America.

Perhaps in no other comparable area on earth are condensed so many contradictions, or manifested so clearly the opposite polarities of all life. The oldest forms of life discovered in this hemisphere, and the newest agent of mass death. The oldest cities in America and the newest. The Sun Temple of Mesa Verde and the nuclear fission laboratories of the Pajarito Plateau. The Indian drum and the atom smasher. Men flying like birds seeding the clouds for rain, while others below them, naked and painted, dancing with rattlesnakes in their mouths. Everywhere the future stumbles upon the jutting past, the invisible gives shape to the visible, blind instinct points the way for reason.

There is no describing it. But it has been symbolized for us in the sand-paintings of Navaho ceremonialism: the plateau-square of the Four Corners inscribed within a circle. We recognize it now as both the crucible of conflict and the *mandala* of reconciliation of the cosmic dualities.

For here as nowhere else has the conflict been fought so bitterly, and have the opposing principles approached so closely a fusion. At that fusion there will arise the new faith for which we are crying so desperately. A faith big enough to embrace all of mankind's experience of the past, all our religious creeds, and all our scientific concepts.

It would not be too great a coincidence if the new symbols of that faith rose out of those of the past, just as mankind itself has risen to successive stages of evolution through the supreme symbol of the *sipapu* epitomized as the Grand Canyon.

An Historical Perspective

Myself, I can't account for the inexpressible fascination that this Hopi *sipapu* holds for me. Whenever things go out of focus, money runs short and the temper rises like a barometer, I always take a squint at Grand Canyon as a down payment on another lease of equanimity.

J. B. Priestly, a noted Englishman, recommends it to us even more extravagantly. "If I were an American," he advises, "I should make my remembrance of it the final test of men, art, and policies. I should ask myself: is this good enough to exist in the same country as the Cañon? How would I feel about this man, this kind of art, these political measures, if I were near that Rim? Every member or officer of the Federal Government ought to remind himself, with triumphant pride, that he is on the staff of the Grand Cañon."

The Hopi, I think would pass this test. Their art, social science and government, the kiva ceremonialism which includes their cosmology and cosmogenesis, their very lives are patterned on it. Some of the rest of us fall a little short. And there are other noted Englishmen who do not seem aware of its existence.

As a matter of fact it is sunset here on the Rim now, an excellent moment to appraise Arnold J. Toynbee's colossal *A Study of History* by the Canyon's own colossal dimensions. We don't need to read the whole first seven volumes, nor even D. C. Somervell's excellent one-volume abridgement. A *Life* artist has recently illustrated his metaphor for us.

Here is the deep, shadowy Canyon itself—the *sipapu* of all life. Up its steep sides come crawling from the depths of subhumanity the twenty-one human figures representing the major civilizations of history. Most of them didn't get very far. Like the Egyptiac, Sumeric, Babylonic, Hellenic, Maya, and Andean, they are lying dead on a low ledge. Stretched out and dying are the primitive societies like the Hopi. Stranded on minor peaks, still alive but unable to climb higher, are five "arrested" civilizations like the Ottoman and Polynesian. Five civilizations are still climbing. Four of them are short of breath and weakening in this altitude: the Islamic, Hindu, Chinese-Japanese, and the Russian. Only one is strong and healthy and has far out-climbed the others: our own Euro-American civilization.

The picture, the metaphor, is apt indeed up here. But at just this instant, in actuality, there comes striding up the Bright Angel Trail from the bottom of the Canyon a grinning broad-faced Hopi. The very same Hopi seen in the picture stretched out and dying as a "Primitive Society." Much later, far behind him, comes "Western Civilization" in the dejected persons of a group of Euro-American tourists astraddle some burros which (in our imagination) are labelled "Machine."

What is wrong with the picture?

It seems strange as we read Toynbee with the care his study warrants, that never, on any page, do we get the sense of surging uplift, of tumultuous upheavals from dark depths, that mark the history of mankind as they do the geologic history of the earth. One doubts that he has ever experienced the tremendous, psychical impact of the upflung Himalayas, the lofty Andes, the rugged Rockies, or this greatest chasm on the face of the earth. He gives the impression of a historian who sees everything from the perspective of a flat Aegean plain washed by the placid Mediterranean.

That indeed is his forte: the Hellenic civilization. It is the keystone by which he measures the structures of all the others. The basis of our own Western civilization, founded on the same rational principle or determinate theoretic component. And so all the great movements of history take place on this comparatively horizontal plane. One after another the ancient civilizations rise like gentle prominences, flower, congeal, and slide forward into the next with a kind of undulatory movement like that of a snake.

There are never any mysterious up-surges of unknown forces from deep in the soul of mankind, no strange cataclysmic plunges into obscurity, comparable to earthquakes, the rise and fall of continents which reflect the same upheavals within the earth. Yet each in some way is related to the other and dependent upon it; both are the sheer utterance of life itself. A life stemming from a common source, whose motion and direction is unpredictable, whose logic is still not deducible. And so in Toynbee's work the great vertical, secular systems of mankind founded upon the intuitional principle or undifferentiated aesthetic component—the Hindu, Chinese, Andean, Maya and Mexic—are sketchily portrayed at best.

The reason for the successive rise and decline of all the twenty-one civilizations is embodied in Toynbee's theme of "Challenge and Response." Society is challenged by environment, war and various other rationalized pressures. As long as it successfully responds to these challenges it continues to expand; when at last it fails to respond, it perishes. But all these expansions are progressively outward, horizontally. Eastward. Southward. Mostly Westward to Europe, to Euro-America. Until now Western civilization has spread around the world. The expansive culmination of the basic Graeco-Roman civilization.

Consistently enough all the four world-religious systems—and all religions are vertical by their very nature—Toynbee sees as products of the merging of the various secular systems. Islam results from the merging of the ancient civilization of Israel and Iran with the modern civilization of the Near and Middle East. Hinduism bridges the ancient culture of the Aryans in India and the modern Hindu culture. Mahayana Buddhism links the history of ancient China with the modern history of the Far East. Christianity rises from the encounter between the Syrian and Graeco-Roman civilizations. . . . All being responses of the various civilizations to the challenge of Graeco-Roman penetration over a period of some 1,600 years.

It is no coincidence that 4004 B.C., the date set by the Christian Church for the creation of the world, is also the approximate date at which began the twenty-one major civilizations. Thus, concomitant with the horizontal spread of Western civilization has been the spread of Christianity. Until now the Christian-Western civilization reigns supreme.

So here too in Toynbee the greatest vertical religions of mankind are but shallowly plumbed. Nowhere do we find in it anything like the intuitive appraisal of Mahayana Buddhism made by F. S. C. Northrop in his penetrative *The Meeting of East and West*. Nor anything to compare with the remarkable exposition of Chinese Taoism made by Richard Wilhelm and C. G. Jung. There is scarcely mention of the basic mytho-religious patterns that still hold sway in Africa and America. In it no continents rise and sink, leaving their vestiges of vanished civilizations engraven on the heart of land and man. The tiny, helpless, prehistoric mammal does not meet the challenge of the great armored dinosaur with the divine biological response attested by the great French biologist, Lecomte du Nouy, in his *Human Destiny*. Mankind has no record of its continuous evolutionary climb through four previous worlds to its present state of existence as attested by Buddhism, Taoism, all ancient mystics, modern psychologists, and the Hopi coming up the trail. That man has a divine destiny which will continue to guide him in his climb, which basic intuitional truth is the core of all valid religions, is not suggested. . .

Without wishing to seem derogatory about Toynbee's work, a study so comprehensive and erudite as to be a classic of its kind, we must yet consider it here on the Rim as a study in two dimensions with little vertical depth.

There is an indication that its writer himself has some misgivings about its thinness. In his later *Civilization on Trial* Toynbee questions his own earlier assumption that these relatively modern civilizations are the "intelligible field" of historical study, the religions serving only as links between them. He now suggests that religion itself may be the "intelligible field" and that the purpose of civilizations is but to spread it among mankind.

This extreme and abrupt volte-face prompts us to ask: But which religion, which civilization's concept of a Divine Plan? The answer is even more surprising. . . .

There will be no reason to suppose that Christianity itself will be superseded by some distinct, separate and higher religion which will serve as a chrysalis between the death of the present Western civilization and the

birth of its children. . . . So far from that, if our secular Western civilization perishes, Christianity may be expected not only to endure but to
grow in wisdom and stature as the result of a fresh experience of secular
catastrophe.*

Q.E.D.

But just at this moment, reassured as we are of the divine inpregna-
bility of our Christian-Western ideology, a gust of wind whips down
from the Rockies. A *Study of History* is blown from our hands. It hits a
gnarled old piñon on the Rim. The ripped off cover tumbles down into a
pack-rat's nest lodged in the roots. We peer down. What an excellent
roof it makes that sub-human little family, bent in the middle to keep
out wind and snow; its jacket title printing vaguely reminiscent of the
letters painted on the tin roof of an old barn.

But we aren't concerned about the mere binding. Where is the text?
One would suppose that the history of six-thousand years would be
quite visible against the background of time. Yes. There they are at last!
Twenty-one paper-thin pages hovering in the blue and purple depths of.
a time 217 miles long, twelve miles wide and a mile deep carven out of
eternity. Twenty-one civilizations floating against the six-thousand year
top layer of an historical record of 2,000 million years. Convoluting like
dry leaves in the air, rubbing together with a dry, brittle rustle. Catch-
ing the bright rays of the sun from above, enveloped by the dark
shadows from below. How small and light they are! Seemingly impervious to the invisible laws of nature.

"Long live the Pharaoh!" echoes one of the pages. Then a down-draft
catches the Egyptiac civilization and sucks it down into obscurity.

"Hail Caesar!" And Pax Romana swoops downward.

"Heil, Fuehrer!" But invisibly the law of gravity reaches up a long
arm and snatches the Third Reich too.

There they go, twenty of them, lost in space, engulfed in time, sinking to rest with the fossilized remains of the brute-animal civilizations of
the prehistoric past.

One remains still ballooned aloft above the Canyon. He can't read it,
the Hopi beside me; he can't read. But we know what it is: the Christian-Western civilization. It sails quite grandly too. But somehow, for
all the up-drafts, the invisible gravitational field draws it down too. Or
maybe it lodges somewhere down there on an undiscovered ledge to
serve as nesting material for a magpie, the bird of augury.

"I go home now," says the Hopi, and a shabby primitive home it is. "I

Civilization on Trial, by Arnold J. Toynbee. Oxford University Press, New York, 1947.

got those work to do. Them kiva duties."

And one remains on the Rim alone. Staring down into the Canyon's sublime depths: at Cheop's Pyramid and the Tower of Ra; at Zoroaster's Temple, Confucius' Temple, and the Krishna Shrine; at the Valhalla Plateau and Woton's Throne; King Arthur's Castle, Gawain Abyss and Lancelot's Point; at Solomon's Temple, Aztec Amphitheater, Toltec Point, Cardenas Butte, and Alarcon Terrace. Washed by seas of flowing color, changing shape in light and shadow, it sees a realm of the fantastic unreal. A world of illusion.

What if Buddhism is right in its assumption that the material world of the senses is non-existent? That all physical matter, as Western Science now proclaims, is but a manifestation of that primordial energy constituting the electron? What if the Hopi is right in persisting to climb through all the successive worlds of his existence by adhering to his kiva ceremonialism in preference to the transient beliefs and material riches of his conquerors? Is the Rock that we shall cling to now the Mountain Around Which Moving Was Done, invisible to us as to the Navahos because its reality lies only within us?

The canyon alone can answer, and it does answer in a mute and guarded tone. Not by its length and breadth But by its depth. For that depth, its third dimension, translates itself into time, the fourth. At the bottom we see the Past; Archeozoic Time. Here at the top we stand in the present; Modern Time. In the stars coming out above the opposite rim we see the Future; Cosmic Time. But suppose they all converge in us in Psychozoic Time, just as we glimpse simultaneously the bedrock of the Canyon, the toprock of its highest wall and the stars above?

Why, then we should know as that stubborn Hopi that we haven't progressed spatially, as Toynbee suggests, at all; we have stood still, doing all our climbing within ourselves. And also, quite naturally, we would not worry about the history of twenty-one civilizations; for as Past, Present and Future are coexistent, we could simply change history now to suit ourselves.

Out of this growing perception of time as the fourth dimension of a world of reality, emerges at last the new symbol which all are seeking.

Time, the Fourth Dimension

"The non-mathematician," says Albert Einstein, "is seized by a mysterious shuddering when he hears of 'four dimensional' things, by a feeling not unlike that awakened by thoughts of the occult. And yet there is no more commonplace statement than that the world in which we live is a four-dimensional space-time continuum."

A continuum is something that is continuous, like space or time. To understand each of these we mark it off in three segments which we label Past, Present, and Future, or Length, Breadth, and Thickness.

Here we are then strolling down the byway of time. Before us a line is drawn across the road. Beyond it is the Future; it does not exist yet. Behind us is another line drawn across the road. Nothing beyond it exists either; it is the Past. What exists, evidently is only the Present segment between the two lines. But part of that segment lies in the immediate Future and part of it in the immediate Past. In fact with every step that we are moving through the Present, we are converting some of it into the Future and some of it into the Past.

Obviously the segment is too large. The two lines will have to be combined into one. For what fixes our location in time is only that one second during which we step across it. And if we start running, that second is reduced to a split-second. That is the only true Present. A split-second of infinity.

Our location in space is just as arbitrary, apparently.

If we step on a train which runs on a straight railroad track according to schedule, our position can be fixed in space at any moment by the mile-post it passes. Two dimensions, however, are required to establish our location if we are on a ship at sea, latitude and longitude. An airplane requires three coordinates: latitude, longitude and altitude.

These three measurements, of length, breadth, and height, constitute space as we know it, just as past, present, and future constitute our familiar concept of time.

But to fix accurately our position on the train, the ship or the airplane in space, time is required: the year, the day, the minute it is at any given point. And to determine accurately our position in time, it is necessary to know our position in space. And both are relative to our movement through them.

We begin to see then that the measurements of space and time are somehow correlated. As Barnett points out, what we call an hour is actually a measurement of space—an arc of fifteen degrees in the daily rotation of the earth. But the earth not only rotates daily about its axis at the rate of 1,000 miles an hour. It revolves annually around the sun at the rate of 20 miles a second. The solar system itself moves within the star system; the star system within the Milky Way; and the Milky Way with respect to the remote outer galaxies.

Our position in time and our position in space are thus relative. Pacific Coast or Eastern Standard Time, Planet Earth Time, Solar System

Time or Milky Way Time. The universe is a four-dimensional space-time continuum with three dimensions of space and one of time.

According to time-space measurement,' a light-year is the distance spanned by light travelling for one year at 186,000 miles a second, or roughly 6 trillion miles. By this measurement the universe is some thirty-five billion light-years in radius. Quite large.

It is also quite old. Geophysicists measure its present age by determining the rate at which uranium expends its nuclear energies. Astrophysicists by estimating the temperature at which the thermonuclear processes in the stars transmute their matter into radiation. And cosmogenicists by calculating the velocity at which the remote outer galaxies are receding from our solar system. All agree that our universe began 2,000 million years ago. As it had a beginning it must have an end. The earth is gradually cooling; the stars are slowly transmuting their energy into radiation; the sun itself, consisting only of free neutrons, is burning out. Eventually, though we may still have another 2,000 million years left us, there will be no light, no heat, no life, and no time. The universe will come to an end.

Yet these spatial and time concepts must be modified. Because, as Barnett points out, the Relativity Theory proves that there is a corresponding distortion of the space-time continuum for every concentration of matter in the universe, "The combined distortions produced by all the incomputable masses of matter in the universe cause the continuum to bend back on itself in a great cosmic curve." Hence a ray of light-energy travelling from the sun at 186,000 miles per second will describe a great cosmic circle and return to its source after 2,000 million terrestrial years.

How strange it is that modern science now defines the cosmos by the same symbol of the circle used by the mathematician-philosophers of ancient Greece, by the religious systems of Buddhism and Taoism, and Pueblo and Navaho ceremonialism.

So wherever and however we travel in space—by foot or horseback, train and ship, plane and rocket—we are bound within this circle. The shortest distance between two points is not a straight line. Every step we take is on an arc of great curvature.

Likewise our journey through time is not a straight line from the past, through the present, to the future. Time too ever bends back on itself in a closed circle. So, as we know, the circle is also the symbol of the human psyche. Our evolutionary Road of Life completes its circuit by returning to its source. The End of our journey is the Beginning.

Man may reach at death the supposed end of his journey. But from the after-death state he is reborn to the life-state. So over and over again within the circle he continues his round of existence. Until finally, through an inner development, he breaks free and escapes from time into eternity.

For a novelist this great theme offers endless, entrancing possibilities. He must hold on to his pen to keep his imagination from running away with it. Think of returning to an indestructible past! *A Yankee in King Arthur's Court!* P. D. Ouspensky, always obsessed with this theme of eternal recurrence, explored it in an early novel, *The Wheel of Fortune*, and developed it in his recent *Strange Life of Ivan Osokin*, who goes back to the same house, the same parents, the same triumphs and failures.

Yes, says Ouspensky, brooding upon the sufferings of people long gone. Mankind cannot leave behind the sins of the past. It must return and destroy the causes of evil, however far back they may lie. Correction, improvement, must take place in the past. Just as psychoanalysts assert that an individual must go back into his past in order to understand and free himself from its evil consequences.

There is nothing frightening and mysterious about this series of phenomena called metempsychosis or reincarnation. A man of sixty is not the little boy he was at six. Every one of the 26 trillion cells in his body has been replaced many times; his thoughts have changed. Yet between the two there is a continuity of consciousness and identity of personality. There is not much more difference between the man when he dies and the child when he is reborn. Death breaks the identity of personality—because he may have another name, live in another civilization—but the causal nexus is still maintained. The continuity of consciousness remains unbroken too; all the memories of his past lives are stored in the unconscious which one day will release them to his conscious mind.

What happens at death is simply that man discards his three-dimensional physical body like an outworn coat, and moves into another dimensional plane. After living a life on this unconscious or after-death plane, he then reenters this conscious plane and immediately puts on another three-dimensional body like putting on a new coat.

Never does he vanish completely, nor does the essential inner identity of any form of life ever vanish. By an immutable spiritual law corresponding to our physical law of the conservation of energy, nothing ever dies, not even places. So as Pueblo kachinas they may be invisibly recalled—not as "spirits" or "ghosts," but as the other-dimensional shapes of mountains, trees, birds, animals, the dead—recalled from a dimensional plane that is not yet apprehended spatially.

But how are we to effect our eventual escape from this synonymous circle of the cosmos and the psyche, and return to the ultimate source?

As Ouspensky, Gurdjieff, du Nouy, Eastern Buddhism, Western science, and Navaho and Pueblo ceremonialism all attest, the inner development or evolutionary journey of man through four worlds or stages coincides with his growing perception of dimensions.

How did things appear to us in the first world or stage of consciousness? Why, much the same as they would to a rock or a plant on a plain. The rock or the plant cannot distinguish whether the plain is rectangular or circular; whether it is near the center or the edge. Being unable to see the horizon and not conscious of time, it cannot establish its position in either time or place. It is one-dimensional.

In the second stage of consciousness, a two-dimensional being like an ant with volition and movement, could distinguish length and breadth. But it perceived everything as a flat geometrical shape. It had no perception of height or depth, of thickness, the third dimension.

In our third stage of consciousness, with the perception of the third dimension, man becomes able to disassociate himself from his environment. He sails over the horizon of the flat world with the new assurance it is a sphere. He flies above it, confirming his location in interstellar space. He also becomes conscious, as a disassociated observer, of the existence of yesterday and tomorrow. But this first perception of time, the fourth dimension, he still sees as three-dimensional: past, present, future; birth, life, death. He cannot conceive it as an actual dimension at right angles to the three he knows.

But gradually as he emerges into the present fourth plane of existence through an inner development, he perceives this fourth-dimensional reality. The faculty of the unconscious develops to correspond with his previous development of the conscious and self-conscious. Through imagination and dreams he enters this unconscious realm of the fourth dimensional past and future. The old oracles we laughed at, as we did Roger Bacon's assertion in the 13th century that there would be flying machines, submarines and astronomical lenses of unimaginable power. We still laugh at our dreams at the breakfast table. Yet there always remains of them a secret reassurance of their ultimate reality. Dunne in his *An Experiment With Time* analyzed many of his dreams over a long period of time, discovering that they were images of the future as well as the past. Rhine, making thousands of tests at Duke University, established as fact clairvoyance, telepathy, and other extrasensory powers. They are impervious to time and distance, penetrate all barriers, and are not even very rare.

Well, why not a fifth and sixth stage of existence, with their corresponding dimensions?

Navaho ceremonialism attests the four successive states or worlds through which we already have climbed, and postulates two more. Buddhism and Taoism confirm this, as does modern psychology, and the late biologist, Vicomte du Nouy. And even some physicists declare that the encounter of two electrons demands a six-dimensional universe in which to actualize their possibilities.

In postulating these further stages of evolutionary development, Buddhism delineates the psychological attributes man will derive from each. That of the fifth will be the unconscious. By it man will be able to recall the complete past. He will have freed himself from time. In the sixth state, the plane of the mind, he will correlate the conscious and unconscious. Man is then perfected and ready to emerge into the last and seventh stage, returning to and merging with the eternal source, undifferentiated from the complete cosmos. So the evolutionary Road of Life is finally completed.

The multi-dimensional universe, then, can be comprehended only as man's own sense perceptions through an inner development are gradually enlarged to encompass it.

As Barnett states, "Yet man's inescapable impasse is that he himself is part of the world he seeks to explore; his body and proud brain are mosaics of the same elemental particles that compose the dark, drifting dust clouds of interstellar space; he is, in the final analysis, merely an ephemeral conformation of the primordial space-time field."

The only world man knows is the world created for him by his senses. What a narrow slit he sees it through yet! In all the vast spectrum he peers through only that tiny aperture between the ultraviolet and infrared rays which we call visible light. Beyond him, on one side, from a wave-length of 10^{-4} cms., extend the heat waves, radar, television and radio waves of 10^{+9} wave lengths to waves of unknown length. Beyond him, on the other side, from a wave-length of 10^{-5} cms., extend the X-rays, gamma rays, and cosmic rays of 10^{-14} wave length to waves of unknown shortness. What realms of majestic color, of unknown vibration, lie there to be discovered beyond his little aperture between the ultraviolet and infrared as our sense-perceptions enlarge dimensionally to encompass them?

Here again, as in Pueblo and Navaho ceremonialism, we have another restatement of the evolutionary process. The colors are chronological as well as directional symbols. Through the seven primary colors of the cosmic spectrum, man finally emerges into the divine sun white which is a composite of all.

So here at last we reach that final recapitulation which synthesizes Navaho and Pueblo ceremonialism with Eastern Buddhism and Taoism, and all branches of Western Science. The evolution of man physiologically and psychologically, his perception of time as another spatial dimension, his correlation of the unconscious and conscious, and the final reconciliation of his own psyche with that of the cosmos—the ultimate meaning of life for all mankind as well as for individual man.

Toward this, mythology, geology, psychology, astronomy, nuclear physics, religion, and metaphysics all travel different paths to the same goal. Only from their common symbols, though expressed in their different mediums, can we read their true meaning.

It is to this meaning that Pueblo and Navaho ceremonialism, which is so uniquely American in sinew, blood and thought, and yet which is so universally the property of all mankind, has so greatly contributed in the idiom of those mountains and rivers, those masked gods of our childhood, whose familiar and loved outlines have shaped our lives and thoughts and hopes.

X

The Woman at Otowi Crossing

In 1956, Waters came to grips with his most serious challenge
in writing fiction when he began work on The Woman at Otowi
Crossing and attempted to dramatize as fiction the themes and
ideas that had been maturing in The Colorado and Masked Gods.
Based on the life of Edith Warner, who ran a tea-room at Otowi
crossing, just below Los Alamos, The Woman at Otowi Crossing
becomes the story of Helen Chalmers, who, in tune with her
adopted environment and nearby Indian pueblo, was also a close
friend of the first atomic scientists. She, herself, forms a kind of
bridge between the two orientations and value systems. On the
one hand, Helen Chalmers understands the passive, intuitive,
docile nature of the Indians; yet she is a product of, and also understands, the power-oriented, aggressive, rational White world.

Early in the novel, a combination of adverse circumstances,
"fear, worry, guilt, dread, shame, financial failure"[15] and the discovery that she is dying of cancer, cause a kind of "psychic implosion" very much like the mystical moment of Enlightenment. A
physicist friend later describes it as if ". . . her essential inner self,
. . . vaporized and transformed into new elements from its old
atomic structure, rose slowly in a new spiritual entity to a new
height of comprehension."[16] In the process of dying, Helen learns
how to live. She becomes increasingly perceptive, receptive, sensitive. She is not a Great Mystic; she is simply "one who knows," a
person of insight into the unity and harmony of all life. In terms
of previous Waters' works, Helen has become "Indianized" in her
ability to perceive universal relationships and mutualities. Thus,

94

the basic assumption of The Woman of Otowi Crossing *is drawn from the conclusion of* Masked Gods.

Since Helen's initial psychic experience occurs early in the book, most of the story consists of her day-to-day living, running her tea-room with the help of her Indian friend Facundo, against the background of the birth of the atomic age. Through the comprehension of her physicist friends, Waters suggests that their scientific theorizing may also eventually lead them to similar states of heightened self-awareness.

This attempt to portray mystical enlightenment in fiction is successful, one critic calling it "a tour de force in fusion."[17] Waters creates an Anglo woman who convincingly demonstrates, as did Maria in People of the Valley, that evolution of consciousness through the synthesis of conflicts is possible.

The Woman at Otowi Crossing *opens shortly before World War II. Twenty years earlier, Helen Chalmers had run away from a wealthy but unhappy marriage in the East. Now, on the edge of an Indian Pueblo, she runs her small tea-room with the aid of Facundo, the Pueblo cacique, a spiritual leader. She has declined the security of marrying her lover, Jack Turner, because she feels she is too old and set in her ways. But the closing of the railroad line, an approaching visit from Emily Chalmers, the daughter she had abandoned, and the onset of financial problems create mounting pressure. Now she has discovered a tumor in her breast. Her first reaction has been one of total panic.*

All that day and night she stayed in the shut up house, withdrawn from life. Then anaesthetized by fear, she rose at sunup, drank a cup of tea, and drove her battered old Ford to Espanola. Dr. Arnold's office was not yet open. She slumped down on the doorstep like a lump of clay.

Eventually he came walking toward her briskly, a little man squinting through bifocals, his thin black overcoat flapping above his worn-down heels. "Not under the weather on a day like this, Miss Chalmers? Well, come in."

He unlocked the door, opened the window, switched on the light. Once in his office, Helen was calm and resolute. Without hesitation she unbuttoned her blouse. "That's it there," she pointed. "I thought you'd better have a look."

Dr. Arnold was a little too old, and practicing in too small a country town, to keep his interest ahead of the great demands made upon him. But he had been reliable enough for years to sew up fiesta knife wounds, deliver babies against the threats and wails of native midwives in nearby villages, and cure all ordinary ills that resisted the effects of native herbs. Also he was honest enough, on difficult cases, to send his patients to specialists in Santa Fe or Albuquerque. All these courageous, commonplace ministrations paraded through Helen's mind as he began his examination.

"All right. Both arms over your head now. Let's see if there's any relative fixation of that left breast...Now, hands on hips"...He held her right hand, placed his left in her armpit....Then he went behind her, placing his hands on her neck to examine the supraclavicular lymph node areas. "Any other members of the family have mammary carcinomas?"

She shrugged without answering and he continued his examination. Finally he straightened and wiped his glasses. "I don't believe there's anything to worry about, Miss Chalmers. I really don't. I've known several women to have similar swellings that disappeared in a short time. Let's give this one a few days."

Helen stared at him with a long, level look of almost indignant disbelief as she put on her blouse. How could she believe him against that secret intuitive self which had soundlessly foretold her fate with incontrovertible conviction?

Dr. Arnold had known her a long time. "Look here, Miss Chalmers," he said quietly. "You've had quite a scare. I can see that. But you're too sensible a woman to panic at a slightly swollen gland that'll probably go down in a few days. If it doesn't, go see a top man. Here." He scribbled out the name and address of a diagnostician specializing in carcinomas and thrust the paper into her pocket. "It could be a small, benign lesion of no significance whatever. But even if it does happen to be malignant there's nothing to be frightened about at this early stage. For goodness sake!"

Without a word, she put down a five-dollar bill on the table and walked out to her jalopy. It wouldn't start. Without annoyance or hurry she went to the garage for a new battery and a Spanish boy to install it. Sitting on the curb while he worked, she took out from her pocket the slip of paper Dr. Arnold had given her, stared at it a long time, then tore it up. It was almost noon when she reached home.

A strange feeling possessed her. It was as if she had gone a long, long distance away, and had been gone a long, long time. Only to come back and find that the calendar pages had not turned, and that everything appeared outwardly as before. The house...The ripples breaking against the sand bar . . . The raucous cries of the magpies, and the silent sweep of a hawk. Yet she seemed somehow disassociated from them. As if she had gone so far and stayed so long from the world she lived in that she was no longer attuned to its meanings.

Listlessly she sat down in a rocker by the window, and thumbed through a stack of newspapers and magazines that seemingly had accumulated during her long absence. Every newspaper screeched the war news in big, black heads. Blood and guts and whining steel . . . She leafed through the slick-paper, fashionable magazines that came from New York. Their over-ripe, ultra-sophisticated advertisements whispered seductively to her with blasé, clichés and aphrodisiacal suggestiveness of a worse death-in-life; whispered of diamond and sapphire pendants, matched furs, lace negligees, and creative headgear for the five o'clock hour . . . Still she sat rocking, unable to escape the mounting pressure of a frantic world being driven to a verge.

Nor could she escape the pressure of her own immediate worries and behind these, still more anxieties: guilt about the Chalmers she had forsaken, the betrayal of her love for Turner, worries about old friends ignored and forgotten till now, and the secret foibles of a youth and childhood she had long repressed. Everything she had done and said and neglected to do or say—her whole life pressed in upon her with an overwhelming conviction of its utter uselessness.

This was the meaning, she felt now, of that swelling over her breast. What did it matter whether it was a malignant growth or merely a swollen gland? It had thrown her life into true perspective. She did not fear death. It was that nullity of not being, of having never really been. That waste of time, of life, that horrible futility. It kept squeezing her. Her breasts ached from the pressure, her back and ribs hurt. She thought she'd choke.

Then suddenly it happened.

A cataclysmic explosion that burst asunder the shell of the world around her, revealing its inner reality with its brilliant flash. In its blinding brightness all mortal appearances dissolved into eternal meanings, great shimmering waves of pure feeling which had no other expression than this, and these were so closely entwined and harmonized they formed one indivisible unity. A selfhood that embraced her, the totality of the universe, and all space and all time in one immortal existence that had never had a beginning nor would ever have an end.

Her instantaneous perception of it was at once terrifying and ecstatic, for it was as if she had always known it and yet was comprehending it for the first time. Like a mote of earthly dust decalmed in the still, dead center of an actual explosion, she continued to sit there long after the blinding glare broke into gradations of color too infinite and subtle to define, and slowly faded and died. Within her now she could feel a strange fusion of body, mind and spirit into a new and integrated entity that seemed apart from the gross elements from which it sprang. Slowly she came to herself enough to realize that it all had happened within her.

Had she died? Suffered an epileptic seizure? A paralytic stroke? Gingerly she moved a hand, a foot. Sensations rushed back into her as into a vacuum. The hammering beat of a clock was deafening. She went into the kitchen and stopped it. A pan of cold tortillas sat on top of the stove; mechanically she broke off a piece. The taste evoked the whole shape, texture and life-cycle of the corn. It was that way with everything she saw and touched: it set off a chain of associations whose ramifications had no end.

Dazedly she wandered outside. The sun was setting in a glow that made her dizzy. Face down, she lay on the little bluff above the river only to feel herself merging into the earth. Like a piece of decomposed granite, whose every grain and particle was separate but which still maintained a curious entity, she sank through the porous, wet sand into the river. Now she knew how a drop of water felt when it dashed against a stone with a queer, cushioned shock and rubbery bounce. How it bubbled up on top; the fun of tossing on the surface; of being lifted up and riding in a cloud! There seemed nothing she did not know and feel—the slow pulse in a stone, the song of the river, the wisdom of the mountains. For the first time she glimpsed the complete pattern of the universe, and knew that everything within it, to a blade of grass, was significant and alive.

It was too much for her. She returned to the house and lay down on the couch without undressing. But she could not sleep for the joy that seemed now to bubble up within her and burst into a fountain at the top of her head, flooding every crack and cranny in the mortal body that held her. All her fears, worries and anxieties were gone. She felt freed of the past: not only from her personal, remembered life, but detached from that pattern of repetitive human passion which long before her time had begot at last her own faulty personal self. It was as if she had just been reborn with all the freshness, purity and innocence of one entering the world for the first time. But one so different—so wonderful and frightening, so joyous and overwhelming—she could hardly comprehend it. A world that was a complete and rounded moment in which she would never die. She was content to lie at its core, watching it revolve about her.

She was still lying there next morning when old Facundo came and tossed his gravel against the window pane. Helen was too engrossed to notice him. In a little while he came back; she saw him standing outside the window with a grave look of compassionate concern on his weathered face. She looked up, and something passed between them. It was as if all that she had experienced was absorbed, understood, and reflected back from the pupils of his dark eyes. Facundo knew. He knew!

"Sun good. Dark no good!"

Helen obeyed him and went out to sit on the ground. In a little while he brought her a cup of tea. It had too much sugar in it, but it gave her a surge of strength.

"*Vegetáble* gone. Berries come now. Pretty soon we catch them pine cones for fire, no?" The old Indian moved off, slowly raking the garden.

The sense of his presence, and of his complete awareness of the moment and all the things that composed it, brought her back to the familiar. She felt the warmth of the sunshine, caught the smell of pine needles, heard the wind in the cottonwoods. Facundo was right. There would be a bumper crop of juniper berries; the grosbeaks were moving in. A pair of blue herons stood motionless in the shallow lagoon at the curve of the river, reflected in the water...A huge pattern that kept spreading illimitably.

She was still not quite herself and kept wondering what had happened to her. It was something strange, indescribable and yet familiar; something that Facundo seemed to understand without being told.

Over two years later, after the secret activities at Los Alamos have begun, the government has suggested that Los Alamos personnel be permitted to dine at Helen's tea-room if she agrees to take no other customers and to ask no questions. While she is weakening from her illness, she is financially secure enough to close her tea-room for a week of camping in the mountains. On her return, she does not hasten to re-open her business.

Early on the morning of the day they returned home, Helen took Turner on her walk. At the entrance to a narrow box canyon they came upon a growth of tiny wild mushrooms in a tangle of rotting logs. She knelt before them with a little cry of delight.

"Don't pick any," cautioned Turner. "They might be toadstools instead of mushrooms."

"There's no difference! It's just an old wives' belief that the edible ones are mushrooms and the poisonous ones are toadstools, and that mushrooms are converted into toadstools when a venemous snake breathes upon them. Almost all of them are good to eat—horse mushrooms, meadow mushrooms, all kinds." Helen picked one and held it up. "But if you ever see one with a little frill around the upper part of the stem—about here—and a bag at the bottom of the stem, look out! It's a Destroying Angel—the *Amanita Virosa*—the most poisonous mushroom known. But so beautiful! Tall and stately, with the satiny whiteness of absolute innocence."

"*Amanita Virosa*," muttered Turner. "The devil with them all! To me they're all putrid excrescences! Parasites living on other plants and dead matter, manure! They're abnormal! They give me the creeps!"

His vehement abhorrence amazed Helen. She suddenly realized that he, as whole races of people throughout the world, was a mycophobe— one who instinctively feared these fungal growths. Helen herself was a mycophile who had always known and loved them, as had all Indian America. There was really something strange about them to have caused this great cleavage between peoples. So many of her rational Anglo neighbors hated them. Yet something about their naked, pale, curious shapes, their earthy smell and musty charred taste, made the Spanish folk and Indians about her ascribe to them an attribute of the mysterious, as had the Aztecs and Mayas long before them. "They got power," Facundo had told her once, but would say no more.

Whatever their strange properties, thought Helen as she walked along in silence, their shapes were repeated by tall rocky buttes and mesas everywhere. Soft sandstone stems eroded away from their hard basaltic caps and softly rounded mesa tops, they stood against the sky like huge mushrooms of bare rock, a primordial motif of this weird and ancient America.

Helen paused suddenly near the upper end of the canyon where the walls narrowed. Before her on the meadow was a large circle of mushrooms. Begun years ago when the spores of a fungus had started the growth of a spawn mycelium, it had spread outward year after year until it now embraced the width of the little valley.

"A Fairy Ring! Jack, look! Have you ever seen one this big before?"

Utterly charmed, Helen jumped into the magic circle and was skipping across the meadow when she was brought up sharply with repulsion and amazement. At the far edge of the ring stood the most monstrous mushroom she had ever seen. The fungus stood nearly two feet high, its cap more than a foot in diameter. Its coarse skin was turning a putrid yellow, splotched with brown; withered gills hung down from the underside of the cap. Bloated, aged, and repulsive, the thing gave Helen a feeling of such overwhelming malignancy that she stood staring at it as if hypnotized.

Turner, a few steps behind her, let out a snort of disgust. He passed her in a flash, running toward it with measured strides. She saw him reach the edge of the clearing, all his weight and momentum thrust forward as he pivoted on his left leg like a football player about to make a drop kick. She saw his right leg go back, his heavy boot swing forward in an arc—and hang there as if fixed in a time whose movement had suddenly ceased.

"Don't! Jack! Oh no!" she screamed, clenching both hands at her breast.

At that instant it happened. With all the minutely registered detail of a slow-motion camera, and in a preternatural silence, she saw the huge and ugly mushroom cap rise slowly in the air. Unfolding gently apart, its torn and crumpled blades opening like the gills of a fish, the fragmented pieces revolved as if in a slow boil revealing a glimpse of chlorine yellow, a splotch of brown and delicate pink. Deliberately it rose straight into the air above the walls of the canyon, its amorphous parts ballooning into a huge mass of porous gray. The stem below seemed to rise to rejoin it; then, shattered and splintered, it settled slowly back to earth.

Not until then, strangely enough, did Helen's sensory consciousness record the impact of Turner's boot tip when he had kicked it apart. She felt rather than heard the slight thud; the slushy rent of senile, decayed tissue; the sharp, suction-like plop when the cap was torn from its stem. The sudden disturbance, still in slow-motion, travelled toward her in a vibratory wave through the earth, shot up her legs and seemed to tap her sharply behind her knees.

When she straightened, the cancerous gray cap was still rising and expanding like a mushroom-shaped cloud in the sky. As she watched, an upper current of air pulled it slightly apart.

Now again she screamed. Crouching down in terror, she vainly covered her head with her arms against the rain of its malignant spores. Countless millions, billions of spores invisibly small as bacteria radiated down around her. They whitened the blades of grass, shrivelled the pine needles, contaminated the clear stream, sank into the earth. Nor was this the end of the destruction and death they spread. For this malignant downpour of spores was also a rain of venemous sperm which rooted itself in still living seed cells to distort and pervert their natural, inherent life forms. There was no escape, now nor ever, save by the miracle of a touch.

Abruptly she felt it upon her. It was Turner, lifting her to her feet.

"Helen! For God's sake! What's happened?"

It was over. The meadow, the far pines, the canyon walls and clear blue sky rushed back into focus. Time released the natural flow of movement. The chirp of a bird broke the preternatural silence.

Helen shuddered, wiping her damp face. "I—I don't know exactly what happened. It was just like a bad dream, a nightmare, that hit me suddenly for a few seconds. That's all. It's gone."

"Are you sure you're all right?"

"Quite, Jack. But just go off for a half-hour. Take a dip in the stream or something. I want to stretch out and relax."

He looked at her with a worried frown. "I don't want to be nosey, Helen. But I don't want to worry about you."

"Don't!" she said as lightly as she could, and with a smile. "There is nothing wrong with me. Really!"

No! Stretched out in the sun, feeling its radiant warmth and life, she kept telling herself there was nothing wrong with her, with mushrooms, the whole world.

Just the same, the vision or fantasy ended Helen's long period of tranquility. If such a thing had happened within her, it must in some way, sometime, happen in the world outside, she told her few friends.

Helen's daughter, Emily, has decided to stay on in New Mexico to complete her doctoral work in anthropology.

Emily had finished the first draft of her dissertation, but before sending it in she asked her mother to go through it carefully, making detailed notes on every point that could be clarified and expanded with knowledge Helen had gained from Facundo. "It's terribly important," she insisted. "I want this *Inquiry* published as an original source book on the subject!"

Helen weakly assented and for nights on end struggled through the long manuscript. The result was disastrous. Early one Sunday morning Emily returned to discuss with her the manuscript and the notes on it Helen had written. Her face was stiff and pale.

The premise of Emily's bulky tome was simple enough. The origin legend of the Aztecs stated that they came from seven womb-caverns to the north, but no one could establish by historical facts that they originated in New Mexico and migrated south. So by parallels between ancient Aztec and modern Pueblo rituals Emily was attempting to prove it.

Helen refuted the premise on the grounds that Emily had missed the real meaning of Pueblo ceremonialism. She insisted that the seven womb-caverns weren't geographical locations and that the migration didn't take place over an actual route of a few hundred miles. The whole thing was really a profound myth or parable outlining in ritual terms the evolutionary journey of all mankind from an ancestral home deep in the womb-caverns of our own unconscious."

"You see, dear, as I tried to explain in my notes—"

Emily blew up like a firecracker. "Hazy generalities, every one! Can't you get it into your head I'm dealing in scientific specifics? You're trying to write off me and my whole work, and I won't have it!" Grabbing up Helen's notes with her own manuscript, she rushed out in a huff.

Emily explained her reaction more clearly in a letter she wrote a few years later to a publisher who had asked her to write a biography of her mother:

"I must decline your kind invitation to prepare for your publication a biography of my mother. As you are aware, I knew her only for a few years before her death. Any material I could offer would not add substantially to Mr. Turner's *Intimate Sketches of Helen Chalmers*, for which I supplied the necessary facts about her family background.

"You will appreciate my disinclination to contribute to the controversial myth of the 'Woman at Otowi Crossing' grown up about her. I cannot comment on the fact that she was seen conducting an Indian rite alone at midnight in her home. I feel it my duty, however, to remark on her use of Pueblo Indian symbolism to express many of her beliefs.

"My mother received only a high school education: one of the reasons why my paternal grandparents objected to my father's marriage to her. She read very little. She was not a member of any church. Her closest friends were the Indians at the nearby pueblo—particularly Facundo, the Cacique or 'medicine man,' who worked for her as a gardener and dishwasher. Through her constant association with them for many years, many persons believed she 'thought like an Indian.' Certainly much of their mythology, kiva symbolism, and ritualism was familiar to her. It was natural that she used them to express her rather abstract ideas. They superseded for her the religious teachings of orthodox creeds; they replaced the intellectual dissertations of our more academic philosophies; and they eliminated her need for wordy explanations.

"My *Inquiry* publicly acknowledges the help I derived from her. I do not minimize this. Yet as an anthropologist and ethnologist, I must frankly state that I adopted from her suggestions only the material I could substantiate by factual research and which contributed to my premise.

"We scientists who work with materials of the past for the benefit of posterity must be so constricted. We must deal with observable facts, not with imaginary conjectures. It is one thing to regard a prehistoric myth as a valuable anthropological record of a primitive people's life-pattern. It is quite another to adopt the same myth as an esoteric experience common to people of all times and races, a blueprint for life today. No. I find it almost absurd to believe that we could live now by the tenets of an almost primitive tribe.

"My mother's death has not mitigated this difference of opinion between us. Yet sometimes I confess to an uneasy feeling when I recall that she who so firmly believed in myth as a living experience is today the subject of a living myth herself."

The allusion in it to the Indian rite which Helen was seen conducting alone at midnight in her house Helen described in her *Journal* as one of the incidents of her friendship with Tranquilino.

Tranquilino had come back from war unable to resume his former life. A tall young Indian with a maimed arm and a tortured face, he lived suspiciously alone in a squalid adobe along the river. Not only did he refuse to work the land allotted him. He rebelled against demands to do his share of community work and ignored his ceremonial duties. All day he sat drinking rotgut whiskey or cheap wine. Then staggering drunk, he lurched down the road venting his hate on everything he met, clubbing dogs and a stray horse, throwing stones at children. The sight of a group of young girls giggling beside an irrigation ditch infuriated him most. He would rise suddenly out of the bushes, shaking his penis at them, and cursing them as they fled in terror.

"That boy no good," said one of his uncles gravely. "Maybe better if he die that time than to shame us all."

This shocking verdict aroused Helen's pity for the condemned. Tranquilino had been such a lovely little boy, shy and sensitive, with big brown eyes. One of those children the world over who saw faces in flowers, in pebbles, in the jutting cliffs. Often he had brought her a stone picked up along the road. "My friend," he would say of it. "I hear him call."

Then one day, still young and proud and innocent, he had gone down to Albuquerque for the first time. The Government had cut his hair short, stuffed him into an Army uniform, and shipped him to a strange land across the water. Here he marched for miles, dug a hole in the ground with a few companions, and lived like a gopher. Why? He did not understand. Early one morning it happened. A blinding, blasting explosion. Blood and guts spewing all over him, dirt pouring down upon him. The salty taste of his own blood, and then darkness. All for no reason at all.

Soon he was home again. His own people shunned him. Spanish boys beat him up. The Anglos put him in jail whenever he went to town. Still for no reason. So now with his maimed arm, his slight deafness and his limp, he nursed his hate for everybody and everything.

One Saturday morning Helen met him on the road to the pueblo. He had already begun drinking and his grimy shirt was splotched with vomit. As she walked toward him his face contorted into a grimace of anger. His right hand crept down to his unbuttoned trousers.

"Stop it, Tranquilino!" Helen commanded, resolutely walking up to him. "What is that you would show to the sun in front of me? Is it the manhood you left behind on the trail of war? A warrior so ashamed of his wounds he must show this thing to make children believe he is a man! Ai!"

The look in his eyes was a terrible thing to see, but remorselessly she went on. "Put down that bottle! That is your manhood now. Put it down!"

Tranquilino dropped the half-filled bottle in the weeds. His face was still frozen in a mask of hate, but he turned it away a little with his best ear toward her.

"Your clothes are dirty, Tranquilino. Your breath smells like a coyote's. The flowers, the stones and the mountains, all your old friends hide their faces from you. They do not see their friend. You do not see them. Tranquilino has not come back from the road of war. Listen then to one who has the power to bring him back. Listen, I say!"

His eyes were wild in their red sockets, but he did not move.

"Go to the river. Wash yourself, your clothes, your hair. Wash the whiskey out of your belly too. Then come to me before the sun has gone into his house-mountain. It is the power in me that says it. Go!"

She clapped her hands three times quickly and softly. Then the fourth time loudly, sharply. With a little cry Tranquilino fled in his sloppy boots.

At sunset he came to her pale and weak, his hair and clothes still damp. She had set the table with her best silver and china. There was a chafing dish full of Spanish rice and chicken, a casserole of beans baked in brown sugar, bread and sauce and butter, a small sweet pudding. Tranquilino ate like a famished dog; she could not bear to watch him. When he was through, he looked up at her with shame and fright.

"Good!" she said sharply, taking down the ancient prayer bowl she had found in the cliffs above, and setting it in front of him. "You know it? From the Old Ones it came. It has power. Facundo would not touch it. No hands have touched it but mine. Pick it up."

Tranquilino stood and lifted it with trembling fingers. Into it Helen poured some cornmeal from a paper sack. "See? My fingers have not touched it either. It has been ground with the proper songs and prayers."

The sun was setting. In its last flicker Helen could see a tiny bead of sweat standing out on his forehead.

"Go now. You will sleep, but you will not dream. I will be making medicine for you. When the moon stands high you will awake as I say," she told him. "You will climb up to those cliffs where the Old Ones lived. There, when Our Father Sun comes out standing, you will greet him with pinches of this prayer meal. To him, to all the directions, to the birds of the air, the fish of the waters, to all the children of the earth, you will empty this bowl. You will empty your heart. Then, because your thoughts are right, you will know that they have heard you. They will know that their old friend, Tranquilino, has come back to them again. I say it! Now go!"

Shortly before midnight she awakened stiff with fright. It was as if a vast, imponderable and implacable black sea of evil was rolling toward her, beating against the house. As she sat up in bed trembling, she seemed to see, with eyes other than her own, a figure riding on the crest. It was crouching as if ready to pounce, holding a pottery bowl high for a weapon. It was Tranquilino, eyes blazing with resentment against her.

She fought to stop him with all her strength of will. Still the black wave kept carrying him toward her. She was wide awake and deathly calm now. This was not the way to do it, she realized suddenly. She was trying to force her will upon him instead of helping him his own way.

Jumping out of bed, Helen lit the lamp and swiftly marked out on the floor with lines of cornmeal the pattern of the four directions. At each corner she molded a little sacred mountain and in it stuck a prayer-feather of eagle-down that Facundo had given her. Through the center of the enclosure she laid with more cornmeal a line of life running from east to west, corresponding to the path of the sun overhead. On this she sat down quietly, head bent.

Almost immediately she felt better, immured within this symbolic pattern of Tranquilino's own world. Her thoughts and feelings cleared. It was as if both of them, Tranquilino and herself, were now embodied within one magnetic thought-field, swept by the same invisible currents of life. Without conscious thought she gave herself to it fully, eyes closed.

How long she sat there, Helen did not know. But when the time came, she got up stiffly, blew out the lamp, and went back to bed.

For a week Helen did not see nor hear anything of Tranquilino. Then one morning on her doorstep she found the old bowl. In it was a small stone. She set them both on top of the mantel. Late that night the stone happened to catch her eye. The lamplight brought out for just an instant the face upon it, then vanished as she went to examine it.

Later, when she saw Tranquilino dancing in the pueblo, his maimed arm covered with twigs of spruce, Helen knew he was on the way back. He still got drunk occasionally and fought with his Spanish neighbors, but he had resumed his ceremonial duties. As he passed her on the turn, she smiled and lifted a finger to him in greeting. Tranquilino did not smile back, perhaps because she was sitting with Facundo and the other old men.

The women sitting around them noticed this sign from the Woman at Otowi Crossing to him she had brought back to life with her power. *"Ai. La hechicera. Cómo no?"* they whispered. So her fame kept spreading among those who recognized her growing power.

Gaylord, one of the atomic physicists, and Emily's lover, publishes after Helen's death a series of papers on psychic phenomena. The series begins:

"If my scientific colleagues find anything strange in an atomic physicist stumbling into the unfamiliar realm of psychic phenomena, they will perhaps not regard it too amiss that he is a man indulging a hobby. Other men play chess; I am interested in trying to discover if the gambits of the supernormal are controlled by any natural laws of universal science. It is a broad field, and in these brief papers I have restricted my remarks to that area embraced by the myth of the so-called 'Woman at Otowi Crossing.'

"Like most scientists, I prefer conclusions that can be reached independently by different observers using the same explicit methods. This approach is not possible here. Everything factually known about Helen Chalmers constitutes one vast paradox. The myth about her is itself controversial. Hence I have confined myself to inquiries as to what is the essential basis of the myth about her; how does it relate, in its broader aspects, to the specific field of atomic physics; and what bearing upon it have those dynamic events and curious incidents which I personally experienced during my too brief friendship with her.

"When then, essentially, is the basis of the myth of the Woman at Otowi Crossing?

"It rests on the strange simultaneity of two events that took place in the vicinity of Otowi Crossing little more than a decade ago; the development and experimental detonation of the first atomic bomb, and the psychic phenomenon experienced by Helen Chalmers. Is there a definable parallel between the objective process accomplished in atomic fission and the subjective process she underwent?

"Nowadays every schoolboy knows the basic principle of the first crude A-bomb. It was explained publicly several years ago when the

New York Times published a *Description of Atom Sabotage Devices* which had been approved by President Eisenhower, the National Security Council and Atomic Energy Commission, with a supplemental letter by J. Edgar Hoover, Director of the Federal Bureau of Investigation. The article briefly defined an 'implosion' as a bursting inward, contrasted with the bursting outward of an 'explosion.' It then explained:

> The scientists who worked on the first atomic bomb needed an implosion in order to compress nuclear material enough to get an atomic 'explosion.' They solved their problem by forming a large sphere of explosive material. In a hole in the center of this sphere they placed the fissionable material they wanted to squeeze.
>
> Then instead of using one detonator to ignite the explosive sphere, they placed many detonators around it. These detonators were connected electrically in such a way that they could be fired simultaneously...
>
> When this fast-burning imploding wave reaches the sphere of fissionable material, this mass has no place to be pushed except in upon itself and is thus compressed.
>
> We have now explained very simply the basic ideas which govern atomic bomb design...

"The similarity of this implosive-explosive process objectively in the A-bomb and subjectively as it happened to Helen Chalmers is at once casually apparent. Fear, worry, guilt, dread, shame, financial failure—all this psychological dynamite accumulated within her, recalled with pain and anguish, and brooded upon, seemed suddenly on a quiet day to be detonated from all directions; to be driven in upon her, implosively, with immense psychological force.

"What happened? We may refer to any description of the explosion of an atomic bomb. The same sensation of blinding brightness, of a great fissioning within her, a sudden fusion of all her faculties; and then an unbroken stillness in which her essential inner self, as if vaporized and transformed into new elements from its old atomic structure, rose slowly in a new spiritual entity to a new height of comprehension.

"If each of these events was preceded by a long period of secrecy and preparation, they were followed by an indefinitely long period during which their effects occasioned frenetic public excitement and controversy. I refer in one case, of course, to the invisible radioactive fallout from the atomic cloud slowly encircling the earth. Helen Chalmers' experience also resulted in a psychological fallout, if we may be permitted to so term it here. What precisely was the nature of the effects engendered by the remarkable psychic energy she released? And to what extent have they affected others?

"The cryptic answers are expressed in the media of all the psychic phenomena with which I was then totally unfamiliar. During my work I also happened to undergo a rather strange experience. It was enough to awaken my interest in an aspect of human nature I had not dreamed existed. With these incidents I began my probing. And with an account of them I began these brief papers . . ."

The novel concludes with this Epilogue:

He was an old, old man with a hairless brown head and a piercing stare. High in a New York skyscraper, he sat at a desk in an otherwise empty room whose door was lettered simply "M. Meru." The desk was bare save for a cheap household ledger labelled "Secret Journal."

For forty-three years he had been investigating psychic phenomena, and as an authority in his peculiar field he was consulted by large foundations, universities, the courts, theatrical agencies, doctors, psychiatrists, and an increasing number of persons compelled to learn of his existence.

"Most of the cases called to my attention are quickly detectable as conscious or unconscious deceptions—outright frauds, professional tricks, spurious age regressions, psychopathic disorders," he began in a gentle voice. "Those remaining take most of my time; they are of growing concern to a large number of my clients. The Throckmorton Endowment Fund, as you know, has supported some of my research. The time is coming when we shall have a National Institute of Parapsychology to take over what some people call my curious hobby. Telepathy, clairvoyance, fragmentary memories of prenatal existence, precognition—such things are no longer rare nor unusual. Even authenticated instances of the experience of creative totality commonly known as 'enlightenment' are occurring at an ever increasing rate. It is a component of our nature derided and repressed so long, I suppose, that under the increasing stresses and strains of our materialistic age it is suddenly breaking forth . . . Or perhaps man is indeed reaching a new phase in his development."

He opened his folded, withered brown hands and gently tapped the household ledger before him.

"To get back to Helen Chalmers . . . Mr. Turner brought me her *Secret Journal* here; he was thinking of destroying it as the product of an unbalanced mind. I found it, on the contrary, to be the most complete and

courageous record of a valid mystical experience in modern times ever
called to my attention. I urged him to publish it. Mr. Turner was unable
to comply with my request. How could he reverse his beliefs of a lifetime and admit that his view of Miss Chalmers had been wrong? No; we
must understand these things too. But he placed it in my care, with the
understanding it would be published after my death."

Mr. Meru paused. "Mr. Turner also kindly persuaded Dr. Emily
Chalmers to allow me to peruse her mother's notes on her *Inquiry*. They
complement the *Journal* in an extraordinary way, restating Helen
Chalmers' own personal experience in the ritual terms of a primitive
people. I was not surprised although I know nothing of the latter.
Granting the universality of such an experience, it can be stated in any
media of expression, ancient or modern. I was, however, unable to secure the doctor's assent to make them public. For a woman so established in her field, she could hardly be blamed for refusing...No, one
must accept both the static and dynamic points of view."

Mr. Meru's gentle voice broke off as he glanced at his watch. He
pulled out a desk drawer, removed a little tin whistle and a bulky paper
sack, and strolled to the open window. A thin whistle sounded, followed by a sudden whir of wings. In an instant the air was filled with
pigeons fluttering around the grain he spread on the sill and flying inside to perch on his bald head and shoulders. A little man in blue serge
enhaloed by white birds, Mr. Meru smiled quietly.

"Suppose that Helen Chalmers' *Journal* and her notes to her daughter's *Inquiry* are never released. Does it matter, really? Do they tell us
anything more than the existing literature of many centuries? The myth
of the Woman at Otowi Crossing, preposterous as it seems to many, is an
ageless myth of deep import."

He erased his winged halo with a slight wave of his arm and sat down
at the desk again. Reaching into a drawer once more, he brought out a
thermos of hot tea, a cup, and a packet of brown wheat crackers. "My
lunch time now. You and my inadequate teeth must permit me to
dunk."

Chewing the end of a wet cracker, he went on. "In this day of over-
rationalization we are inclined to disparage myths. We depend on science which is a record of observable facts. We treat even theology as a
body of historical facts which outweighs its essential metaphysical
meaning. Yet myth expresses as no other medium the deepest truths of
life. No one consciously creates a myth. It wells up spontaneously

within us in the same involuntary processes which shape the mind, the foetus within the womb, the atomic structure of the elements. So it is with the myth of the Woman at Otowi Crossing. We ourselves created it—we of a new age, desperately crying for a new faith or merely a new form that will model old truths to useful purpose. Helen Chalmers affirms our mistrust of the neuter and negative materialism of our time. In the image of a warm and pulsing human being, she embodies the everlasting Beauty combatting the Beast, the spirit versus the flesh, the conscience of man opposed to the will of man. Helen Chalmers is dead and will be forgotten, but the myth of the Woman at Otowi Crossing is woven of a texture impervious to time. We ourselves, each one of us in turn, simply tailor it anew for successive generations."

He opened the *Journal* and pushed it across the desk. A stray pigeon flew in, lighting on his shoulder. Mr. Meru began feeding it crumbs from his cracker, some of them falling on the excerpt he had pointed out:

> So all these scribbled pages, Jack, are to help you understand that an awakening or Emergence, as the Indians call it, is more than a single momentary experience. It requires a slow painful process of realization and orientation. Just like a new-born child, you get it all and instantaneously in the blinding flash of that first break-through—the shattering impact of light after darkness, of freedom after confinement. Then the rub comes. The learning how to live in this vast new world of awareness. The old rules of our cramped little world of appearances won't work. You have to learn the new ones. The hard way too, because everything you've known takes on new dimensions and meanings. This process of awakening with new awareness, a new perspective on everything about you, of perceiving the "spherical geometry of the complete rounded moment" as Gaylord once called it—this is the wonderful experience I've been going through.
>
> How many thousands of obscure people like me all the world over are having the same experience right now? And for no apparent reason, like me. Keeping quiet about it too, because they can't quite understand it at first or their friends might believe them mentally unbalanced. That's why some day you'll get this Dime-Store ledger. To reassure you it's a normal, natural experience that eventually comes to every one of us. So when your turn comes, Jack, don't be afraid. Be glad! It's our greatest experience, our mysterious voyage of discovery into the last unknown, man's only true adventure. . .

XI

Book of the Hopi

In 1959, Waters began his Book of the Hopi, *living much of the next three years on the Hopi Indian Reservation. His purpose was to record not only the traditional religious beliefs and their accompanying rituals, but also the Hopi "...instinctive perception of life processes which our rationally extroverted White observers still ignore."[18] Waters calls it "their book of talk."[19] The words of some thirty Hopi spokesmen were tape-recorded, translated, then edited and organized by Waters, who added his own eye-witness accounts of the rituals as well as a history of the Hopi people. The result is a complete view of both the literal and mystical aspects of Hopi ceremonialism.*

According to the Hopi, our present world is the Fourth World, the preceding three having been destroyed because of the divisiveness, selfishness, greed, and/or materialism of its inhabitants. In each case a few survivors were permitted to emerge to the succeeding world and were re-instructed in proper behavior. After emerging into the present world, they were instructed to divide into groups and undertake a series of migrations before finally settling down in their chosen land. That the chosen land was in a barren, arid desert is not incongruous, for in the preceding worlds comfort and material wealth were inevitably accompanied by spiritual disintegration. According to Hopi prophecy, our Fourth World is in rapid decline, heading for destruction, after which there will be a turn upward and a new age.

The focus of Hopi ceremonialism is on the harmonious unity of all forms of life. Their dances symbolize the interactions of the opposing and conflicting life forces in all creation, perpetuating "the primal harmony of cosmic forces" and literally "holding the world together."[20] *To the Hopi, the ultimate evil is—like Martiniano's in* The Man Who Killed the Deer—*the illusion of separateness. In his introduction, Waters comments:*

> . . . they speak not as a defeated little minority in the richest and most powerful nation on earth, but with the voice of all that world commonwealth of peoples who affirm their right to grow from their own native roots. . . . They remind us we must attune ourselves to the need for inner change if we are to avert a cataclysmic rupture between our own minds and hearts. Now, if ever, is the time for them to talk, for us to listen.[21]

The following account reflects Waters as both observer and interpreter of Hopi ritual.

THE SNAKE-ANTELOPE CEREMONY

Commonly known by its most spectacular ritual, Chu'tiva [*chu'a*, snake; *tiva*, dance], the Snake-Antelope ceremony has gained worldwide fame as a public spectacle. Indians dancing with live rattlesnakes in their mouths!—a "loathsome practice" the United States Indian Bureau once threatened to stop. Still it goes on year after year, and from the four corners of the earth people come to see it. Undoubtedly it is both fascinating and repulsive. Certainly it is the least understood of all Hopi ceremonies. Embodying two dances, two races, and rituals in two kivas, the full ceremony has been more meticulously reported in detail by professional observers than has any other. Yet its deepest meaning lies hidden within a dark and primeval mystery perhaps unfathomable now even to its modern participants.

The Snake-Antelope ceremony, as stated in the preceding chapter, alternates with the Flute ceremony and is held every other year. Like the latter's, its beginning date is determined by observation of the sun rising over the Munyá'ovi cliffs; it lasts sixteen days; and its immediate purpose is to bring rain for the final maturity of the crops. The Snake Dance itself is given on the sixteenth day.*

The well-reported details of preparation include those common to all ceremonies: the announcement, planting of the standards on both the Antelope and Snake Kivas, ritual smoking, making of *páhos*, immuration of society members, and setting up of the altars. The Antelope Society is the more important; its functions precede those of the Snake; and

---

* Hotevilla and Shipaulovi, August 21; and Shongopovi, August 27, 1960.

to its kiva the Snake chiefs go each morning and evening to smoke and pray. The Snake altar is set up at night, contrary to usual custom. It is very simple, featuring the images of two Snake Maidens. The Antelope altar is more elaborate. It is set on a sand painting about four feet square, bordered with lines of directional colors, and at each corner is a "cloud mountain," a small cone of sand in which is stuck a hawk feather. On it are placed a Corn Mother and four ears of corn pointing to the four directions, and several bowls of water from Flute Spring. The backdrop of the altar, representing a house, is decorated with buzzard feathers. Against it is stood the *típoni*, about two feet high, made of eagle-wing feathers and with downies tied to the tips, and wrapped with red buckskin thongs. The whole altar complex represents the world as it was formed by earth, air, water, plant life, and mankind; and each step of its construction is accompanied by songs that describe the formation of the world and its occupation, and by purification with the sacred water. The songs are secret, no outside person being allowed to hear them. Upon completion of the altar on the eleventh day the Antelope members go without salt for four days. The next day, the twelfth, the Snake members begin their most important preparation—their four-day gathering of snakes.

Gathering the Snakes

White Bear's maternal grandfather, Koahwyma [Animal Skin Reflecting the Sun] of Oraibi, brings out several little-known facts in relating his own experience. As a young man, a member of the Badger Clan, he became seriously ill. The medicine man whom he called could not help him, advising him that he could be cured only by the power of the Snake Society. Koahwyma asked a man named Siyowma [One Who Carries a Flower] to be his godfather and to intercede for him. The Snake Society, upon being consulted, agreed to help Koahwyma if he would join it and participate in its rituals for four years. He agreed, and with the medicine from the Snake Society and help from his own medicine man he began to improve. By spring he was well and strong, able to work in his fields.

That summer upon returning to his home he found on the path a snake sack and a snake whip, and knew it was a signal for him to go to the Snake Kiva and participate in the rituals according to his agreement.

"There was fear within me," he related. "I could not understand what only those born into the Snake Clan understand: why do our people perform a ceremony with snakes that other men fear, and call them their brothers? But my grandmother prepared food for me to take to the kiva with the snake sack and snake whip, and I walked up the trail to Oraibi on trembling legs. It was getting dark and no one was near the kiva, for according to custom a line of cornmeal had been drawn around the kiva which no one could cross except a member of the Snake Society. Then I saw the *na'chi* hanging on the kiva ladder. It was made of long hair dyed red to symbolize the rays of the sun, and with it hung the skin of a *kolichíyaw* [skunk]. Fear paralyzed me. Then something said to me, 'You are alive and walking on the good earth,' and I realized I would not have recovered from my sickness if I had not given my life to the Snake Society for four years and promised to help with their rituals. So I said back to that which had spoken to me, 'Yes, I did promise and I am here.' At that moment strength came back to my legs. I stepped across the cornmeal line and entered the kiva."

Koahwyma as a Tuwálanmomo [Watchful Bee] was welcomed and seated on the raise during the preliminary rituals. Next morning he went out with all the members to gather snakes. The snake hunt lasts four days: first to the west, to the south, to the east, and finally to the north. There were a number of initiates. Each carried a water jar, a sack of cornmeal, and a *kwáwicki* of two buzzard feathers tied together. These wing feathers of the buzzard, Koahwyma was told by his godfather, have gray spots underneath which possess a strange odor and the power to soften the anger of a snake, when they are waved over its head. The snakes are not actually afraid or angry at man; they only coil to strike "when they see what is in man's mind and heart." One, then, must be of good heart and not afraid. He must never try to pick up a coiled snake. He must wave the snake whip over him until he uncoils.

Koahwyma was afraid of finding a rattlesnake or sidewinder, which are poisonous, and hoped to find a bull snake or gopher snake. But he learned that every godfather prayed in his heart that on the first day of the hunt his initiate should first pick up a rattler rather than a bull snake. This was because a bull snake was far more dangerous, being able to suck the life out of a man's body without striking.

There was a sudden call across the desert. A track had been seen and Koahwyma was called to gather his first snake. They hurried up to follow the track of a large racer into the hole of a field mouse. This was fortunate, for the snake had eaten the mouse, and when he was dug out he was too heavy to run. Koahwyma, however, was instructed to be careful not to hurt him, his brother. So he blessed the snake with cornmeal, with the sun, and with the earth, and then picked him up. When the snake began to fight, Koahwyma held him behind the head with his left hand, spat in the palm of his right hand, and began to brush the snake full length. The snake soon hung limp as a length of rope. Everybody was happy at Koahwyma's luck with his first *pókoi'ta* [pet]. That day the hunting party returned home with about twelve snakes, and when the four-day hunt was over there were about sixty snakes, which meant a long and successful dance and a good crop at harvest.

Every night in the kiva Koahwyma remained seated on the raise. Early in the evening the Snake chiefs left to smoke and concentrate in the Antelope Kiva, where the deepest and most sacred part of the ceremony was conducted. It seemed a long time before they returned. Koahwyma could look up through the ladder opening and see the Milky Way stretching north and south across it. Mostly he sat looking at the large jars on the lower, altar floor. Their tops were covered with buckskin punched with holes to let in air. In them were the snakes. Every day they were given pollen for food—usually corn pollen, sacred in all ceremonials, and containing life itself, *talásiva* [flower-producing life from sun]. Then about midnight the chiefs returned. It was the time for *pavásio* [deepest concentration], for blessing and entertaining the snakes.

"First sand was spread on the altar floor," continued Koahwyma, "then my godfather showed me how to smooth it out nice with part of a weaving set. This was so we could see the tracks in the sand and know which way a snake was moving. All members of the society seated themselves in a circle around it, each sitting cross-legged and touching the next man's knee. Then one of the men untied the buckskin tops of the jars and let all the snakes loose on the sand. At the same time the singing began, soft and low.

"There were all kinds of snakes: rattlesnakes, big bull snakes, racers, sidewinders, gopher snakes—about sixty all tangled on the floor. The singing stirred them. They moved in one direction, then another, looking over all the men in the circle. The men never moved. They just kept singing with a kind expression on their faces. The snakes began to roll on the sand, taking their bath. Then a big yellow rattler moved slowly toward an old man singing with his eyes closed, climbed up his crossed leg, coiled in front of his breechcloth and went to sleep. Pretty soon this old man had five or six snakes crawling over his body, raising their heads to look at his closed eyes and peaceful face, then going to sleep. It showed they had found their friend, looking within the heart of this one upon whose body they chose to rest. That is the way snakes show who are good and kind men with pure hearts, for some members of the society had one snake on their laps and some didn't have any. So I sang carefully and tried to keep my heart and thoughts pure till dawn, when the singing stopped and the snakes were put back into their jars. Then some of us went out to the spring to bathe ourselves, and others were given special duties to perform before we ate our morning meal."*

The Mystic Marriage

Meanwhile the same four-night *pavásio* of sacred songs and *nánapwala* [purifying from within] is carried on in the Antelope Kiva. Its concluding ritual begins before midnight of the eleventh day of the ceremony when the Snake chief brings in a young girl, the Snake Maiden, who is the living counterpart of the two wooden images, the *chu'manas*, on the altar in the Snake Kiva.

She is a virgin who has been initiated into the Snake women's society. The upper half of her forehead, her chin, and her throat are painted white with *tuma* [white clay]. The rest of her face is painted black with *mánanha*, a substance taken from a diseased ear of corn. Over her woven black dress, the customary *manta*, she wears a Snake dancer's kirtle and a woman's white and red cape. Her hair is loose and to it is tied a small eagle down feather. A necklace of turquoise and shell is hung around her neck. She carries an earthen jar containing prayer sticks and corn, melon, squash, and bean vines.

The Snake Maiden and the Snake chief are met by the Antelope chief with a young man, the Antelope Youth, who carries a *típoni* and a snake. His hair is also loose, with a small downy feather tied in front, and he wears a white ceremonial kirtle. His face and body are painted ash-gray with *páskwapi* [decayed clay] taken from the edge of a spring and not from under the water. His chin is painted white with *tuma*, and with the same white clay zigzag lines are drawn on his body, arms, and legs.

The Snake Maiden is seated on the south side and the Antelope Youth

---

* Contrary to popular belief the fangs of the snakes are not extracted nor are their sacs of venom emptied. Many instances have been recorded when men have been bitten without any effects whatever. One precaution is taken, however. A concoction named *chu'knga* [snake medicine] is given to all Snake members, who drink a little and rub their hands with it before going out on the snake hunt. If a member is bitten in the kiva while entertaining the snakes, he rubs a little of it on the wound and continues singing. *Chu'knga* is made from the leaves of the large male and the small female plant called *hohoyawnga* [stinkbug plant]; to which are added the root of *chu'si* [snake flower] and leaves of the plant *chu'öqwpi* [snake vertebrae]; all being boiled in water which has been blessed.

In Old Oraibi *povolsi* [butterfly plant] was taken before the dance. Added to the medicine water, it was called *lugupna*. *Kungyna* was also chewed during the gathering of the snakes. *Kunya* [water plant] and *wiqupi* [fatty-looking plant] were added to the emetic.

on the north side of the altar level. Between the fire-pit and the altar is set an earthen bowl containing soapy water made from yucca roots. In front of the altar is placed a woven plaque full of many kinds of seeds. Girl and boy are now brought to the bowl by their chiefs, and a wedding ceremony is performed according to Hopi custom. The Snake Maiden's hair is washed in the milky seminal fluid of the yucca root by the Snake chief, and the Antelope Youth's by the Antelope chief. The two chiefs exchange places to wash the hair again, then twist it together while it is still wet to symbolize the union. The couple is then conducted to the seating ledge on the north side, the girl being seated upon the plaque of seeds which has been brought by the Antelope chief. The seeds signify food for the birds of the air, the animals of the earth, and man.

It is now midnight and the *pavásio* begins—the period of concentration and the singing of songs. It lasts until the stars in Orion's belt are hanging above the western horizon. Snake Maiden and Antelope Youth remain seated together until it is finished, being careful not to fall asleep. Then they are blessed and the girl is taken home by her godmother, the boy by his godfather.

The obvious meaning of the ritual is the union of the two societies which jointly carry out the Snake-Antelope ceremony. But as the immediate purpose of the ceremony, like that of the Flute, is to bring rain for the final maturity of the crops, the marriage also signifies the fruition of all life. The snake is a symbol of the mother earth from which all life is born. The antelope, because it usually bears two offspring, symbolizes for the Hopis fruitful reproduction and increase in population. Hence the union of the two is symbolic of creation, the reproduction of life.

Looked at more closely, it has a still deeper meaning. For as the bodies of man and the world are similar in structure, the deep bowels of the earth in which the snake makes its home are equated with the lowest of man's vibratory centers, which controls his generative organs.* The antelope, conversely, is associated with the highest center in man, for its horn is located at the top or crown of the head, the *kópavi*, which in man is the place of coming in and going out of life, the "open door" through which he spiritually communicates with his Creator.** The

---

* Similarly in Hindu mysticism the goddess Kundalini, personified as the feminine aspect of the universal force latent in man, is envisioned as a sleeping serpent coiled within the lowest center, the *muladhara cakra*, corresponding to the *sacral plexus* and *plexus pelvis*, which stand for the whole realm of reproductive forces.

** Hindu mysticism also uses the horn to symbolize the outgrowth of the highest psychical brain center, and the horned antelope pictured on Buddhist temples is emblematic of the peace of mind attained through divine consciousness.

two then symbolize the opposite polarities of man's lifeline, the gross or physical and the psychical or spiritual which supersedes and controls the functions of the former, just as the Antelope Society supersedes and controls all functions of the Snake Society. Their mystic marriage is thus a fusing of man's dual forces within the body of their common ceremonial for the one constructive purpose of creation.

If this meaning is true we may look for its development throughout the later public rituals, remembering that the Antelopes always first posit the purposeful end, the Snakes following to show the means.

The Races

The Antelope Race is held on the morning of the fifteenth day, and the Snake Race on the morning of the sixteenth. The two races are substantially alike, members of both societies participating in each.

This year, 1960, we see them at Hotevilla. The sun is just coming up. House roofs and cliff top are crowded with people, most of them huddled in thin cotton blankets against the thin wind of dawn sweeping up from the desert below. Directly below in the curve of the cliff lies the spring which gives Hotevilla its name. The spring gushes out of a small cavern, now enlarged, which formerly scraped a man's back as he stooped to gather water. Hence the name of Hotevilla from *hote* [back] and *villa* [scratch]. Below the spring the steep side of the mesa is neatly terraced for tiny fields, which give way to larger fields planted between great dunes of encroaching sand. Beyond, far to the west, stretches the empty desert, now yellowing under the rising sun.

For a while there is no more to see. Gradually in the paling shadow of the cliffs one distinguishes at the curve of the trail below a group of Snake and Antelope priests patiently waiting, the Snakes painted dark brown, the Antelopes ash-gray. Farther away more dim and diminutive men emerge on the trail, carrying green cornstalks, squash, and melon vines. Then an old Hopi nearby points to the horizon with his chin. "They comin'."

A friend has a pair of binoculars. They are less sharp than the old man's eyes, but one distinguishes out on the sunlit desert a moving spot and then another. The racers are coming in.

The starting point is about four miles out. Here an Antelope, a Snake, and a Qaletaqa draw with cornmeal a line running east, encourage and bless all the runners. This talk by the starters is called *Mónglavaiti* [Priest Talk]. The starter then waves his *pahómoki* [cornmeal sack], and the race begins. It is not exciting at all, for the wait is long. But gradually, one at a time or in small groups, the racers appear over the dunes or between the trees.

Meanwhile an Antelope priest stationed about two miles out is jogging along in front of the runners. He is an old man who can't run very fast. His hair is flowing loose, he wears only a breechcloth, and he is carrying a bunch of prayer sticks and a small jar of water blessed in the kiva. With him is another Qaletaqa to protect the blessed water. Suddenly the leading runner sprints up. The old priest hands him the *páhos* and water jar. "Thank you and bless you, my son. Carry this on to our home." Then the runner heads for the foot of the cliffs. He keeps looking back; for if another runner can catch up with him, he must in turn hand over the *páhos* and water jar and bless his successor.

A tremor of excitement ripples through the crowd. The other runners are trying hard, urged on by the men along the trail waving their cornstalks and vines, and loudly encouraged by the Snakes and Antelopes waiting at the foot of the cliffs. It is no use. The runner is a young boy of perhaps sixteen, said to be the fastest runner in the village, and none can catch him. Reaching the foot of the mesa, he begins clambering up the steep, rocky trail, urged on by the Snake and Antelope Qaletaqas whirling their *tovókinpi* [rolling thunder] or bull-roarers—sticks whirled on strings to simulate the roaring sound of low thunder.

He reaches the kiva before the rest of the runners begin panting up the mesa, accompanied by all the Snakes and Antelopes and the men carrying cornstalks and squash vines. Often a tired runner, his body streaked with sweat, stops to rest his bruised bare feet. There are ribald calls from the crowd on top, jokes and laughter. The warm August sun is up; everybody is in good humor. When all reach the top of the mesa the fun begins: everybody—women and children, even a scattering of tourists—rushes to grab a stalk or vine, a leaf, a tendril, to carry home.

In the midst of the excitement the winning runner, having been blessed in the kiva, slips quietly back down the trail to plant his prayer sticks and jar of water in his family's fields out on the sandy plain.

The races are this simple—deceptively simple, for they are also rituals in a long and involved ceremony, bearing their share of its progressively developed meaning. Just what do they symbolize beneath their charming and colorful aspect on a sunny August morning?

The mystic marriage of Snake Maiden and Antelope Youth stated the purpose and end: the union of man's two life forces, the physical embodied in the lowest center at the base of the spine and the spiritual residing in the psychical center at the crown of the head. But what is the path between them, and how can they be made to fuse?

The channel, as explained by Eastern mysticism, is the main median nerve, known as the *sushumna*, extending through the center of the spinal column. Around it, crossing to the right and left at intervals, are two other psychic nerve channels coiled like snakes, forming the symbol of the caduceus of Mercury. That on the left, Ida, is regarded as "feminine," being the conduit of the negative lunar current; Pingala, on the right, as "masculine" and the conduit of the positive solar current of universal energy residual in man. Up these subtle channels flow and fuse the life forces of man when aroused.

The analogy presented by the Snake-Antelope races is at once apparent. The long racetrack, a mere trail ascending from far out on the desert to the kiva on the crown of the cliff, is the median nerve. It is crossed and recrossed at intervals where prayer sticks are planted and other priests are stationed. These mark the successive centers vitalized by the ascending life force when it is called up. It has two aspects: the feminine or lunar force symbolized by the dark-brown Snakes, and the masculine or solar force symbolized by the ash-gray Antelopes. The full ceremony began when the Antelope chief planted his *na'chi* on the kiva. For it is he, representing the masculine power of the divine, who takes precedence over the feminine and sanctions the awakening and loosing of its power. Throughout the whole ceremony it is always the Antelope which takes precedence over the Snake, and day after day the Snake chief dutifully presents itself at the kiva of the Antelope chief—the lower self before the higher. So in the races the Antelope Race comes first—not with snakes but with the fruits of the later transmutation, the green cornstalks, squash, bean, and melon vines.

If the mystic marriage of Snake Maiden and Antelope Youth expressed the purpose and end of the ceremony, the Antelope and Snake Race symbolize the means. They lay out in a simple, beautiful and strikingly original imagery the pattern of a wholly subjective concept that, if it is not original with the Hopis, is still as ancient as their own prehistoric rites. With the end of the races it is time now for the actual, climactic union.

The Dances

The Antelope Dance is given at sunset on the day of the sunrise Antelope Race, and the Snake Dance follows the Snake Race on the next day. The two dances, like the two races, are similar, save that the familiar squash, melon, and bean vines are used in the Antelope Dance, the snakes being danced with only in the concluding Snake Dance. There are few spectators for the former, some Hopis even referring to it as *nátwanta*, a "practice dance." Yet, as in all the preceding rituals, it has its purpose and sets the pattern for the Snake Dance to follow. Running Antelopes make the sound of thunder whose vibration stimulates the clouds to come out of their shrines. Hence the Antelope Dance first draws the clouds. The bull snake has the power to suck out life and rain from the clouds. So on the following day the Snake Dance brings rain.

The focal point at Oraibi was the always significant *típkyavi* [womb], the plaza in front of the Snake Kiva containing the *sipápuni*, the small hole representing the place of Emergence from the under-world. Into this during Powamu, it will be remembered, the *kachinas* Eototo and Áholi poured water from the jars on their *mongkos* to purify man's routes of Emergence from all his successive stages of evolutionary existence. Here in Hotevilla and in other villages a similar small *sipá-puni* is dug in the open plaza. Over this is laid a cottonwood plank to serve as a sounding board or resonator, the *pochta*. Behind it is con-structed the *kísi* [shade house], a bower of green cottonwood branches over whose opening is hung a blanket or strip of canvas. Into this, early in the afternoon of the sixteenth day, the great day of the celebrated Snake Dance, are carried all the snakes from the kiva.

Already the crowd is arriving for the spectacle—dudes from guest ranches, boys and girls from summer camps and schools, tourists from the world over, government Indian Bureau agents, Pueblo Indians from the Rio Grande, lots of Zuñis, and hordes of Navajos, everybody swarming the sandy little plaza of Hotevilla, fighting for places on the flat Hopi roofs, jamming terraces and doorways. All are broiling and perspiring under the blinding sun and sultry clouds gathering on the ho-rizon, patiently waiting, hour after hour, to see Indians dance with live snakes in their mouths.

Meanwhile in the kivas the participants are getting ready. The Snake members paint most of their bodies with a composition of *suta* [red min-eral] and *yalaha* [deep red mineral]. A large oval over breasts and shoulders is painted white with *tuma* [white clay]. White is also used for a strip covering the upper part of the forehead and the front of the throat. The rest of the face is blackened with *monha*. Each member wears a reddish-brown kirtle, carrying in black the design of a snake, and brown fringed moccasins. On both are sewn seashells.

In contrast the Antelope members paint themselves ash-gray with white zigzag lines running up from their breasts to the shoulders and down the arms to the fingers, and down the front of the legs to their big toes. The rattle which each will carry is a gourd covered with the skin of the testicle of an antelope. Each wears a white kirtle and embroidered sash. As a final touch the chin is outlined by a white line from ear to ear.

By now it is after four o'clock and the crowd massed in the plaza is getting restless. A wind has come up, whipping clouds of sand and dust over the rooftops. A little girl strays to the *kísi* and starts to go inside. One shudders to think of her toddling into that mass of writhing snakes, but no one shouts warning; perhaps no one realizes what is inside. Very casually an old Hopi walks up, takes her by the hand, and leads her away.

Meanwhile something more important is happening. We are watching it from a rooftop, White Bear and I, where we are squeezed in a mass of Navajos. The broiling August sun has disappeared and the wind is driving a flock of somber black storm clouds northward along the horizon. Other Hopis are watching too with looks of anxiety on their placid faces. It has been a summer of drought and despair. Niman Kachina brought no rain; for some reason the ceremony was improperly performed in some villages; in others another dance was substituted for the Home Dance. Nor did the Flute ceremony bring rain. The corn is stunted in the fields. Old Chief Tawákwaptiwa died in April, and a successor is not yet appointed. An undercurrent of strife and evil runs through all the villages. This Snake-Antelope ceremony is the last hope, and it always brings rain. So, above as below, the sky reflects this battle between good and evil. And while the crowd, now shivering with cold, becomes restless with the long wait, the Hopis patiently watch the increasing tempo of the battle.

There comes a driving blast of sparse raindrops, each hard and cold as a pellet of ice. White Bear patiently squeezes out from the packed rows of Navajos, climbs down the ladder, and goes to the car. Down in a narrow street one can see him listening to a group of older Hopis. All are looking upward. The black storm clouds are being driven northward past the village. The rain does not come. Instead, the sky gets blacker, the air colder. White Bear returns with a coat to wrap around my thin shirt. The Navajos begin to smell, so closely we are packed together. Still we sit wordlessly, watching the storm clouds turn west across the desert.

Then suddenly they file into the plaza—two rows of twelve men each, like a pair of prayer sticks for each of the six directions, the Antelopes ash-gray and white, the Snakes reddish-brown and black. The appearance of the Snake chief strikes the keynote of the somber scene. There is something neolithic about his heavy, powerful build, his long arms, his loose black hair hanging to his massive shoulders. At the end of the line trudges a small boy. Silently they encircle the plaza four times—a strange silence accentuated by the slight rattle of gourds and seashells. As each passes in front of the *kísi* he bends forward and with the right foot stomps powerfully upon the *pochta*, the sounding board over the *sipápuni*. In the thick, somber silence the dull, resonant stamp sounds like a faint rumble from underground, echoed a moment later, like thunder from the distant storm clouds.

This is the supreme moment of mystery in the Snake Dance, the thaumaturgical climax of the whole Snake-Antelope ceremony. Never elsewhere does one hear such a sound, so deep and powerful it is. It assures those below that those above are dutifully carrying on the ceremony. It awakens the vibratory centers deep within the earth to resound along the world axis the same vibration. And to the four corners it carries to the long-lost white brother the message that he is not forgotten and that he must come. There is no mistaking its esoteric summons. For this is the mandatory call to the creative life force known elsewhere as Kundalini, latently coiled like a serpent in the lowest centers of the dual bodies of earth and man, to awaken and ascend to the throne of her Lord for the final consummation of their mystic marriage.

The power does come up. You can see it in the Antelopes standing now in one long line extending from the *kísi*. They are swaying slightly to the left and right like snakes, singing softly and shaking their antelope-testicle-skin-covered gourds as the power makes its slow ascent. Then their bodies straighten, their voices rise.

The Snake chief at the same moment stoops in front of the *kísi*, then straightens up with a snake in his mouth. He holds it gently but firmly between his teeth, just below the head. With his left hand he holds the upper part of the snake's body level with his chest, and with the right hand the lower length of the snake level with his waist. This is said to be the proper manner of handling a snake during the dance. Immediately a second Snake priest steps up with a *kwáwiki* or feathered snake whip in his right hand, with which to stroke the snake. He is commonly known as the guide, for his duty is to conduct the dancer in a circle around the plaza. As they move away from the *kísi* another dancer and his guide pause to pick out a snake, and so on, until even the small boy at the end is dancing with a snake in his mouth for the first time. It is a large rattlesnake, its flat birdlike head flattened against his cheek. All show the same easy familiarity with the snakes as they had with the squash vines the day before.

After dancing around the plaza the dancer removes the snake from his mouth and places it gently on the ground. Then he and his guide stop at the *kísi* for another snake. A third man, the snake-gatherer, now approaches the loose snake. It has coiled and is ready to strike. The gatherer watches it carefully, making no move until it uncoils and begins to wriggle quickly across the plaza. Then he dexterously picks it up, holds it aloft to show that it has not escaped into the crowd, and hands it to one of the Antelopes singing in the long line. The Antelope, smoothing its undulating body with his right hand, continues singing.

So it goes on in a kind of mesmeric enchantment in the darkening afternoon. There is nothing exciting about these men dancing with snakes in their mouths—only a queer dignity that reveals how deeply they are immersed in the mystery, and a strange sense of power that seems to envelope them. The seashells with their slight, odd sound are calling to their mother water to come and replenish the earth. The song of the Antelopes is describing the clouds coming from the four directions, describing the rain falling. All the Hopis know that if it does not rain during the Home Dance of Niman Kachina rain will come with the Snake Dance. For this is the consummation of the union of the two universal polarities, the release of that mystic rain which recharges all the psychic centers of the body and renews the whole stream of life in man and earth alike.

It is dusk now. The battle between the elements is over, and the sky is covered by low-hanging clouds. Out of them fall a few drops of rain. It is enough. The last of the snakes has been danced with and a group of women are making a circle of cornmeal beside the *kísi*. All the Antelopes bring their armloads of snakes to deposit within the circle. Then quickly the Snake members grab up as many snakes as they can carry and take them out on the desert, some each to the west, the south, the east, the north. Here they are blessed again and released to carry to the four corners of the earth the message of the renewal of all life, as it is known that snakes migrate back and forth across the land.

When the men come back each drinks a bowl of strong emetic called *nanáyö'ya*.* The men then stand on the edge of the cliff to retch. Otherwise their bellies would swell up with the power like clouds and burst. The women help them clean off the paint on their bodies, after which they return to the kiva for purification.

The Snake-Antelope ceremony is the last major ceremony in the annual cycle which began with Wúwuchim, Soyál, and Powamu and carried through Niman Kachina and the Flute ceremony. It is a great ceremony and a subtle one. For if the first three symbolize the three phases of Creation and the next two carry through in some manner the evolutionary progress on the Road of Life, the Snake-Antelope ceremony cuts through the past to the ever-living now, and its stage is not the externalized universe but the subjective cosmos of man's own psyche. Whatever its meanings, and they are many to many students, it shows how the interplay of universal forces within man can be controlled and made manifest in the physical world. That this is accomplished within the framework of what is commonly regarded as a primitive and animistic rite is a great achievement.

---

* The principal ingredient is the leaf of the plant *tikus musli*, identified as *Gila Aggregate*, to which are added the roots of the plants *casung* or *sue grappi*, the *Curotia Lenta*, and *hohayungua*, the *Pislostrophe Spareiflore*.

XII

Pumpkin Seed Point

*The evidence presented by the Hopi elders seems to have con-
firmed and stabilized Waters' previous theories. More importantly, it seems to have promoted his own increased personal
integration. The evidence for the latter is to be found in his next
work,* Pumpkin Seed Point, *the highly subjective story of his personal experience while living among the Hopi. This work, which
Waters began in 1965, two years after publishing* Book of the
Hopi, *records the psychic and spiritual growth he had been experiencing through* The Colorado, Masked Gods, *and* The Woman
at Otowi Crossing. *It reveals Waters' own developed synthesis as
he attempts to make personal reconciliation of the multitude of
dualities presented by the Hopi teachers. He recognized that the
true meaning of the Hopi myths and legends would have to be
presented from within, integrated into a personal philosophic system, and in* Pumpkin Seed Point *he records his experiences as he
further evolved this philosophy of fusion.*

> Little wonder that we Whites, with our desperate reliance upon sur-
> face physical reality, seldom perceive that in this Indian sub-stream lies
> an America we have never known, yet embodying the truths of our own
> unconscious, the repressed elements of our darker, deeper selves.[22]

*That Waters is not completely successful in reconciling the Indian
and White worlds is not surprising. But the record of his attempt—and the implications of that attempt—are of much importance. As a reader follows Waters through various stages of
growth, he is led to the conclusion that Western Civilization it-*

126

self, in order to survive, must find "a viable fusion between the two great worlds of industrial-mechanical-rational and the organic-spiritual-intuitive,[23] *and that the overall movement of our history does seem to be in that direction. Waters suggests that the function of the Hopi teachings can be to show us, by revealing what they have, what it is that we do not.*

The following three essays from Pumpkin Seed Point *reflect Waters' commentary on the White/Indian dichotomy, his intense awareness of Indian ritual, and his ever-increasing subjective involvement.*

TWO VIEWS OF NATURE

Contemporary Hopi, Zuni, and many other Indian tribes, as well as the prehistoric Toltecs and Aztecs, believe in the myth that they lived successively in three previous worlds before coming to this one. What root race of mankind these Indians of Mesoamerica belonged to, what vanished or still-existent continent they came from, when, and how, no one knows. Their origin is lost in a time that is being continually pushed back to the edge of the one great mystery of life. Yet these documentary questions need not trouble us. The great myth of their Emergence, as the Hopis most aptly call their arrival upon this continent, is the dramatized story of the emergence of consciousness from the great pool of the unconscious—the evolution of that consciousness of object and self which has enabled man alone to distinguish himself from the rest of nature. It is one of the great awakenings along the Road of Life. By it man gives the world its objective existence and so partakes himself in the process of Creation.

How wonderful it must have been, this ancient and unknown America, this new and promising Fourth World, when man first saw it through Indian eyes! So glistening fresh with the dawn's dew on it. So pristinely pure, so virginly naked in its beauty. How enchantingly diverse the land was with range upon range of snowcapped mountains, shimmering deserts lying below the level of the seas that gnawed at its shores, arctic tundras merging into illimitable plains of waving grass, rising into high-level plateaus, and sinking again into fetid tropical jungles. All teaming with life in every form, tiny plants and dense forests, birds, reptiles and insects, and countless animals of many unique species now extinct, like the buffalo whose vast herds blackened the tawny plains. A land with its own great spirit of place, its own brooding destiny hovering over it with invisible wings.

The Hopis, like other branches of their race, knew themselves as privileged newcomers to this great new world. So upon their arrival they first asked permission to live upon it from its guardian spirit and protector. The spirit gave his permission, telling them, however, that they were not free to wander over it rampantly, using it as they wished. They were to make ordered migrations, north, south, east, and west, to the four *pasos* where the land met the sea, before settling in the place prescribed for their permanent home. There they were to establish those annual ceremonies which would recapitulate their wanderings and reclaim the land for its Creator.

The meaning of the myth is clear. The emergence of consciousness does not set man entirely free. He is still obligated to the dictates of the unconscious which embodies all his primordial past. He may travel to the limits of his mind and will, but he must always observe those thaumaturgical rites which acknowledge his arising from the one great origin of all life and which keep him whole.

Such a tradition, like many other versions of its kind, marked the relationship of the Hopis to the land. If the directional peaks and boundary rivers to their tribal homeland were stained with the blood of a virginal youth and maiden, the memory of their sacrifices was perpetuated through uncounted generations by male-and-female prayer-feathers planted on ceremonial altars to remind all men of the sacred foundation of their tenure. The land was not tangible property to be owned, divided, and alienated at will. It was their Mother Earth from which they were born, on whose breast they were suckled, and to whose womb they were returned in a prenatal posture at death.

The earth-mother had many children other than man: the stem of long wild grass that developed into a stalk of maize, the lofty spruce, all the birds of the air, the beasts of plain and forest, the insect and the ant. They too had equal rights to life. They supplied the needs of man, but they were not sacrificed ruthlessly and wantonly. A deer was killed only after obtaining his ceremonial assent to the killing that enabled all life to endure in its ordered pattern. Eagles were needed for their down and feathers. But first their heads were washed to signify their adoption into the tribe. Then their lives were snuffed out (bloodlessly) with a blanket and their stripped bodies were carried to an eagle burying ground. The tall and stately spruce furnished its trunk, branches, and tufts of needles. The tree was asked also to consent to its necessary sacrifice, and it was given a special drink so that it would not feel pain from the axe. How remarkably similar these still-observed rituals were among widely separated tribes throughout the Southwest and Mexico.

They may seem curiously sentimental to those of us who are accus-

tomed to think of matter and spirit as antithetical. Yet they conform to
the common belief, held by all American Indian tribes, in a mysterious
force or dynamic energy, an impersonal spirit of life, pervading and
uniting every entity in nature—the living stone, the great breathing
mountain, plant, bird, animal, and man. It was the *orenda* of the Iro-
quois, the *maxpe* of the Crows, the Sioux *mahopa,* the Algonquin
manito. And their belief is validated by the mystery teachings of the
East which assert that everything is alive to the degree in which its consciousness is dormant, sleeping, or awakened. Hence the Indians did not
set themselves apart from all other physical forms of life. They regarded
themselves as a part of one living whole.

Each entity in nature, then, possessed not only an outer physical form
but an inner spiritual force. Man was free to utilize the fleshly form for
his own bodily needs. But he was ever aware that its spiritual component remained alive as a source of psychical energy which could be invoked to manifest its benign powers for his need.

These spiritual components the Hopis called kachinas, "respected
spirits," and they are invoked each year still. Spirits of plant, bird, animal, and human beings who have died; of all the invisible forces of life,
they manifest themselves in the physical forms of men wearing masks
imbued with the powers of the spirits they represent. So they come
dancing into the plazas, uttering their own strange cries, singing from
dawn to sunset.

Such a ceremony is a profound mystery play which if produced in
Europe would draw thousands of Americans in an annual and fashionable pilgrimage. Still there are pitifully few people here who appreciate
it as a superlative, indigenous art form whose anthropomorphic masks,
stylistic dancing, and subtle rhythms of song have no equal throughout
the world. This superficial artistic consideration, however, is validated
by the basic truth and meaning of the kachina. However unique and
complex it may seem, the Hopis have created with it a form for the everlasting formless; a living symbol for that universal spirit which embodies all matter; and which speaks to us, as only the spirit can speak,
through the intuitive perception of our own faith in the one enduring
mystery of life.

This primitive, animistic view of nature, as we are accustomed to regard it, emerges in true perspective only when we compare it to our
own Euro-American view of nature.

It too, like the Indians', springs from a long religious tradition. One
reads in the first chapter of Genesis, in our Judaic-Christian Bible, that
man was created in God's own image and divinely commanded to subdue the earth. The connotations of the word "subdue" cannot be lightly

disregarded. For in this view of the dualism of man and nature perhaps lies the real beginning of human tragedy in the Western Hemisphere.

The Christian-European white race, from its first discovery of this pristine New World of the red race, regarded it as one vast new treasure house of inanimate nature that existed solely to be exploited for the material welfare of man. So one sees the Spanish spearheads of conquest thrusting into Peru under Pizarro and into Mexico under Cortés. And one watches closer home the Anglo course of empire sweeping like an engulfing tide across our own America from sea to sea. How little time it took to subdue the continent! It was a rapacious achievement whose scope and speed have not been equalled in all history. Year by year, and mile by mile westward, the white conquerors leveled whole forests under the axe, plowed under the grasslands, dammed and drained the rivers, gutted the mountains for gold and silver, and divided and sold and resold the land itself. Accompanying all this destruction was the extermination of birds and beasts, another aspect of nature inimical to man. Not for sport or profit alone, but to indulge a wanton lust for killing that wiped out vast herds of buffalo at a time, leaving tens of thousands of carcasses piled in a heap to rot in the sun.

The results of our savage onslaught against nature are now all too evident. We have so denuded the grasslands and forested mountains that the topsoil is washing down the drain into the sea. The underground water level is lowering so rapidly that we are being forced to develop means for purifying sea water for our use. The very air we breathe is becoming dangerously toxic in all our large cities, and radioactive fallout from our latest technological triumph is laying to waste wide swaths around the whole planet.

Yet it is not enough to have subdued a continent and exhausted its natural resources. There still remains a vast domain of untouched nature in the universe—the other planets in outer space; and to reach them we have already committed ourselves to exploratory voyages. Is it naive to ask if the purpose of our national space effort is to subdue, colonize, and exploit them also for our material ends? Or is it simply because we are caught in the maelstrom of a technology that cannot be stopped?

In the field of inquiry which these questions pose lies the human tragedy of America, both ours and the Indians'. For accompanying the rapacious destruction of nature from the very start was the virtual extermination of all Indians. These savages, as often viewed by the whites, were not human beings. Like wild beasts which possessed neither souls nor reason, they too were an inalienable part of that vast body of nature inimical to man and hence an embodiment of evil.

History has documented the tragic massacre of tribe after tribe across the continent throughout our "Century of Dishonor" far beyond the need to comment on it here. But when at last the holocaust was over, there were left throughout all the land scarcely 200,000 Indians penned up in ever-dwindling Reservations.

Chief Seattle, for whom one of our cities was named, spoke the epitaph of his race:

> We are two distinct races with separate origins and separate destinies. To us the ashes of our ancestors are sacred and their resting place is hallowed ground. You wander far from the graves of your ancestors and seemingly without regret. . . .
>
> But why should I mourn at the untimely fate of my people? Tribe follows tribe, and nation follows nation, and regret is useless. . . .
>
> But when the last red man shall have become a myth among the white men. . . when your children's children think themselves alone in the field, the store, upon the highway, or in the silence of the pathless woods, they will not be alone. In all the earth there is no place dedicated to solitude. At night when the streets of your cities are silent and you think them deserted, they will throng with the returning hosts that once filled them and still love this beautiful land. The white man will never be alone.
>
> Let him be just and deal kindly with my people, for the dead are not powerless. Dead?—I say. There is no death. Only a change of worlds.

These noble sentiments did not mitigate the cumulative effects of this fateful disaster upon us all. They perceptively forewarned us of the ghosts that now stalk our streets, the burden of guilt under which our national conscience is beginning to stagger, and the racial prejudice against people of all colored skins engendered in us. Yet when we view the decimation of the red race within the context of white belief, our retrospective compassion loses much of its emotional intensity. For the tragedy was not only the Indian's, but the white man's too.

Man was not created apart from nature, as he thought, but out of nature whose unconscious forces and instinctual drives still swayed him. So we, the whites, while subduing nature, also tried to subdue the aspects of nature within ourselves—the secret and shameful desires of "natural" man, the appetites of the flesh, all the instincts so incompatible and hostile to the mores of rational man. Our own minds and bodies became the battleground of man against nature, man against God, and man against himself, divided into two warring selves: reason and instinct, the conscious and the unconscious.

The outcome was never in doubt, for the white newcomers had committed the one sin against which the great spirit, Masaw, had warned the arriving Hopis. They had cut themselves off from the roots of life.

With the phenomenal rise and spread of Western civilization we have now become the richest materialistic nation that ever existed on this planet. The monstrous paradox is that while we have created untold benefits for all mankind, we have impoverished ourselves spiritually in the process. In achieving what seems to be a complete triumph over nature, we have established a machine-made society so utterly devitalized that it is anticipating the synthetic creation of life within a laboratory test tube. What could be more reasonable, then, than to enthrone the machine as its deity?

The refutation is expressed by nature itself—that one great unity of all Creation, imbued with one consciousness and infused with one power, of which everything in the universe is an embodied part. Everything is alive, differentiated not in kind but only in the degree of sentiency with which it reflects this all-pervading life in the ascent from mineral to man. The life of the whole is an unconscious process illuminated by consciousness. But pragmatic consciousness is limited. It lights up not the whole, but only a fact-section of it. Hence man's viewpoint is partial. He selects only that part which seems useful to him, ignoring and disowning the rest.

That part, to rational Western man, has been constantly decreasing. It has been successively reduced to that small segment of humanity comprising the white race, to Western Europeans, and now with excessive nationalism largely to American-dominated political entities. The trend is against the evolutionary tide of nature, by which he must constantly extend his frontiers of consciousness. Not only to include all the races of humanity, primitive as they may be; but to establish a living relationship with the animal kingdom, the plant kingdom, that of the living earth itself, and finally the whole of the universe of which he is in reality an enfranchised citizen.

These then are the two pictures broadly outlined by our opposite views of nature. The extrovert view generally held by white Europeans and the introvert view traditional to the colored races of the Far East as well as to Indian America are complementary sides of the same coin. If rational man came from nature in order to stand apart and see nature objectively, nature came to itself in man in order to see itself subjectively. The comprehensive view, it would seem, must come from a perspective that includes both instinct and reason. How are we to reach it?

This problem of means and ends seems strangely acute to a man not too well informed of current events by the Village Crier here in New Oraibi. Like many undeveloped countries it stands on the perimeters of two worlds, owing full allegiance to neither. Which way is New Oraibi to turn? It cannot remain in the primitive Hopi past. Nor can it go forward into a technological future so threateningly sterile. Western civilization also stands at a major crossroads. Its hard-won consciousness cannot sink into the unconscious. Nor can it persist in its rational, willful alienation from life. We both have reached an impasse that the H-bomb may well solve for us.

The Village Crier does not, of course, keep us posted every morning on the steadily rising fallout rate. But almost daily we are informed of the widespread trend of Hopi prophecy. It suggests a way out of our present tragic dilemma. Long, long ago when the Third World became evil and sterile, preparations were made for mankind's Emergence to a new Fourth World. The people were told simply to keep open the *kopavi* at the crown of the head. Through this "open door" to the Creator they would receive guidance to the shore of their new world and then to their homeland, during their fourfold, continental migrations. So it was they were led by the voice of their guardian spirit, by kachinas, by a star—by all the voices, shapes, and symbols through which intuition speaks to our inner selves.

Today, says Hopi prophecy, mankind is ready for an Emergence to a new Fifth World. Once again we must strive to keep open the door. Through it we will hear a new voice, glimpse a new star to follow. It will be Sasquasohuh, the Blue Star, far off and invisible yet, but to appear soon. We will know when it appears, for Sasquasohuh, the Blue Star Kachina, its manifested spirit, will dance in the *kisonvi* for the first time.

We whites also stand on the threshold of a new epoch in the evolution of mankind. Nearly 2,000 years ago a new star appeared to the wisest of our kind also. It led them to the manifested spirit of a new urge within man, to a new faith that for century after century embodied all our needs. The meaning of Christianity is not antiquated today, but it has been distorted into moral precepts by a church community which has deteriorated into a social-political institution. Excessively rational man now reads its mythical parables as mere historical events, substituting knowledge for faith, forgetting that the seat of faith is not consciousness but the unconscious. It is from this only source of religious experience that we too must look for the appearance of a new star, a new symbol to rejuvenate our faith in life itself.

By it we must chart our course through the great, unknown interstellar spaces within us, the new world of the future. Even modern science, in its reduction of material units to smaller and smaller size, recognizes that matter does not exist. It consists only of electrical fields unified by the attraction of their opposite polarities—the invisible kachina forces envisaged by our generally ignored Hopis. Is it impossible to concede that beneficent psychical energy may be evoked from them as well as the destructive physical energy released by the hydrogen bomb?

So it seems to me as I lie here in the little house below Pumpkin Seed Point that our two views, ours and the Hopis', are not too divergent after all. Extravagantly pessimistic and suspicious of each other as we are, we are both curiously imbued with the same unfounded belief in the mysterious continuity of life that will raise us to a level on which we will see reconciled in fuller perspective the opposite and complementary sides of our common coin. Already we have come a long way from the speck of green scum in that fetid pool beside the dinosaur tracks imprinted on the rocky floor of Shalako Canyon. But the journey ahead, like that behind us, lies through the subjective realm of time and love; there is no short cut through outer space by mechanical travel.

TIME

That the Indian concept of time is far different from our own is a truism asserted by every perceptive observer. Just what this difference is, none of them adequately explains. Nor is it fully illustrated by the *koshare* or Pueblo Indian clown I once saw dancing into a tourist-crowded plaza, pointing derisively to an alarm clock strapped on his arm and shouting, "Time to be hungry!" I cannot quite explain it myself, for time is a great abstraction that cannot be expressed in rational terms. Yet sometimes I awake in the silence of the night with an intuitive feeling of its mysterious context. It is as if I am no longer caught in a moving flow, but becalmed in a placid sea that has depth and content, a life and meaning all its own. At these moments of utter peace I feel absolved from the necessity of hurrying through space to reach a point in time; or, yes, of becoming hungry at the stroke of a clock. For time seems then a living, organic element that mysteriously helps to fashion our own shape and growth.

It is the same feeling engendered by the great ruins of ancient America—the ceremonial complexes of pyramid and observatory, temple and tomb, still compelling our wonder in the jungles of Yucatan, in the Valley of Mexico at San Juan Teotihuacan, and on the summit of Monte Alban in Oaxaca. Here, 1,500 years before Christ, 3,000 years before this continent was known to Europe, the Indians of Mexico erected the first observatory in the New World and evolved the calendar which became the basis of their religion. The deeper meaning of these great stone edifices is unknown to us, so foreign are their shapes and proportions, the very inclination of their planes—the terms by which they exalted the journey of the spirit out of matter, and equated the invisible dimensions of time and space with eternity.

Nowhere is this more apparent than in the Toltecan sacred city of

Teotihuacan, The Place Where Men Became Gods, some thirty miles outside Mexico City. Dating from the first century B.C. and not yet wholly excavated, this sacred city was the oldest and largest metropolis in Mesoamerica—fifty-five square miles in area. The heart of this immense and majestic ruin, completely paved and covering seven square miles, was divided into two sections. The lower section comprised a vast quadrangle composed in horizontal lines of masonry. Within it was set the Temple of Quetzalcoatl, its sides decorated with 365 heads of the Plumed Serpent carved in high relief, one for each day of the year. The name derived from two Nahual words: *quetzal,* a bird of resplendent plumage, and *coatl,* a snake, signifying the union of heaven and earth, of matter and spirit. Quetzalcoatl, then, was a god of self-sacrifice and penitence who redeemed man through the conflict of opposites; the supreme deity, the Redeemer.

The upper section to the east, toward the rising sun, was architectured with vertical lines and dedicated to Heaven, counterpointing the lower, horizontally laid-out section dedicated to Earth. It was dominated by two great pyramids, one each for the sun and the moon. The Pyramid of the Sun was immense, rising 210 feet high from a square base whose sides each measured 726 feet. Its east-west axis deviated seventeen degrees north from the true line in order to orient the pyramid to the spot at that latitude where the sun fell below the horizon on the day of its passage through the sky's zenith.

Linking the two sections was a noble avenue, one and a quarter miles long and forty-four yards wide, called Miccaotli, the Street of the Dead. It led past terraced buildings in which religious neophytes probably underwent ceremonies signifying their ritual death to the world of matter before they ascended the Pyramid of the Sun to attain the luminous consciousness of spirit. This was the ritual path taken by Quetzalcoatl before he was transformed into the planet Venus. It is the same path still followed by Venus, which first appears in the western sky, disappears below the horizon for several days, and then reappears in the eastern sky to reunite with the Sun.

Hence the Pyramid of the Sun, as Laurette Sejourne points out, was dedicated to the Fifth Sun or Fifth World in which man, synthesizing all the elements of his past, must now by a reconciliation of opposites make his final ascent out of matter into spirit. All the great stone monuments along the longitudinal axis of the sacred city were oriented in terms of it. Teotihuacan was thus astronomically laid out with geometric precision in the shape of a vast stone mandala, a quincunx with four cardinal points and a synthesizing center symbolizing the sun, the light of consciousness within man himself.

How little we know about these vast ruins, so many of which are still covered by the rubble and drifted sand of a thousand years. And still less of the meaning that once imbued them with life, that gave birth to a great civilization on a continent unknown to the savage tribes roaming the forests of Europe. We can only stand appalled before this conception in stone of universal wholeness, of cosmic balance, which expresses above all the mystery of a space-time continuum alien to our own pre-occupation with a linear, flowing time.

Perhaps more than any other people these Toltecs and Zapotecs, Aztecs and Mayas were obsessed with the flux of time, with the relationship of every individual to it as an element in their own natures. Still today all Indian America lives in the element of time as livingly real as the elements of fire, air, water, and earth.

We Euro-Americans must question our own concept of time as a medium of linear measurement. The lives of a star and stone are measured by millenia; the evanescent life of a moth is measured in hours. Yet nothing on our scale indicates that vertical dimension of time in which the life-cycle of each is completed in accord with its own unique design of being.

To us time is a shallow, horizontal stream flowing out from the past, through the present, into the future. We are increasingly obsessed with the sense of its constant movement as it increasingly loses all relation to astronomical time. The clock ticks ever faster. Every tick converts a segment of the distant future into the present, yet this present is swept so swiftly into the past that we have no present left to experience in its fullness.

This conception of time as a flowing horizontal stream, an unwinding scroll or ribbon, accounts for our fascination with histories and biographies. They enable us to watch the scroll unwind. What we see marked on it, nevertheless, are largely the spatial locations and astronomical dates fixing man's entrance into the stream and his exit from it, with the jutting landmarks observed during his linear journey. The history of a nation or an individual, it seems to me, consists of far more than these events that protrude above the surface like the visible tips of submerged icebergs. Deep below lie the invisible forces in which they have their true being. All the great movements of history—the Crusades, revolutions, and the present world unrest—are impelled by the laws of some inner necessity as instinctive, inexplicable, and certain as those that dictate the migration of swallows to San Juan Capistrano. The historical events are empty cocoons discarded by the spirit that moved through them.

We are no less obsessed with the portion of the unrolling ribbon we call the future. We keep dividing it into ever smaller segments, marking each with an entry. Perhaps no other people have been so infernally pre-occupied with programs, schedules, budgets. "I have no time!" This is the despairing cry of twentieth-century man, panicky with unrest, as he rushes ever faster from the past to the future over the knife-edge of the unlived present.

Fortunately there are a few who are beginning to have uneasy qualms about our "objective" view of time. Could it be possible that time is subjective, existing only in the mind? For behind us stretch geo-logic eras of ever-lengthening time-spans into the immeasurable archeo-zoic which as it recedes merges into azoic time, and it into cosmic time that curves back into the psychozoic time to come. The magic circle in which the past links with the future, without beginning or end. The im-memorial snake of the ancients, swallowing its own tail.

Indian time—what is it, really, abstract as it seems?

Benjamin Lee Whorf in his profound analysis of the Hopi language calls it a "timeless language." It has no three-tense system like our own. It contains no imaginary plurals like a period of ten days; a Hopi at-tending a ten-day ceremony says simply that he stayed until the tenth day. His time always has zero dimension; it cannot be given a number greater than one. The Hopi language thus avoids the artificiality of ex-pressing time by linear relation, as units in a row. Our "length of time" is expressed by the Hopi not as a linear measurement, but as a relation-ship between two events. These events reflect the intensity of the ob-server, for time varies with each observer. Hopi time, then, is a true psychological time, Whorf insists. "For if we inspect consciousness we find no past, present, future; everything is in consciousness, and every-thing in consciousness *is*, and is together." Hence the Hopis' time is not a motion. It is a duration, a storing up of change, of power that holds over into later events. Everything that ever happened, still is—though in a different form. A constant anticipation and preparation that be-comes realization. A sense of ever becoming within a duration of im-movable time.

This supreme time which has no beginning or end, no stages or breaks, and which is motionless and boundless, is also known as Dura-tion or *Parakála* in the religious philosophy of the East, Shakta Vedan-tism. It has two aspects. It may be statically condensed into a point (now) which is the pivotal center of every event. And it may expand dy-namically into a boundless continuum (always) which is the experience of Duration involving past, present, and future.

Space, like time, has the same twofold aspect, shrinking to a center (here) and swelling in a boundless continuum (everywhere), the evolu-tion and involution being the pulse of life itself. Nor do the Hopis have our concept of static three-dimensional space. The distance between events includes time—not as a linear measurement, but as a temporal relation between them. For the realm of objective events stretches away to the realm of mythical events which can only be known subjectively. Hence the immediacy and emotional strength of mythical happenings as enacted in Hopi ceremonialism. May we question whether time and space comprise one single continuum? And may it be equated with what we call the all-embracing Self?

In this conception of time lies the secret of the power and validity of Hopi ceremonialism. There are nine great ceremonies in the annual cycle: three in the winter, three in the summer, and three in the fall.

The first group portrays in a profound three-act drama the three phases in the dawn of Creation. In Wuwuchim all forms of life are germinated—plant, animal, and man; and the creative fire with which life begins is lighted. Soyal, the second phase, lays out the pattern for life's development. The wide and naked earth is solidified; the sun is turned back on the night of the winter solstice to give warmth and strength to budding life; and the kachinas arrive from their other-world homes to consecrate its growth. Powamu, which follows it, purifies the life-pattern laid out by Soyal. During it the life germinated by Wuwuchim makes its first appearance in physical form, and mankind as children are initiated by the kachinas into its spiritual meaning.

The second group of ceremonies—Niman Kachina, the Snake-Antelope, and Flute ceremonies—is held during the period of the summer solstice. Time has not moved. But within its immovable duration, the anticipation and preparation embodied in the winter ceremonies now become realization. Their stored up power transforms potential events into manifest form—into the full development of all life forms, the summer rains, the growth, maturity, and fruition of crops. With this, the host of kachinas have done their work and return again to their other-world homes.

The third group of ceremonies follows in the fall, concluding with the harvest. They are ritually concerned with the harvesting not only of the crops but of the prayers planted during the winter. Lakon, Maraw, and Owaqlt are women's ceremonies and hence they have another meaning. For now the earth is hardening again, the days are growing shorter. It is time to make ready for germination of life anew. Hence the accent on sexual symbols, woman being the receptacle and carrier for the seed of mankind which will link the concluding cycle with the new one to begin.

There is no mistaking the meaning of these nine intricate and interlocked ceremonies. They form a web of relationships that includes not only man but the sub-orders of the plant and animal kingdoms, the super-orders of spiritual beings, the kachinas, and the living entities of the earth and planetary bodies above. Interrelated in an ecological pattern of correlative obligations, they dramatize a creative plan whose power supersedes that of the limited human will. A plan that has no beginning and no end in time. For Creation did not take place, once and for all, at a certain time—at precisely nine o'clock on a morning in 4004 B.C. as Archbishop Usher once maintained. The creative plan is repeated endlessly outside and within man himself.

These ceremonies, we must observe, do not constitute a formal Sunday religion of moral tenets exhorted by priest and preacher for the benefit of the laity. The Hopis have no priests, no consecrated or professional intermediaries. Each Hopi man participates in his turn in one or more of the ceremonies; and each ceremony lasts from nine to twenty days. Nor is the observance of Hopi religion restricted to them. All Hopis are abjured to pray, to hold good thoughts. For thought is power; it is the seed planted to bear fruition in durational time, the anticipation that becomes realization.

All history, as well, is embodied in the ever-living present. I have been repeatedly annoyed and perplexed at the Hopis' complete disregard of dates and chronological sequences. They have related incidents which apparently occurred during their own memory but which, as I found out later, actually happened a century or more ago. The importance of such events is not measured by their relative significance in historical time, but by the emotional intensity they created—as the hatred of the white Slave Church which impelled the destruction of Awatovi. Hopis at Oraibi still persistently point out great ruts scraped into the rocky mesa top by the ends of huge logs. These logs, it will be explained, they had been forced to drag from the mountains nearly a hundred miles away for use as roof beams in the mission church. A casual visitor, looking vainly for the church, may learn with surprise that the ruts were made three centuries ago.

The European conquest of all Indian America illustrates this on a continental scale. Seldom has one race been so completely subjugated by another for so long. Yet after four and a half centuries, white domination is still a surface veneer. A story once told me in Mexico City by Anita Brenner is not unusual. A little village church in the remote mountains of Michoacan was noted for years for the devout attention it received. From miles around, Indians trudged in over the steep trails to kneel at its altar and bank it with flowers. Even the simple young rural priest in charge was baffled at this mysterious devotion on the part of such usually ignorant and obstinate Indians. . . . Until a slight earthquake overturned the altar, revealing a squat stone Aztec idol underneath. The story happens to be true, but it could well be an apt parable in which the altar signifies a religion made rationally conscious, under which lies the mythological content of the unconscious, that one great pool of life and time.

I first became aware of this subterranean quality of land and people many years ago when alone on horseback I rode down the length of Mexico. Small clusters of adobes or *jacales* were the only villages in these remote sierras. A man plowing a small corn *milpa* with the crotch of a tree. A barefoot woman grinding the kernels on a concave stone, the Aztec *metatl* now called the *metate*. Patting the dough into *tortillas*, the Aztec *tlaxcalli*, and cooking them on a griddle, the *comal* or *comalli*. A group of naked children leading my horse to their mother's hut. Here I asked permission to sleep on the floor with the family, rolled in my own *serape*. Then I waited a day or two until someone could accompany me to the next village.

A guide was necessary, for in this unmarked wilderness there were no roads and only an Indian could follow the dim trails trod by the bare feet of his father's fathers. I always tried to obtain for the day's journey a young boy or an old man; not only because they could be better spared from the fields, but because they talked more freely. With them trudging beside my mule, the land and people took on meaning. My guides unveiled the hidden names and spiritual meanings of physical landmarks, the peak, the gorge, the secret spring; and they explained the medicinal use of unknown herbs. It was not unusual to encounter an isolated shrine in which had been placed small clay idols like those planted in the corn fields. I remember my surprise at seeing one young boy gathering flowers and carrying them to deposit on top of a small hill. When I asked him why, he simply scraped off the rubble of sand and pebbles from its sides to reveal the pyramidal outline of cut stones.

It was an old charcoal burner who finally summarized the meaning of my journey of three months and a thousand miles. He had guided me to the top of an abysmal gorge in the mountains to show me the trail leading down to the village below. It was late afternoon and the tenuous mountain mist was lifting. In a moment it all spread out with the incomparable beauty of an immense intaglio. The great mountain walls still shrouded with mist. The tiny valley below. And in it the ancient village—a great, empty cathedral of blackened stone mounted in a central plaza and surrounded by adobe houses, huts, and corrals. A village, he explained, whose people still spoke Aztec.

"How beautiful! A man could live here forever!" I exclaimed in a burst of extravagant praise.

The old Indian turned to me an impassive face still blackened with charcoal. Neither his eyes nor his voice betrayed an ironic amusement. "*Pues.* How long are *you* staying?"

That is the story of the Spanish conquest. Of a race of foreign in-
vaders who built their cathedrals in these tiny villages, imposed their
tongue and customs on the people, and spread their veneer of conquest
over all the land, but never reached its roots. The cake is still iced with
baroque and mosaic decorations, still bejewelled with the great cities
they founded. But the land and the people remain unchanged. The
pulse of life is not echoed by the church bell and the factory whistle. It is
still the pat-pat-pat of earth-brown hands shaping a *tortilla* from Indian maize shaped by the earth itself.

The Mexican revolution against Spain was not the result of Napo-
leon's crossing the Pyrenees. Nor can the new tremors of unrest now
shaking the Sierra Madres and the Andes be attributed to political and
economic stresses. These but explain their effects, not their causes. For
they are subterranean movements rising from deep within the soul of
man and land. The present resurgence of ancient Toltec, Aztec, Maya,
and Inca values in modern architecture, art and music show how
deeply they are rooted, and they are but a prelude to the re-emergence
of Indian values in all fields. I cannot but believe that the final flowering of civilization throughout the Western Hemisphere is yet to come
and that it will reflect its own indigenous shape and meaning. Like the
greatest mountain and smallest insect, it is an organic life-pattern
planted in that durational time which mysteriously ensures its growth
within its own cycle.

We who are frantically racing against the flow of horizontal time, engulfed in its flood of external materialism, fear there is not enough time
left for humanity to improve before the world's self-destruction by thermonuclear war. Yet becalmed in a motionless moment of silent night,
we may take some comfort from the belief in another dimension that
gives us all the worlds and time we need. In it we too may find the
power to simply *be*, secure in the faith that the past and the future form
one organic whole within us.

THE DREAMS*

Among the events that helped to break the ice for us that first winter
was a series of strange dreams that came to me. They began in a curious
manner soon after the mysterious incident of gravel being thrown
against the window pane.

Entering the two Bears' apartment late one afternoon, I saw an old

*Readers will notice discrepancies between the spelling of Hopi words and names in this
selection and that in subsequent selections. The early attempt at precise phonetic render-
ing was later replaced with more simplified forms. For example, Old Dan's last name,
here spelled *Qochhongva* is later spelled *Katchongva* in *Mountain Dialogues*. [C.A.]

man in his late seventies sitting on the couch with White Bear. He was dressed in a ragged red sweater and baggy pants, his straggly gray hair falling in bangs to his chin and tied with homespun cotton into a chignon in back. Tears were streaming down his dark, wrinkled face. He would wipe them off with a hand still darker and more wrinkled, and continue talking into the tape recorder. He gave the impression of a man torn by a wracking sincerity. His words, interpreted by White Bear, bore this out.

"I don't blame the white people for their genius to transmit power through their many kinds of machines. But I am not impressed with these machines. They are crude mechanical contraptions that may break down. We Hopis don't need them. We know how to manifest our powers—the same powers—without machines. I will tell you about these powers and how the stars help us. It won't do any good. For our First World was destroyed because the people became evil, then the Second World, and the Third World. Now we are on the Fourth World and we have become evil too and it will be destroyed. But let me tell you. Without my people, without any people left in the world at all, I will still conduct my ceremony, singing and praying to the sun to project his power by silent vibrations so that we may continue our life on the next, Fifth World. Thus I will fulfill my ordained duty."

He stayed for dinner and gratefully accepted a package of cigarettes before White Bear drove him home. White Bear returned elated. Dan Qochhongva, he said, was the chief religious leader in Hotevilla. He was going to tell us all he knew. Moreover he was going to persuade all the other religious, kiva, and clan chiefs to help us too. Our worries were over!

"I told him about that gravel. He trusts you. He said to tell you that you will now have four important dreams. You will see!"

A couple of nights later the first one came.

I was suddenly aware that there were two men in the room. My first impulse was to jump out of bed and throw the catch on the door as I had been told. But the men were already inside and looked quite harmless. They were probably two traveling salesmen, old-fashioned drummers of the sort who occasionally drove through the Reservation peddling knickknacks from house to house. One was dressed in a reddish-brown suit with one coat button off, and the other in a rumpled dark blue suit.

"Don't be alarmed," said the man in the reddish-brown suit. "We're ghosts, and you should know that ghosts are just like people except that they live in a world invisible to you. We travel in great migrations, something like wild geese, along a traditional route from way above

Bering Strait down to the tip of South America. My own home base between trips is northern Alaska. My partner here hails from the lower Argentine."

The one in the dark blue suit was just as sensible and friendly although his voice sounded a little more stern.

"We've dropped by to tell you that this place is directly on our route back and forth between the poles. You're on the line now. Mind what I say. Stay on the line now."

Next morning I related this occurrence to White Bear at breakfast. He was curiously excited and demanded full details.

"No, I don't remember their faces at all," I explained. "Just their clothes. I couldn't tell their race or nationality. So it must have been a dream. Anyway the light was out when I awoke this morning."

White Bear rushed over to Mama Bear's house and then drove up to see old Dan Qochhongva. When he came back, he assured me that my visitors had been the sacred Twins, Palongawhoya and Poqanghoya, one of whom was stationed at the north pole of the world axis and the other at the south pole. Their duties were to keep the earth properly rotating and to send out calls for good or warning through the vibratory centers of the earth.

"See? You're on the line to receive their vibratory messages," White Bear told me. "You must be careful to stay on the line as they told you."

The second dream came within a week.

I dreamed that I was driving my car back from Hotevilla on the high northwestern tip of the mesa. The downhill grade was very steep, swinging around the bend of the cliff walls. This semicircle of sheer rock escarpments enclosed a high valley sloping down to the flat desert below. It was barren and forbidding, littered with huge boulders and debris from the talus slopes of the cliffs. But suddenly it filled with a glowing pink light beautiful beyond description. As I swung closer round the bend I saw that the valley was completely filled with a thick orchard of cherry, peach, and apricot trees whose branches and blossoms filtered the sunlight with the strange pinkish glow. At the same moment, I could feel the warmth of the glow suffusing my whole body.

When I told the two Bears about the dream next morning, Brown Bear exclaimed at once, "Isn't that the place, Bear, where you said some geologists found oil but couldn't get permission to dig? Oil wells are going to sprout there, all right. It's Bear Clan land too, isn't it? You better see that your claim to it is established right away!"

"A good dream!" said White Bear, his face beaming like a full Hopi moon. "That's the place where the racetrack and stone piles of the Twins are, the shrines of the Oaqol and Lalakon maidens, and all the rock writing. Everything is going to blossom out for us. We will ask Old Dan!"

Old Dan Qochhongva, I had found out, was generally considered the foremost religious leader not only of Hotevilla but virtually of all other Hopi villages. This mantle of leadership had been won with difficulty. Back in the 1880s, Chief Lololma of Oraibi had been taken to Washington where he was persuaded to cooperate with the government. Opposition developed under the leadership of Yukioma, Old Dan's father, who accused Lololma and his followers of being too friendly to the government and too progressive. Yukioma and his followers insisted that all Hopis, like themselves, adhere to their own traditional way of life. As evidence of their faith, they refused to send their children to school. Thus there developed two factions: the Friendlies under Chief Lololma and the Hostiles or Traditionals under Yukioma.

Trouble developed when a troop of Negro cavalry arrived to enforce Americanization of all Hopis. Lololma, shamed and betrayed, died of a broken heart. Tawakwaptiwa assumed leadership and continued the quarrel with Yukioma. It came to a head in the famous Oraibi Split when the two factions, in order to avoid bloodshed, agreed to a tug of war to decide the issue. Yukioma and his Traditionals lost. That night they left Oraibi forever—nearly 300 men, women, and children—and camped on the site of what soon became the new village of Hotevilla.

During the fierce but bloodless battle, Old Dan, then a young man, was struck on the head and lay unconscious and unheeded, for his father had decreed that if anyone were struck down he was not to be touched. Finally he regained consciousness, swearing an oath that he would always uphold his people's traditions. This religious enlightenment stood him in good stead.

More cavalry troops arrived to dig naked and frightened children out of their hiding places and to cart them off to school. Yukioma resisted and was carried off to the Keams Canyon agency where he was jailed for seventeen years. Despite the imprisonment of this "American Dalai Lama," as the agent called him, the contentious village of Hotevilla prospered under his son's obdurate traditionalism. As fast as the ceremonies were given up at dying Oraibi, they were adopted at Hotevilla. By 1929 Oraibi's eight centuries of rule were over. Hotevilla had become the center of Hopi ceremonialism. Yukioma had died and Old Dan had assumed leadership. Now approaching eighty, he still held the reins in his aging, wrinkled hands.

There was something deeply significant about this historic Oraibi Split, as I found out, for it brought to surface for the first time the inner schism that had been developing since the arrival of the first white men.

I began to sense in Old Dan an unusual man for trusting to the guidance of his inner promptings against forceful outside opposition, as a result of his religious enlightenment while he was unconscious. I was eager to hear what he might say about my second dream.

It was not yet eight o'clock in the evening when White Bear and I drove up to see him, but Hotevilla was already dark and lifeless. How eerie it was to grope through the narrow, sand-drifted, and refuse-littered streets behind the beam of a flashlight! The gloom was not dispelled when we found and entered his house. Five or six persons were squatting on the floor, shelling corn on a blanket. The process looked simple, as they merely scraped the kernels off with an empty cob. The trick was to keep the kernels from flying all over the room. It might have been a homey, jolly scene, but in the dim light of a smoking kerosene lamp that no one turned down it took on a somber aspect. No one laughed or talked or sang. When Old Dan came in all stopped working, the women crouching in the corner, the men sitting quietly with bowed heads.

Old Dan dominated the room with an hour of steady talk. Head thrown back, eyes half-closed, hands clutching his ragged red sweater, he never stopped for breath. I began nudging White Bear to translate. He ignored me.

I was reminded of the story of an attaché who accompanied an American woman visiting in Germany to hear, in the Reichstag, a speech by the Chancellor, a famous orator. Minute after minute went by without a word of translation from the attaché. In desperation the lady finally poked him in the ribs and whispered, "What is he saying?" The attaché flung her a look of annoyance. "Madame! I am waiting for the verb!"

Like the lady, I finally gave White Bear a stiff poke and demanded, "What does he say?"

"He said your dream was good and the third one will come soon. He has all the leaders lined up to help us."

As we drove home an hour later, White Bear added another bit of information. Old Dan was going to enter the kiva next day to begin the purification rites for the coming ceremony. "If my heart is right during my duties tomorrow," he had said, "the clouds will gather above me." His name, Qochhongva, meant in English "White Clouds Above Horizon." The next evening for the first time in many days the clouds were piling up in a rosy flare at sunset.

It was now late in November and the first of the great ceremonies in the annual cycle was beginning. Wúwuchim was a solemn and important ceremony. It recreated the first dawn of Creation and was a ceremonial supplication for the germination of all forms of life on earth—plant, animal, and man. No white man, and no Hopis save its participating members, were allowed to witness its major ritual. It was so sacred and so secret that people referred to it only as Astotokya, the Night of the Washing of the Hair—a night of terror and mystery. Old Dan conducted the ceremony as the chief of the Two Horn society. Its symbol of two great curved horns which the priests wore on their heads designated their knowledge of the three previous worlds as well as this present Fourth World. Old Dan was now immured in the kiva to conduct sixteen days and nights of secret rituals before the public ceremony on the last day. We were fortunate indeed to have the promise of his support, and I looked forward to the third dream or vision he had foretold for me.

It came while he was still in the kiva and took the shape of a vivid fantasy.

I was awakened one night by the sound of someone walking around the house. A measured, steady tread, accompanied by a curious, faint rattle at every step. As I listened, the pace of the steps increased, the rattling grew louder, until it seemed as though the house were encircled by running figures. I flung out of bed and rushed to the window. No one, nothing moving, was visible in the moonlight. The sound increased in pace and volume, rising in pitch to a steady whine. The feeling suddenly struck me that I was encircled by a swiftly revolving ring at once invisible and impenetrable. What it might be I could not imagine. I dared not open the door and stick my head outside; I felt curiously safe within the house. I went back to bed. A moment later, with a last shrill and hollow whine, the sound suddenly stopped and I fell asleep.

Old Dan interpreted it later when he taped an explanation of the entire Wúwuchim ceremony. At the beginning of the ceremony a line of cornmeal was drawn on the ground around the kiva to seal it off from all trespassers. On the dread Night of the Washing of the Hair all roads were also closed by cornmeal, and villagers living in houses close to the kiva were evacuated. To further protect the initiates from all worldly contamination, Two Horn and One Horn guards kept encircling the kiva. Each carried a long lance and wore on his left leg a turtle shell rattle which sounded the stamp of his measured tread. As the crucial hour approached when the initiates went through a re-enactment of the Emergence, other-world spirits then came to encircle the kiva with whirling rings of invisible power.

If there were any doubts as to the astounding similarity between this ritual and my own fantasy, they were dispelled on the last day of the ceremony when I saw the Two Horn and One Horn priests come out of the kiva, stamping their rattle legs as they successively encircled the kiva, the plaza, the village, and surrounding shrines. A weird and barbarically beautiful procession of fantasmal shapes gliding from dusk into the darkness of an immeasurable past.

My fourth dream followed in ceremonial sequence as preparations were being made for Soyal, the second ceremony, whose major rite was timed to coincide with the winter solstice. Soyal was one of the greatest of all Hopi ceremonies. It symbolized the second phase of Creation at the dawn of life, when all the life germinated during Wúwuchim made its first appearance in living forms and man was initiated into the mystery of his being.

I knew nothing about the rites as yet, but I dreamed that I was sitting in a kiva on a low bench in the middle of the floor. The light was dim, but I could see that the bench was placed on a cornmeal line that ran from east to west as if marking the path of the sun's journey overhead. An altar loomed before me. I paid no attention to it, for someone was behind me. All I could see were the hands that reached around me to unfasten the belt at my waist. They were old and dark and wrinkled. They took off all my clothes—every stitch. Then they washed my hair in soapy water. I could tell by the smell that the suds were made by *amole*, the roots of soap-weed yucca. When this was done, a tiny hawk feather was tied to the hair at the top of my head and over my shoulders was thrown a beautiful cape—pure white, hand-woven, a little coarse but soft as cotton.

All this time I was sitting with my bare legs stretched out before me and with my hands in my lap. Those strange dark hands now lifted my feet to the bench, and placed my own hands under my armpits so that my elbows stuck out on each side. It was an uncomfortable position.

In a little while the hands reappeared with a bowl of queer-tasting liquid which I was given to drink. I didn't like its faint odor either; it took me some time to drink it down. After this I was left alone, still sitting in that awkward, winglike position.

My arms and legs began to cramp. Then I began to feel ill from the bowl of liquid I had drunk. It made me want to vomit and to go to the toilet. This I seemed to know was impossible; there just wasn't anywhere to go. So I sat there, gagging, cramped, and uncomfortable. Waiting for what? A taxi to arrive and drive me off in a hurry! A New York taxi with a little yellow light on top and a meter clicking away inside! It didn't come, and the next thing I knew I was awake in bed feeling quite comfortable....

Old Dan seemed pleased by the dream, but made only one direct comment. The liquid given me to drink was *ngakuyi*, a medicine-water made from bones of fierce animals such as the bear, mountain lion, and

wolf, ground and mixed with water. It was drunk for inner purification, reacting on the nervous centers of the body. Ordinarily it did not
make anyone sick, he said, but to one of a different race like myself it
might possibly act as an emetic.

As Soyal was predominantly a Bear Clan ceremony, we also went to
Papa Bear for an explanation of its rituals. He confirmed the use of *ngakuyi* by all participating members and described how a path of cornmeal was drawn from east to west, symbolizing the Road of Life for all
plants, birds, animals, and men on earth. All these forms of life were
symbolically hatched by a woman who was escorted into the kiva and
seated on a specially woven plaque filled with seeds and prayer feathers. Here she squatted like a setting hen during the ceremony, patiently
hatching the germinated seeds and prayers of her people. She was commonly called Hawk Maiden because the young neophytes or initiates
were always called *kekelt*, fledgling hawks. Naked save for a white cotton *manta* thrown over their shoulders, and a tiny hawk feather tied to
the hair at the top of their heads, they were made to sit with their feet
up, hands tucked under their armpits and elbows sticking out. This sig-
nified that they were fledglings too weak yet to fly with their spiritual
wings. How often I saw them later in the kivas! Little boys patiently
squatting in their cramped positions, watching with mesmeric wonder
the strange masked shapes dancing before them.

This series of dreams that had come as foretold by Old Dan had a cumulative effect upon me. Not only were they dreams about an esoteric
religion I was yet unfamiliar with, but they had portrayed aspects of its
rituals in advance of the ceremonies themselves. How progressively they
had built up! The first dream of two ghosts had told me that I was "on
the line" to receive knowledge. This had been followed by a glowing
promise of fruition. I had then been symbolically immured in a kiva,
and later I had been given my first initiation as a fledgling hawk. All
four were so literal that they left me only one interpretation. Old Dan,
in some manner, had led me to a dream-initiation into the mysteries of
the ceremonies upon which we were then working. I felt a strange and
warm attachment to this obdurate old mystic in his ragged red sweater,
and looked forward to more dreams under his guidance.

They never came. For suddenly the coin of his nature, like that of
most Hopis, flipped over to reveal its obverse side.

Things had been building up step by step to the climax. White Bear
kept relying on Old Dan's promise to obtain prominent spokesmen for
us. Old Dan kept putting him off. Finally he agreed to call a meeting of
kiva and clan leaders at which we would explain to them the purpose of
our study and ask their cooperation.

One night they all came down from Hotevilla—Old Dan and a half-dozen of his leaders. For three hours they sat talking, listening, talking some more. Finally they left, saying they would think it over and let us know.

A week later Old Dan sent word that one of his leaders had turned against us, saying we were being paid by the government to ferret out Hopi secrets to use against them. The meeting, explained Old Dan, had been merely a ruse by which he could find out which one of his leaders was disloyal to him. Now he knew and would drop him.

His rival we knew as "Mister Hopi." Feared and mistrusted by many Traditionals throughout the reservation, he had two traits distinctly non-Hopi: an aggressive lust for power and an itch for publicity. Openly declaring himself a staunch Traditional, he yet curried favor with the younger faction of Americanized Hopis and members of the government-sponsored Tribal Council which rubber-stamped the decisions of the agency on all secular matters. He dressed well, spoke excellent English, and was constantly writing letters datelined the "Hopi Empire." At the same time he was not above letting out tidbits of religious tradition to visiting ethnologists, government officials, and prominent tourists who would quote him as a spokesman.

Finally the matter came to a head. White Bear and I were called to another meeting in Mister Hopi's own home. Here he blatantly informed us that it had been determined we were either government or church spies, and that none of the leaders would be permitted to give us any information. Old Dan did not utter a word in our defense during the long harangue. He sat, head tilted back, eyes half closed, his thin wasting body visibly shrinking before our eyes. Feeling too ashamed of him to be sorry for him, we left without a word.

His betrayal of us shook White Bear badly. After a sleepless night, he came to me pale and defeated. "It's all over! We can't go on. We must drop the project! It has been prophesied."

"Not on your life!" I shouted back just like Dodagee, the Dictator. "We're not going to be stopped by that cowardly old reprobate or Mister Hopi either! We're going out and find other spokesmen, loyal Hopis who are sincere in what they believe!"

A great deal more lay behind this incident than was apparent—the whole complex web of Hopi traditionalism. The Bear Clan was the leading clan, but there were no Bear Clan members in Hotevilla, for its dissenting founders, when leaving Oraibi, had been largely members of Yukioma's Fire or Ghost Clan. Since by tradition leadership should pass from the Bear Clan to the Parrot Clan and then the Tobacco Clan, many Hopis refused to accept the leadership of the Fire Clan. If this tradition of clan succession seemed complex, another factor beclouded matters still more.

Old Dan, being Yukioma's son, was not of the Fire Clan; according to custom he belonged to his mother's Sun Clan. Hence Yukioma's rightful successor was the son of his sister, a man known as James, who belonged to the Fire Clan. James, however, had been away for some time and in trouble. So Old Dan had assumed leadership during his absence. Now that he was getting old and his power was waning, Mister Hopi emerged as a would-be contender for leadership. Mister Hopi, however, belonged to a minor clan without a ceremony or any standing whatever. He needed something with which he could nudge tottering Old Dan off his insecure throne. That, I saw now, was Old Dan's disgraceful sponsorship of us two spies under the bountiful pay of the government or a white church. It had worked. We were out, and it looked as if Old Dan were out too. Still, one never knew. Old Dan was not the son of the indomitable and irascible Yukioma for nothing. In the intricate game of Hopi politics he might merely have sacrificed White Bear and me to · gain more worthy ends. The incident, tragic-comic as it was, turned out to our advantage. But I missed Old Dan.

It was months before I saw him again. A public meeting was called in the abandoned schoolhouse near Shongopovi on Second Mesa. Mister Hopi and his cohorts were there in a vociferous body to protest the acceptance of state welfare benefits by any impoverished Hopis because such dependence would destroy their faith in the Creator. After the meeting was over, I happened to see Old Dan come limping up the road in his ragged red sweater. Mister Hopi and his other former leaders had not offered to bring him. So Old Dan had walked and hitchhiked the twenty miles. He did not speak, but I saw in his sweat-filled eyes a look of warm recognition and ironic amusement.

What an admirable old rascal he was! Dispossessed in the field of secular affairs, like Yukioma, he functioned only in the mystic realm of rituals, dreams, and visions—a true Hopi.

I thought a great deal about dreams that winter. Most dreams seemed to me no more than unconscious reflections of the day's surface happenings of which we had been aware; one could attach little significance to them. Such an attitude was typical of the average white. To almost all Hopis, on the contrary, constant dreams, visions, and fantasies were a commonly accepted part of their daily lives. They depended upon them for personal guidance and to foretell future events for their people. These "voices of prophecy" were ancient gods, archetypal symbols and images speaking from the lowest level of the unconscious. C. G. Jung termed this bottom level the impersonal or "collective unconscious" because it embodied the contents of the primeval past common to all humanity, distinguishing it from the upper level of the personal unconscious distinctive to each individual.

Reading the many studies of both Jung and Neumann, I began to understand the origin of these psychic dream components in the unconscious and the layers through which they rose to consciousness. I began to perceive the differences between casual top-level dreams and these dreams at depth. Rising into consciousness, their forms were of course molded by the psychology of the individual dreamer. But before they reached the perimeter of consciousness, something else, I was sure, helped to shape their forms. It seemed to me there must be a layer or level in the unconscious not postulated in any of the studies I had read: a layer interposed between the impersonal or collective unconscious and the personal unconscious. A filter that somehow embodied all the predispositions or inherited tendencies of the race to which the individual predominantly belonged.

Jung, who named the collective unconscious, was a Swiss-European. All his vast body of work reflected his own racial and cultural background, particularly the archetypes of ancient alchemy on which he was an authority. India's archetypal images and symbols he strangely refused to accept, considering the universality he imputed to any archetype. "Shall we be able to put on, like a new suit of clothes, ready-made symbols grown on foreign soil, saturated with foreign blood, spoken in a foreign tongue, nourished by a foreign culture, interwoven with foreign history, and so resemble a beggar who wraps himself in kingly raiment, a king who disguises himself as a beggar?" he asked.

I, for one, on the contrary, have never had a dream in my life with a medieval European or alchemical background, although since childhood I have had dreams whose forms and backgrounds reflected the ancient pasts of both Asia and Africa. Nor have I ever known in my long acquaintance with them an American Indian or a Mexican Indian whose dream backgrounds were the Arthurian cycle and the quest of the Holy Grail, however universal is the meaning of their symbolism.

This difference seemed quite natural if one accepted, as I did, the fact that prenatal predispositions or inherent tendencies are embodied in each one of us on the basis of our own evolutionary past—that accumulated prehistory of causal effects termed karma by Eastern philosophers. We carry not only an individual karma, but a karma of the race and of the land mass to which we are attuned. All the past of all humanity lies stored in the collective unconscious of each of us. But in the rise of its archetypes into consciousness they are filtered through a racial layer which transforms them, *with unchanged meaning*, into familiar indigenous forms.

My dreams that lonely winter, then, posed a number of questions I could not answer. I was pleased to believe that I had soaked in enough Hopi ceremonialism for my four dreams to reflect it, aided by my own part-Indian heritage. But still I understood that these dreams referred not so much to the world of Hopi ceremonialism as to my own inner world. What were they trying to tell me?

Weeks later I had another strange dream. I was slowly climbing down a flight of stone stairs in the dark interior of what I felt was a pyramid. One flight terminated at a small level only to give way to another flight leading to one below. By the light of a candle I finally reached the bottom, a subterranean chamber closed off on all sides by solid dark walls.

Possessed by a growing uneasiness, I noticed imbedded in the floor a great bronze slab peculiarly shaped like a rectangular keyhole. Looked at more closely, it revealed the engraving of an ancient head, Egyptian or Mayan, wearing large earrings of the same shape as the slab itself. Around this was a border or frieze of similar, smaller heads. Suddenly a voice spoke. "Don't just stand there and look! Why don't you pull it up?"

I stooped, took hold of one of the large earrings, and pulled. It was the handle for the bronze slab which lifted easily as if it were on hinges, revealing an opening below. Just then I woke up.

White Bear, when I told him the dream, interpreted it literally, for the slab had the keyhole shape of many doorways found in prehistoric ruins throughout the Southwest and Mexico. For days thereafter he kept reminding me of other similar shapes we had not thought of before: the floor plan of many Hopi kivas; the visible portion of the kiva protruding above ground, the *kivaove*, "the part above"; the inlaid earrings worn by the Flute Maidens during the re-enactment of the Emergence of this Fourth World; and finally the outline of every Hopi man's head with his square-cut hair bangs falling down over his ears.

Uniquely Hopi as it seemed, the design was but a variation of the four-square, sacred symbol expressing a religious experience of wholeness common to all mankind. I myself, then, interpreted the dream as applying to me personally rather than exclusively to Hopi mythology. My lonely stay here among alien people was leading me, as my dream showed, deeper and deeper into my own inner self. The very keyhole shape of the bronze slab indicated something that needed to be unlocked. What lay beneath it?

So every night after looking at the stars above Pumpkin Seed Point, I would settle in bed to view with great wonder that vaster, unexplored realm within us—man's last, greatest, and most mysterious frontier.

XIII

To Possess the Land

As previously noted, Waters had, in 1971, completed Pike's Peak, *the rewrite of the Colorado trilogy, sharpening the focus on its central theme of a man's alienation from the land. Waters next turned to a* historic *example of such alienation in* To Possess the Land, *the biography of Arthur Rochford Manby. Manby was one of the most unscrupulous, intelligent, immoral, and mysterious figures of the American West. In his final degeneration we see a historic illustration of the attitude of all White settlers who regarded the land as "an inanimate treasure house to be exploited for their material benefit"[24]—and perhaps of their inevitable fate also.*

While Waters modestly suggests in his Introduction that it would be impossible to construct a book that would synthesize three possible story-telling points of view, that is precisely what he accomplished. And, with typical Waters time-sense, he begins the story with the Epilogue.

INTRODUCTION

The story of Arthur Manby's incredible life and mysterious death or disappearance can be recounted from three widely divergent viewpoints.

From one, it is a story of violent action and events that exceed the wildest imaginations of Hollywood producers of Western thrillers and mystery horror-films. In approved tradition, it opens on the frontier of the Wild West with a cowboy feud and a shoot-out. Fantastic incidents, unequalled in pure fiction, mark the career of this brilliant promoter,

153

ruthless land grabber, and art connoisseur—a legal contract drawn for the disposal of $827,000,000; a forged U.S. government gold certificate for $1,000,000; a secret society terrorizing towns and villages. And the story ends with Manby's horrible murder or mysterious disappearance, which, with its international complications, remains the greatest unsolved mystery of the West.

From a second viewpoint it is a detailed, documented history of the devious methods by which one of the numerous Spanish land grants was individually acquired during the era of American occupation of New Mexico following the Mexican War. The United States government made no effort to observe the provision in the Treaty of Guadalupe Hidalgo insuring the preservation of the rights of the conquered people. Greedy promoters, land grabbers, lawyers and politicians, corporations and railroads, moved in swiftly to take possession of the newly acquired territory. Their virtual theft of the land and its vast natural resources from the commonwealth and public domain is an aspect of history not yet thoroughly documented and made public. Recently it has emerged to national prominence through the issue of the ownership of the vast Tierra Amarilla Land Grant: the storming of the courthouse in the village of Tierra Amarilla, the arrest and conviction of Tijerina, and the formation of his *Alianza* to assert the rights of Spanish Americans. Hence this account of Manby's acquisition of the Antonio Martinez or Lucero de Godoi Land Grant is a significant part of the overall political, economic, and social picture and of historical importance.

The third approach differs greatly from its extroverted Western-mystery aspect, and its impersonal and historical aspect. The story of Manby can be recounted from a wholly introverted, psychological viewpoint. No antecedents in the genealogy of his distinguished English family can account for his deviation as a curious blacksheep. Even to the members of his immediate family he was a mystery. His life might well constitute a psychological case history: apparently that of a man finally and completely possessed by his "shadow," that negative and usually repressed aspect of the dual nature of each of us.

It is obviously impossible to narrate Manby's story on all three of these widely different levels in a book that is required by usual literary standards to adhere strictly to one point of view. Yet each approach is essential. To solve this dilemma without subterfuge, I have deliberately ignored all literary pretenses to form, letting the chips fall where they may. I have simply presented here, for the first time, all the facts known about him, the conjectures, the tantalizing clues to his enigmatic character. From this primary source material can be developed later fiction, historical papers, and psychological studies.

EPILOGUE

On a hot morning in the summer of 1929 United States Deputy Marshal Jim Martinez from Santa Fe, driving a dust-covered jalopy, crawled out of the dark gorge of the Rio Grande. Taos Valley spreading out before him was a long-familiar scene. His historic family had lived in northern New Mexico for generations. It included the famous Padre Antonio Martinez who had helped to organize a bloody revolt against American occupation in 1847, probably for the very good reason that in 1716 a preceding Antonio Martinez had been awarded a large land grant below the shoulder of the lofty peak ahead and saw no reason why it and the rest of the country should be taken over by gringos. Now, two centuries later, the marshal's brother Malaquias was still living on a piece of the grant although the rest had been stolen by the old man the marshal now had been sent to see.

He was in fact carrying papers to serve on A. R. Manby in renewal of a suit brought against him by a woman in 1922. The court had awarded her a judgment, but it had not been paid. Now after seven years the suit would expire unless it was renewed, and Marshal Jim Martinez had been instructed to serve the papers without fail.

He puttered through the familiar straggle of small adobes which surrounded the massive, buttressed Mission Church of San Francisco at Ranchos de Taos, and rumbled into the town of Don Fernando de Taos. Old Manby's large hacienda-style home was only a few buildings away from the central plaza and surrounded by a high adobe wall. The front gate was locked and several people stood uneasily in front of it.

"*Que pasó?*" he asked.

A bystander shrugged—an eloquent answer.

It was the sweltering noon of July 3; and fearing that the old man might have gone off for a Fourth of July celebration before he could serve his papers, the marshal returned to the plaza. The sidewalks were jammed with a holiday crowd: Spanish villagers, Anglo merchants, cowpokes, farmers, gamblers, Indians wrapped in their white sheets despite the heat, a few artists, loafers of all kinds. The marshal went inside the courthouse. His brother Malaquias, the deputy sheriff, was talking to another idle group in the hall. The marshal explained his errand.

"Something must be wrong," answered Malaquias. "George Ferguson here tells me he thinks Manby is dead."

Ferguson nodded assent. "Flies are swarming all over the back screen door."

How Ferguson could have looked through two high walls and seen flies on the back door, the marshal didn't know or ask. He simply accompanied both men back to Manby's house.

A crowd was beginning to gather at the front gate by now, probably drawn by rumors spreading from Ferguson's assertions. Several people the marshal knew; others Malaquias identified in a low voice. They included Doc Martin who lived next door; big-boned Milton A. Spotts, a county commissioner; Teracita Ferguson, George's aunt; Carmen Duran, with whom Teracita was now living; her friend, a large woman named Mrs. Felix Archuleta who operated a restaurant in town; a *político* by the name of Des Georges; and several others.

Led by Carmen Duran, the group walked around the high adobe wall to the far side, climbed over it, and walked through the back patio to the front wing of the house. Here Duran discovered that he had a key to the door. Unlocking it, he led the group inside.

Following a terrible stench and the swarm of blue bottle-flies, Marshal Martinez entered one of the front bedrooms. There on a cot beside the wall, he confronted an unpleasant sight: the decapitated body of a man dressed in heavy underwear, a red sweater, and a khaki coat. The body was swollen in the July heat but not decomposed, and maggots were crawling around it. Beside the cot lay Manby's large German police dog.

"Here Lobo!" Carmen Duran, taking the dog by the collar, led him out into the patio where Malaquias shot him. Another dog was howling and jerking at his tether, and this one Malaquias tied up to take home later.

When the men returned to the house, the group was standing in the adjoining bedroom where Deputy Marshal Martinez had discovered the decapitated head, the right side of the face obliterated.

A coroner's jury was formed immediately, with Des Georges as foreman. Without hesitation it pronounced that Manby had died from natural causes and that Lobo had then gnawed off his master's head.

"That's that!" grunted Doc Martin. "The crazy old coot's dead. Let's git him under!"

Within an hour the group had placed the old man's head and torso in a wooden box and buried it on the back of his property which adjoined the small cemetery in which the famous scout Kit Carson was buried.

For Deputy Marshal Martinez the matter was ended; he got into his car and drove back to Santa Fe.

For the town it was just beginning. A few persons confidently asserted that the old man had been murdered, and darkly hinted that they could offer proof. This was vociferously denied by others who claimed the decapitated body found was not Manby's. Still others swore they had seen Manby the day after his alleged body had been buried. All agreed there was something strange about the whole business, and their wild conjectures, allegations, and suspicions were echoed by the press.

So there began to mushroom one of the greatest unsolved mysteries of the Southwest, and of America, with international complications. Yet the manner of Manby's passing did not equal the mystery of his long life. Who he was, what manner of man he was—this disreputable old recluse in his enormous, nineteen-room Spanish hacienda who had been taken for granted for so many years—no one knew. They only knew that from the day of his mysterious death or disappearance, his squat, wide-shouldered figure cast a shadow long in time and substance. Like a headless body, it stretched from the somber black gorge of the Rio Grande, over the corn *milpas* around the little adobe town, to the blood-red peaks of the Sangre de Cristos. For more than forty years it had lain dark and heavy upon them all. The poor Spanish folk seeking relief in the charms of native *brujas* from the evil he cast upon them. The Indians lifting their hairless eyebrows and growing elaborately dumb at the mention of his name. And the Anglo artists and newcomers volubly probing the undying speculations about him.

No one, perhaps, ever really knew him. Always unpredictable, he exceeded everything told about him. Yet, image and shadow, all that he was and did reflected the monstrous immensities of the land that had been his one great passion—the great bulks of the heaving mountains, the grassy *vegas* sere under drought, the flat-topped mesas and the buttes weirdly carven as his own fantastic dreams and schemes, all the richness and poverty, the beauty and cruelty of the land that was at once his great dream and his folly. The mystery of Manby, if one would seek its ultimate meaning, is still embodied within the mountain below which lies his alleged grave.

XIV

Mexico Mystique:
The Coming Sixth World
of Consciousness

*Almost all of Waters' themes and theories are brought together·
in his next work,* Mexico Mystique: The Coming Sixth World of
Consciousness *(1975). Here he synthesizes an enormous mass of
knowledge about the people of ancient Mexico, their history,
myths, symbols, archetypes, cosmology, and astrology, noting in
particular the dualities:*

> The antinomy is expressed in many ways: light and darkness, male and
> female, good and evil, spirit and matter, instinct and reason, God and Sa-
> tan, the conscious and unconscious. The conflict between these bi-polar
> opposites and the necessity for superseding it is the great theme running
> through the mythology, symbology, and religious philosophy of pre-Co-
> lumbian America—the Mexico mystique.[25]

*He then goes beyond usual academic integration to relate this
material to numerous theosophical systems, to Jungian psychology, to astrology, and to world mythology in general. He suggests
that his conclusions*

> ...tend to show that the ancient civilization of Mesoamerica was basi-
> cally religious; that its spiritual beliefs still constitute a living religion per-
> petuated by the contemporary Pueblos of the Southwest; and that this
> common religious system of all Indian America embodies the tenets of a
> global belief expressed in terms of Christianity, Buddhism (and other reli-
> gious philosophies of the East), and in modern Western analytical psy-
> chology.[26]

A large part of the work is focused on explaining and interpreting the ancient Mesoamerican calendar system which measured time in Great Cycles of 5,125 years, each marking the duration of a world era. According to the astronomical calculations of the Mayas, their last Great Cycle and the present Fifth World began in 3113 B.C., and its end was projected to 2011 A.D. This date also marks the end of the present great 25,920-year cycle of the precession of the equinoxes. At this time, the Aztecs and Mayas believed the present world would be destroyed by a cataclysm and replaced by a sixth world.

According to Waters, these "worlds" are but dramatic allegories for the successive states of man's ever-expanding consciousness. Other apocalyptic interpretations also allude to what he calls the "coming sixth world of consciousness" as "a new beginning through a convergence of past and present, East and West, the archaic and the civilized."[27] At that time, Waters hopefully suggests, the resolution of our universal paradoxes will begin at a higher level.

It is impossible to illustrate synthesis of this scope by excerpting selections. However, perhaps the following chapter suggests the interweaving of themes and perception of relationships typical of Mexico Mystique.

MAYAN GOD-POTS AND CROSSES

Many similarities and parallels between ancient Mesoamerican and contemporary Pueblo rituals and beliefs have been given throughout these pages to point out how obdurately these still persist as far north as the American Southwest. I have neglected to mention, however, how deeply they are rooted in the soil and people of Mexico and Guatemala themselves. The omission will not be missed, for the subject has been covered by hundreds of documented studies. But it comes very much alive in the highlands stretching from Chiapas in southern Mexico down into Guatemala. Here and in Yucatan live more than two million descendants of the ancient Mayas.

In these relatively remote, mist-covered mountains, life follows the old pattern with few adaptations to encroaching progress. Even the dress of the people trudging down the trails to market, with variations to distinguish each village, reflects ancient styles and designs. The men wearing a cape *(capixaiji)* or blanket *(ponchito)*, and carrying a *bolsa*, or bag of woven cloth. The women in a *huipil* (blouse), a skirt secured by a *faja* (belt), with a *tapado* or *rebozo* and *cintas* of colored ribbons. The brilliant colors of the textiles range from deep purple and violet through red and orange to yellow, all made with native dyes. The round hole in the neck of the *huipil* represents the sun, with its rays of colored stitches. Of the embroidery designs that of the Plumed Serpent is most common, the *huipiles* of the Quetzaltenango region carrying two rows of serpents banded above and below by rows of small birds. The double-headed eagle, so noticeable at Chichicastenango, is another duality symbol. Lilly de Jongh Osborne also distinguishes designs of many *nahuales.** A variation of the Aztec *ollin*, symbol of movement, appears. The cross is common, and deserves study.

The cross is so prevalent among the Chamulas and Zinacantecos of Chiapas that many observers refer to their "Cult of the Cross." Chamula, about ten miles from the town of San Cristobal de Las Casas, is not properly a village, although it has a huge church. It is a *cabecera*, or ceremonial center, for the forty thousand or more Chamulas living in *parajes*, or remote hamlets, around it who come here for the observance of great religious ceremonies such as that of San Sebastion on January 20. Thousands massed in the plaza in front of the church, in a cup of the forested hills, with milky white clouds rising from the pines. All wearing the *traje tipica*. The men wearing white or black woolen ponchos, knee length, belted by a *cincho* around the waist, their hands tucked inside against the cold; heads wrapped in white scarfs like Oriental burnooses, their hats hanging down over their shoulders with streamers of colored ribbons. The women dressed similarly in black *rebozos*, most of them barefooted. A vast somber landscape of land and people in stark black and white.

The usual horseplay of all Mexican fiestas takes place in the great courtyard: bursts of rockets and fireworks, followed by a parade of dancing men bearing the *toro*, a wooden framework covered with canvas in the shape of a bull. But inside the massive church all is oppressively silent.

Outsiders are rarely permitted inside. Occasionally, after a formal interview with the *presidente* and *principales*, one is accompanied inside by the *presidente* to insure safe conduct. The emotional impact of the eerie scene is overpowering. Immense, long, and lofty, the room is bare of furniture and decoration save for two streamers of colored cloth suspended overhead and a dozen life-size Catholic saints propped against the two side walls. The floor is strewn with fresh pine needles. On it are

*Lilly de Jongh Osborne, *Indian Crafts of Guatemala and El Salvador*

squatting a hundred or more women with candles mounted on flat stones and with braziers of burning copal. Presumably they are praying to the saints along the walls, their lips almost imperceptibly moving, but giving forth no sound. From time to time small groups of men arrive from other remote *parajes*, led by a *jefe* carrying the immemorial cane of office, his men carrying handmade guitars and curious triangle-shaped harps. Finding a place to stand, the musicians begin plucking their strings in monotonous, muted tones. The music is part of the silence, the candle-lit clouds of burning copal.

Through the dim light wreathed by spumes of the sweet-smelling incense the *presidente* gingerly leads us through the mass of huddled women to a wooden box up front. In it we dutifully stuff a five-peso note. This, with the *presidente's* sponsorship, validates our presence. The flag-bearers standing at the altar do not seem to notice our presence. The flags they bear are simply large squares of colored cloth attached to long pine poles. The *presidente* leaves us to stand in the swiftly filling church.

The fireworks and horseplay out in front have ceased. Not a sound enters the great closed doors. The immense dimly-lit room is packed with people and filled with silence, the heavy Indian silence, impregnated with the ancient perfume of burning copal. There is nothing here suggestive of the patina of Christianity. There is no formal worship. Only the mute and eerie observance of the archaic mystery, the mystery of life itself.

Little by little the church empties, the Chamulas massing in front of a row of high crosses beyond the courtyard. All are decorated with crude designs of trees and branches. What is there in this ancient symbol that holds silently entranced so many thousands of people?

Some fourteen miles away the same fiesta is being observed by a crowd of the eight thousand Zinacantecos from fifteen outlying *parajes*, or hamlets, in their *cabecera*, or ceremonial center, of Zinacantan. It lies in a great open meadow in front of a church. In contrast to somber black-and-white Chamula, Zinacantan is cheerful pink and white in the bright sunshine. The color tone is given by the dress of thousands of Zinacantecos, the men wearing *serapes* or *ponchos* of fine-woven wool with narrow pin-stripes of pink and white, from which protrude their white shirt sleeves. Around their necks they wear a scarf of delicate blue, hanging down in back with brilliant red tassels tied to the corners. The woman's dress is similar, but in form of a *manta* fastened in front.

The cheerful scene belies the Nahuatl name of Zinacantan, "House of the Bat," given it because of the great stone bat once worshipped here. Everywhere in the meadow are huge piles of tangerines, sugar cane, peanuts. People are sitting on the grass eating tortillas and bits of meat purchased from a stall off to one side, or idly strolling about. Under a shelter sit older men, the new office holders, San Sebastion being the first major fiesta they have celebrated. The previous year's officers have visited the church to pray forgiveness for their misconduct during their term of office. Their wives are not exempt from censure. And this gives rise to a great deal of buffoonery.

Two men, faces painted black and wearing hats and tails of jaguar fur, appear. They are the *Bolometic,* the Jaguars. Each carries stuffed squirrels with genitals painted red, which he pokes with a stick and throws at persons in the crowd. They are said to represent wives of the outgoing office holders, shameless, oversexed women who interfered with their husbands' performance of duty. Late in the afternoon they climb a bare red tree, the Jaguar Tree, *Bolom Te,* and throw their stuffed squirrels and food to the crowd. More groups of masked clowns file in from a hamlet a mile away, indulge in horseplay, and vanish in the swelling crowd. Despite the church and modern innovations, one sees in both Chamula and Zinacantan vestiges of the ancient Mayan· past. One is reminded of the great Navajo Sings of years ago: the tiny cooking fires, the massed crowd encamped on the snowy plain, the same Indian silence and absorption into the same mysterious spiritual realm.

As at Chamula, there are wooden crosses everywhere throughout these highlands—at the foot and on the summit of sacred mountains, beside springs and waterholes, in caves, and in the patios of houses. A most imposing array stands near the remote and primitive hamlet of Romerillo, high in the mountains above Las Casas. Rising starkly on top of a deforested hill stands a row of twenty-one huge wooden crosses some twenty feet high, with tree branches planted between them. On the barren hillside below lies the Campo de Santo with innumerable burial mounds. Each is marked by a foot-high cross and a planted twig.

From the appearance of all these crosses everywhere, as the anthropologist Vogt observes, one has the impression this is one of the most solidly Catholic communities in the world. "But while these crosses may look like contemporary replicas of the classic Christian cross on which Christ was crucified in far off Jerusalem, they have no such meaning to the Zinacantecos. . . . The Zinacantecos are not Catholic peasants with a few Maya remnants left in the culture, but rather they are Maya tribesmen with a Spanish Catholic veneer—a veneer that appears to be increasingly thin as we work with the culture."*

Some observers assert that the four-pointed cross represents the Maya

---

*Evon Z. Vogt, *The Zinacantecos of Mexico*

four-fold rain god Chac. Others that the cross decorated with designs of trees, branches, and flowers is the Tree of Life, represented for the ancient Mayas by the sacred ceiba tree which is rooted in earth and tips the heavens, its arms signifying the four directions. Vogt offers another interpretation. The hundreds of *Kalvarios* at mountains, springs, and caves where crosses are erected are the meeting places of ancestral gods. The crosses are "doorways" or channels of communication with these gods, opened by processions of men offering prayers to the crosses, decorating them with pine boughs and flowers, lighting candles, burning incense, and depositing offerings of rum and black chickens. The *krus*, then, is an avenue of communication between the "essence" or "inner soul" of man and the gods.

Underlying all these interpretations is a common meaning. From the earliest ages of man, the cross has been a universal symbol. If the extension of its four arms in opposite directions represents conflict and division, their point of intersection signifies reconciliation and unification. It is the meeting point of the conscious and unconscious, the mystic center identical with the creative principle of the universe. Immemorially it has been shown surrounded by a circle, as often has been the entire cross. Now to leave the circumference of the circle for the center, as Cirlot reminds us, is equivalent to moving from the exterior to the interior, from multiplicity to unity, from form to contemplation. And it is here on these crosses that the Chamulas and Zinacantecos carve circles and hang flowers. The cross then is a Tree of Life, for life develops only from the conflict and reconciliation of the opposites; the "doorway" of communication between men and gods; and between our unconscious and conscious selves. It was to its mystic center that Quetzalcoatl journeyed. And so it is in these multitudinous, stark crosses in the Chiapas highlands we see reconciled ancient and contemporary Indian belief.

One can journey still farther back in time by visiting the Lacandones. A surviving remnant of the ancient Mayas, the Lacandones refused to submit to the conquering Spaniards and hid in the depths of the tropical rain forest to carry on the life of their forefathers. Today, numbering only a few hundreds, they live in two small settlements on the Mexican side of the great Usamacinta River: one on the shore of Lake Naja, the other on the banks of the Lacanhá River.

They are difficult to reach except by a chartered plane which sets down on a narrow runway in the midst of the towering *selva*, the dense rain forest. At the edge of the clearing is a camp periodically occupied by a few guests (like ourselves) of Trudy Blom, widow of Franz Blom, the archaeologist. The compound comprises five *chosas* with palm-thatched roofs but without walls, the large one serving as a kitchen and the smaller ones provided with posts and hooks from which we can sling our sleeping hammocks.

From here two Lacandones, Old Chank'in and K'in, paddle us in a huge dugout canoe hollowed out of a mahogany across Lake Naja. Across this incomparably clear and beautiful jewel in its green setting lies the northern Lacandon settlement, or *caribal*, of Naja. It consists of some twenty or more *chosas* scattered at random in a clearing interspersed with small corn *milpas*, clumps of banana and orange trees. Life is still primitive. The men raise corn, fish in the lake, and hunt *cojolites*, the crested guan, the pheasant *curassow*, and an occasional deer with bows and arrows. The long bow is made of *guayacán* wood, the string of *ixtle*, or agave, fibers, and the arrows are tipped with parrot feathers. The women grind corn on stone *metates* and boil it in huge pots, and weave cotton cloth for their garments on small back-strap, horizontal looms. Each man has several wives, each wife having a separate fire in their common *chosa*. Men and women alike wear only one garment, a loose, white, knee-length gown down which hangs their long, uncombed black hair. Walking barefoot in file through the dank, dark jungle they resemble nightwalkers in nightgowns or pale, noiseless ghosts.

The Lacandones are said to the be the most primitive Indians in all Mexico, although the Tarahumaras in their isolated Chihuahua canyons seem far more wild, shy, and secretive. But certainly the Lacandones with their short powerful bodies, broad feet, and childlike faces always breaking out in smiles, are true creatures of nature. There is a simple dignity about them; they are not abashed by strangers and meet them on equal footing. Their greeting is simple: *"Utz im pusical"*—"My heart is good." And no man enters another's *chosa* unless he is invited.

Their religious observances are simple. There are no chiefs or priests. The head of each family is responsible for conducting rituals, praying, and teaching his sons. Their common "church" is the God-house, an open thatched-roof hut like all the others save that on a shelf under the roof stands a row of God-pots. They are incense pottery bowls striped red, white, and black, and shaped on the rim into crude faces. Each represents a god, and holds a small stone effigy of the god or a bit of jade from an ancient temple ruin. Rituals are conducted for the birth of a child, to insure one's safety on a journey, to ask for a long life, to aid an ill patient. Old Chank'in permitted us to watch him conduct a healing ceremony for one of his wives. Making little palm wands, he squatted down in front of a God-pot in which he burned copal. Chanting and praying in a low tone for a long time, he blackened the wands in the smoke of the sweet incense. Then he left the God-house to touch them to the body of his ill wife.

Every spring there is held a long renewal ceremony during which all the people of Naja gather at the God-house. New God-pots replace the old ones which are carried away and hidden in caves. Women prepare *posole*, a corn gruel, and *balché*, a drink made from the bark of the balché tree mixed with water and sugar cane, and fermented. Copal is lighted in the new God-pots which are given food and drink while the men in unison pray and chant that the fumes of the incense may carry the essence of their offerings to the real gods above.

Remnants of similar God-pots have been found in ancient Maya ruins, possibly indicating that the great mass of common folk may have observed the same simple rituals, leaving the priests and nobles to carry out the intricate temple ceremonies. The dwindling Lacandones have forgotten the great religious structure of their ancestors, but they still believe in three heavens—Chembeku, Kapoch, and Hachakyum, and one underworld, Yaralum, whose lord, Kisin, is evil. Trudy Blom reports the names of four of their many gods: Hachakyum who made heaven and earth; Akíinchob, his son-in-law; Itzanoku; and K'ak, god of fire.

The birthplace of all the gods was said to be Palenque, the loveliest of all Mayan cities. Price reports that the Lacandones knew of the ancient tomb deep in the heart of the stone pyramid of the Temple of Inscriptions long before it was discovered by archaeologists.* They also venerate Bonampak, now famous for its gorgeously colored temple murals, not far from Lacanhá. But the holiest of all was Yaxchilán. It was built as a new city for the gods of Palenque by Ak'inchob, the corn god, upon instructions from Hachakyum.

Here the gods met and manifested themselves. On the Acropolis was the temple or earthly home of Hachakyum, where was carved a great stone statue of him. To this now ancient ruin the Lacandones used to make frequent pilgrimages. Old Chank'in and one of his sons walked there a few years ago with offerings of copal.

Their trip through the jungle must have been long and arduous. Even for us it poses some problems in transportation. One takes a small plane over the *selva*, so dense that from above it looks like a solid growth of moss often obscured by a sea of clouds. This makes plane travel uncertain; a jungle pilot has to wait hours for the mist to clear before take-off, and may have to turn back if he cannot see to land on the narrow strip

---

*Christine Price, *Heirs of the Ancient Maya*

at Agua Azul. The three buildings there lie on the high bank of the great Usamacinta River which marks the boundary between Guatemala and Chiapas, Mexico. In years past Agua Azul was a *centrál* for mahogany lumbermen and *chicleros* who gathered sap from the *zapote chico*, or sapodilla, for chicle or chewing gum. From here the massive mahogany logs were floated downriver to Tenosique where they were tied into rafts and floated on down to the Gulf of Mexico for shiploading.

From Agua Azul a long mahogany dugout with an outboard motor takes the few of us downriver. The two or three hour trip, aided by the current, is magnificent. The great Usamacinta is flanked on each side by an almost impenetrable wall of rain forest: giant mahogany trees growing to a height of 150 feet; ceibas with tall straight trunks leaved at the top like umbrellas; sapodillas; the balché whose bark is used with sugar cane, honey, and water to make the Lacandon drink of balché; the *chechén* exuding a poisonous sap from its leaves; rubber, bamboo, palms. Orchids are everywhere. Begonias grow waist high. It is a glimpse of a virgin world just after Creation.

Then at the site of Yaxchilán the river makes a wide U-bend, the land jutting out like a peninsula with twenty-foot-high banks up which the river rises during the rainy season. There is a sandy spit for the dugout to beach, and up above a clearing containing a compound of a half-dozen *chosas* roofed with thatchings of palms. Two families live here, the headman being caretaker of the ruin. In two empty *chosas* we ate by lamplight, hung our hammocks, and lay listening to the howler monkeys.

The jungle begins a dozen yards away; one dare not go far alone. The ruins begin at once, but to reach them two men have to cut a path through the dense growth. Yaxchilán was one of the most beautiful and important of all Maya cities, and its ruins long have been famous. The Spanish saw them in 1696, Maudsley and Charney in 1882, Maler in 1895, and many late archaeologists have studied them and then left them to be eaten up by the jungle. Why Yaxchilán has not been preserved and restored, in preference to far later Chichén Itzá for one, is a mystery. Maler's map of 1897 shows an Acropolis Grande, an Acropolis Pequeña, and rows of majestic temples in front and behind, a total of some forty structures. Today it is impossible to detect the architectural plan. The encroaching growth surrounding the structures is so dense that the caretakers have to cut it every two months to make them visible. Even so, huge trees and tree-size roots extend down through roofs, walls, and subterranean chambers, tearing apart the cut stones.

Yaxchilán's pyramid-temples are not high, but their upper facades and roof combs are decorated with figures carved in stone. The stone here is said to be harder than at Palenque whose panel frescoes are so marvelous, so Yaxchilán's sculpture is among the best; it is famous for its carved stone lintels. Lintel 8 records a Calendar Round date of 755 A.D. The huge stelae are magnificent. Most of them have fallen and are covered by moss. Others that have been studied have been turned face down to protect them from the weather.

So it remains today, one of the jewels of classic Maya civilization, long abandoned and neglected save for venturesome pirates who have snaked out a stelae for sale to private collectors.

What the purpose was of the Lacandon pilgrimages to this holy city of their ancient culture, this place of brooding mystery, we did not realize until we saw the headless statue of Hachakyum in front of the middle doorway of the great temple. It had the shape of a humanized feline figure in a posture of worship that instantly recalled that of the Olmec semi-humanized jaguar sculpture in the museum at Villahermosa. Many years ago mahogany cutters had broken off the head which lay on the ground below. Here the Lacandones burn innumerable little pyramids of copal and offer their prayers to the time when the head and body will be reunited. It will mark the destruction of this world and the beginning of a new era, with the rebirth of the old gods, and a final flowering of the ancient Maya culture.

According to the precisely calculated, astronomical-astrological prediction made by their ancient forefathers, we shall see that that time is not far off.

XV

Mountain Dialogues

*In 1981, Waters published a collection of personal essays enti-
tled* Mountain Dialogues. *The title of the book comes from two
mountains located near Waters' home in Arroyo Seco, New Mexico. The nearby Sacred Mountain of Taos is described as "benign"
and "motherly"; the other, El Cuchillo Del Medio, as "malign"
and "masculine." These bi-polar mountains, like the biblical Mt.
Ebal and Mt. Gerizim, ". . .imprint their forces both on the physical and inorganic world, and on organic life. . . ." Waters says:*

> [Arroyo Seco] had a distinctive aura, a rhythm, a flavor of its own.
> There were so many feelings between opposite poles! All these invisible
> forces helped to mold me into their pattern, whatever that is. Gradually
> they began to speak to me with the voice of the living land, and its chief
> spokesmen were the two great peaks that rose from the mountains
> above. . . .
>
> Our communication with the spirit of a place, with its constituent
> voices of a stream, a rock, a tree, confirms the truth that this interrela-
> tionship is necessary for our continued existence as one species of organ-
> isms dependent like all others upon the same eternal powers that inform
> the universal whole.

*At first glance the collection seems to deal with unbelievably
disparate topics—ranging from his next-door neighbors to* The
Nature and Meaning of Man. *On closer examination, however,
one becomes aware that the book is very carefully crafted—as
tightly woven as a Navajo blanket. Themes introduced in one essay constantly emerge, disappear, and re-emerge in others. The
meaning of each of the separate essays thus becomes ultimately
dependent upon what has been said before and after its appearance in the book. In the opening paragraph, for example, a little*

neighbor girl asks Waters, "How does this dirt make our garden grow?" The question gives rise to the ensuing essay entitled "The Living Land." In the tenth essay, "Ley Lines," the question again surfaces, as Waters says, "And here perhaps we have an answer to the question asked by the little girl of my neighborhood. . . ." In addition, what the reader learns from the essay on ley lines and from the opening essays on "The Sacred Mountain" and "El Cuchillo Del Medio" is related directly to the material covered in the next to the last essay, "The East is Red," in which Waters, continually enlarging the scope of this book, writes of his 1976 visit to mainland China. By the end of the book, the scope has been so enlarged that he can observe with validity:

> The nature of the world and [the nature of] man as perceived by the great civilizations of the past in Egypt, India, Tibet, China, and Mexico have already been briefly outlined.

Perhaps the most prominent of the book's many unifying themes is Frank Waters himself. For in this work Waters reveals more about his own interests and experiences, about his own nature, than he has in any of his previous works.

In Mountain Dialogues, *Waters acknowledges his sources, the major writers and thinkers and places which have influenced him. He weaves together the threads of these influences, adds his own additional thought, and presents a truly cosmic overview.*

THE HOPI PROPHECY

It is curious how an odd idea from an obscure source, long unknown, ignored, or considered irrelevant, suddenly emerges to general public notice. The idea itself cannot alone account for its sudden spread and wide acceptance. Nor can the media of books, magazines, and newspapers which report it. Relevant though it may be, an idea first requires a fertile ground in which to take root and grow. And this must be the unconscious level of those who at last find in it something akin to their own deeper feelings.

The Hopi Prophecy is such a phenomenon. When I recounted it in the *Book of the Hopi* published some years ago, it was as generally unknown as the Hopis themselves. Today the Hopis are prominent in the news, and their prophecy has caught the imagination of people everywhere.

The Hopis, when I lived among them for three years, were a small tribe of five thousand people confined to a desert Reservation of four thousand square miles in northern Arizona. They lived in nine ancient villages built on top of three high mesas, with a tenth some fifty miles away. Oraibi on Third Mesa, dating from 1200 A.D. or earlier, was the oldest continuously occupied settlement in the United States. Just below it lay Kiakochomovi, New Oraibi, historically a new village without tradition, a "government town." The nearest modern towns on the transcontinental highway—Flagstaff, Holbrook, and Winslow—lay a hundred miles south by narrow dirt roads. Impoverished farmers, the Hopis subsisted mainly on the sparse patches of corn they grew in the sandy desert below their mesas. Isolated and neglected, they were but a fragment of the nation's ignored Indian minority.

The Hopis themselves, however, maintained an inner life as rich and meaningful as their outer life seemed shabby and meaningless. They perpetuated the tradition of a mythological past and a prophecy of the impending future. The fecundant past was embodied in their Creation myth and migration legends, and dramatized in their nine great annual ceremonials, the only true Mystery Plays indigenous to America.

These recount that the Hopis had lived in three previous worlds which were successively destroyed when mankind ceased to follow the plan of all Creation, depending instead upon materialistic desires and technical inventions. Yet there was always a small minority who adhered to the divine plan, and escaped to the next world. Such were the Hopis who emerged from the annihilation of the Third World into our present Fourth World, reaching the shores of southern Mexico or Central America. Here, they were directed by its caretaker and guardian, Massau, to make ordered migrations by clans to the four directions— *pasos* to the north and south, to the Atlantic on the east and the Pacific on the west—before they settled in their permanent home, Túwanasavi, the Center of the World. Túwanasavi was not the geographic center of the continent, but the spiritual or magnetic center at the junction of the north-south and east-west routes of their migrations. The area corresponds generally with what we today call the Four Corners region, the only place where four states touch—New Mexico, Arizona, Colorado, and Utah. Here in this harsh desert heartland they would have to depend upon nature for their simple livelihood, and so maintain the Creator's divine pattern of life instead of becoming profane and materialistic.

This is the difference between the world view of the Hopis who would preserve nature, and the later pragmatic arrivals who would destroy nature for material gain. When the destruction by the latter reaches a climax, the Hopis believe a cataclysmic rupture takes place to restore the balance of forces. A new world is created to replace the old, and to it emerge those devout Hopis who seek to re-establish the sacred plan of Creation. Each such Emergence of man to a new world is thus a new step of human consciousness sanctioned by the enduring moral laws which govern the revolutionary process. This pattern had been followed three times before, and would be followed again.

This continuity of life throughout the previous worlds, whose events, although contents of the unconscious, are still felt as consciously immediate, reflects the Hopi conception of time. The past and the future are too entwined in the present to be separated into tidy compartments as they are in our own rational White culture.

Benjamin Lee Whorf, in his perceptive *Language, Thought, and Reality*, calls the Hopi language a "timeless language." It has no three-tense system like our own. Our "length of time" is expressed not as a linear division of past, present, and future, but as a relationship between two events. Hopi time, says Whorf, is a true psychological time. "For, if we inspect consciousness, we find no past, present, future; everything is in consciousness and everything in consciousness *is*, and is together." Hence, Hopi time is not a motion. It is a duration, a storing up of change, of power, that holds over into later events. A constant anticipation and preparation that becomes realization.

In this mode of thought lies the power and validity of the nine great, interlocked, annual Hopi ceremonials. They re-enact the Emergence from the three previous worlds as if they were in the immediate present. And in preparation for a fourth Emergence to another new world, the Hopis pray and hold good thoughts during each of the nine to twenty-day ceremonies. For thought is power. It is the seed planted to bear fruit in durational time, the anticipation that will become realization. The immediate purpose of their collective effort during ritual after ritual is to help maintain the balance of all the forces of nature. What a cosmic scope it covers! A vast web of relationships that includes not only human beings but the sub-orders of the mineral, plant, and animal kingdoms, the super-orders of the kachinas, those spirit beings, and the living planetary bodies above. All are interrelated in the spiritual ecology of one universal pattern which supersedes that of the human will.

But the Hopi Prophecy is not as simple as this bone-bare skeleton might suggest. It is fleshed with an intricate maze of symbols, archetypal images, and ceremonial interpretations that we must try to understand in light of the historical events which it projected.

It relates that when the first Hopis arrived on this new Fourth World, three stone tablets were given to the leading Bear Clan. The cryptic markings outlined the boundaries of the Hopis' sacred land, the areas to be apportioned to the various clans, and the figures of six men representing the leading clans. One of these ancient stones was still in the custody of Mina Lansa, the *kikmongwi*, or village chief, of Old Oraibi, who showed it to me some years ago.

The time would come, however, when the Hopis would be overcome by a strange people who would take much of their land and try to force them into a new way of life which deviated from the sacred path. If the Hopis did not comply, they would be treated as criminals and punished. The Hopis—a People of Peace, as their name implies—were not to resist. Help would come, as shown by a fourth stone tablet given to the Fire Clan by Massau, its deity. On one side were engraven a swastika and a sun. On the other side was the figure of a man without a head, and the *nakwach* symbol of the brotherhood of man. One corner was broken off. Massau explained that the missing fragment had been given to the Hopis' elder brother, Pahána (derived from *pásu*, "salt water"), who had been directed to go in the direction of the rising sun. Eventually he would return to his younger brother, the Hopis, carrying the missing corner of the tablet to identify him as the Lost White Brother. Some of the Hopis would have been contaminated by the materialistic way of life of their conquerors. On the Day of Purification they, with all the world, would be destroyed. Only those people who still adhered to the divine plan would be saved. With them, Pahána would initiate a new universal brotherhood of man, beginning a new cycle and mankind's Emergence into the Fifth World.

The Hopis interpreted the events of recorded history as confirmations of Prophecy, and confirmed the difference between the world views of the Hopis and Whites. The westward march of empire by the Whites bore out the prediction of a conquering race whose members usurped much of their land and confined them on a government Reservation. American soldiers broke into Hopi homes, captured their children, and sent them to distant schools to learn a new language and a new way of life. The People of Peace offered no armed resistance, as did their neighbors, the 8,491 Navajos who were finally defeated and marched into a captivity which lasted four years.

The sacred Fire Clan tablet showing the figure of a man without a head indicated how these evils could be dispelled. If a Hopi leader assented to having his head cut off, he would save his people. The two tribal leaders at the turn of the century, Lololma—friendly to the Whites—and Yukioma of the Hostiles, both declined to fulfill the Prophecy.

When Lololma, shamed in front of his people, died of a broken heart in 1901, he was succeeded as village chief of Oraibi by Tewaquaptewa, his sister's son. Tewaquaptewa adopted Christianity, established good relations with the Whites, and became leader of the Friendlies. Armed conflict between the two factions was averted by a "push of war" on September 8, 1906. A line was marked across the rocky top of Third Mesa. The two forces massed on each side. It was agreed that the faction which was pushed over the line would leave Oraibi forever. The bloodless struggle of the People of Peace ended when the Friendlies of Tewaquaptewa pushed Yukioma's Hostiles across the line. That night, Yukioma and his followers packed their belongings and trudged north to čamp at a spring, founding the village of Hotevilla.

The Hopis' way of life had withstood three hundred years of Spanish and Mexican rule, and fifty years of United States aggression. This Oraibi Split was more than a social schism between factions friendly or hostile to the encroaching Whites. It constellated the psychological split in the Hopi soul between good and evil, and the cultural rupture between the old way of life and the new.

Now in 1934 came the passage in Congress of the far-reaching Indian Reorganization Act, also known as the Wheeler-Howard Act. It announced a new era in the relationship between the federal government and Indians. The Act, as it was explained to the Hopis, offered economic aid and federal support through their adoption of a Hopi Constitution and the establishment of a Tribal Council which would function as the sole representative of all the Hopi villages. Acceptance or rejection of the proposed system was to be decided by popular vote.

The man engaged by the Bureau of Indian Affairs to campaign for Hopi approval was Oliver LaFarge, the well-known anthropologist and author of the Navajo novel *Laughing Boy*, which had won a Pulitzer Prize. From the start, he ran into trouble. The *kikmongwis*, religious and clan leaders, saw no reason why their traditional form of self-government should be replaced by one devised and controlled by the federal government under the BIA. The general mass of Hopis showed their ingrown habit of shying away from anything that smelled of government control. Hence they did not attend the meetings called by La Farge, in village after village, to organize them into a federation under a new Constitution and Tribal Council. Their abstention from all meetings and discussions, rather than participating in argument, clearly expressed their opposition in the traditional Hopi manner.

The final election was held on October 24, 1936. In the traditionalist stronghold of Hotevilla, only thirteen persons voted out of a population of two hundred—twelve votes for, one vote against. This vote was federally reported as a landslide victory for the proposed IRA-BIA system, ignoring the two hundred and thirty-seven persons who had showed their opposition by staying away in their fields.

The overall vote throughout all villages showed only 755 votes cast by the 4,500 Hopis—651 for acceptance and 104 for rejection. This total of 755 votes from 4,500 people represented only sixteen percent of the people. Yet the BIA and the Department of Interior expressed satisfaction that it reflected the will of the people. The vote was officially approved in December 1936, and the Hopi Tribal Council established.

The Tribal Council, as set up, was to comprise one member from each of the villages. This White concept of "democracy" was utterly foreign to the Hopis. For ages, each village had existed as an independent sovereignty headed by its spiritual leader, the *kikmongwi*. He and other religious clan leaders governed not only the religious but the secular life of the villages. Property rights were determined by clans in a hierarchical order in a system of matrilineal descent. Yet property rights of clans were regarded as communal rights; no Hopi land could be alienated or expropriated by foreign powers.

In one sweep, the Tribal Council erased this traditional system by negating the function of the *kikmongwis*, the ancient structure of the clans. Hence the leading traditionalist villages, viewing it as merely rubber-stamping the dictate of the Bureau of Indian Affairs, thereafter refused to send representatives from their villages. This, in effect, made the Council illegal, for it was not representative. A few progressives, however, supported it in order to gain prestige, favor with the government, and whatever benefits they might receive.

Still the Redeemer, Pahána, the Lost White Brother, did not return. But there were hopeful signs when World War II broke out.

On the gourd rattle used by kachinas in their ceremonies are painted two prime Hopi symbols, the swastika, surrounded by a red circle representing the sun. The significance of the swastika was accentuated when the Nazis adopted it as their emblem. For a time, some Hopis believed the Germans were the people who would return with Pahána. Then, with the defeat of the Hitler regime, came Japan's drive for world power, climaxed by the bombing of Pearl Harbor. The national emblem of Japan was the rising sun, the other primary Hopi symbol. So now the Hopis transferred their hopes to the Japanese.

These two beliefs were mentioned in my *Book of the Hopi*, but they were editorially deleted. And wisely, I think, for the references clearly implied a political disloyalty to the United States when it was hoped the book would help to better the Hopis' relations with the government and their economic conditions.

The dropping of atomic bombs on Hiroshima and Nagasaki confirmed another phase of the Hopi Prophecy which related that a gourd full of ashes would be dropped from the sky, bringing destruction to man and earth. In a letter datelined "Hopi Indian Empire, March 28,

1949," and signed by six chiefs, four interpreters, and sixteen other Hopis, these spokesmen wrote the President of the United States. They warned him that the Hopis and White men now stood face to face at the crossroads of their respective lives, at the most critical time in the history of mankind. "What we decide now and do hereafter will be the fate of our respective peoples. . . . We are talking now about the judgement day. In light of our Hopi Prophecy it is going to take place here in the Hopi Empire."

No answer was received, nothing was done. Events marched on toward the final Day of Purification.

Immense deposits of coal were discovered beneath the surface of Black Mesa. This great tableland of 3,300 square miles lay partly within the Hopi Reservation and partly within the immense Navajo Reservation which surrounded it on all sides, and was considered sacred by both tribes. Lease of the Hopi land to the Peabody Coal Company, a member of the consortium of the country's twenty-two greatest power companies which had already devastated Appalachia, was granted by the Department of the Interior without Congressional or public hearings. Neither the traditionalist leaders, nor the Hopi people, were generally informed of the terms of the contract which was signed on May 16, 1966, by the Tribal Council, acting through its Interior-approved tribal lawyer, John S. Boyden of Salt Lake City.

Three weeks later, on June 6, a similar contract was signed by the Navajo Tribal Council for a thirty-five-year lease on the Navajos' portion of Black Mesa. The contracts provided royalty payments of twenty-five cents a ton for the coal. The Hopis would eventually receive an estimated $14.5 million, the Navajos $58.5 million, while the Peabody Coal Company profits would amount to about $750 million.

Strip-mining of 45,000 tons a day of Black Mesa coal by Peabody Coal began immediately. Its colossal, coal-fired Four Corners power plant spewed daily 1,300 tons of gases, pollutants, and particulate matter into the air, covering 10,000 square miles. The five million tons of pulverized coal a year were mixed with water and pumped through a slurry line to the Mohave Plant, near Bullhead, Nevada, 273 miles away. The water for this—between 2,000 and 4,500 gallons per minute—was pumped from the underground water table upon which the Hopis depended to supply their springs and sparse corn patches. A third great power plant, the Navajo Plant, was erected near Page and Glen Canyon Dam in Arizona. The 8 to 10 million tons of Black Mesa coal it required yearly were shipped by a new railroad 78 miles across Indian land; and the plant's 70-story smokestacks poured still more pollutants into the air.

This colossal "Rape of Black Mesa," with its devastation of the land, depletion of water resources, and pollution of the air, in order to promote the sale of power to Las Vegas, Los Angeles, Phoenix, and Tucson, was widely publicized. Public resentment against the great power companies and the federal bureaus supporting them was voiced by the Native American Rights Fund, the Environmental Defense Fund, the Sierra Club, the National Wildlife Federation, and the Black Mesa Defense Club. "Save Black Mesa" posters appeared everywhere. The National Environmental Policy Act of 1969 was enacted, requiring the preparation of environmental impact statements. Yet despite attempts to impose emission standards, nothing stopped the extension of still more strip-mining and plans to erect still more power plants by private interests backed by the federal government.

The lease of Black Mesa land now precipitated a century-old dispute between the Hopis and Navajos.

In 1882, the government had set aside a large desert wilderness of 4,000 square miles, some 2,500,000 acres, for the "Hopis and other Indians as the Secretary of the Interior may see fit to settle thereon." This tract, nominally the Hopi Reservation, lay in the center of the immense Navajo Reservation of 25,000 square miles. The 5,000 Hopis were a sedentary people living in their mesa-top pueblos and growing corn in sparse desert patches below. The Navajos were pastoral grazers of sheep. As they increased to more than 100,000 people, and their flocks overgrazed the land, more and more families drifted into the Hopi Reservation.

The federal government now designated a small central area of 631,306 acres (about 2,500 square miles), known as District 6, for exclusive grazing by the Hopis. Nevertheless, Navajo encroachment upon the Hopi land outside its boundaries kept increasing; fights between Hopis and Navajos grew more bitter.

In 1962, three federal judges then ruled that the Hopis still had exclusive right to the District 6 area of 631,306 acres; and that the remaining 1,800,000 acres or more, designated as the Joint Use Area, were to be used jointly by both tribes. There was little "joint use," for the ever-increasing Navajo sheepherders kept encroaching on the area. The federal government was finally forced to pass legislation in 1974 partitioning the area, each tribe getting 911,000 acres. Out of this decision came lawsuits between the two tribes and against the government; and the still pending problem of where to relocate 3,500 Navajos and some Hopis. The net result was a reduction of 911,000 acres from the original 2,500,000 acres established for the Hopis in 1882.

The Hopis' last hope of ever regaining the sacred land granted them by Massau was extinguished when they were offered $5 million in payment for all original or aboriginal lands they had lost. Application for the settlement had been made to the Indian Claims Commission by the Interior-approved Hopi attorney. In approving the claim, the Commission held that the United States took the Hopi lands when it created the Hopi Reservation in 1882; and that the Reservation constituted all the aboriginal Hopi lands. The Hopis, however, asserted that the land had been taken from them in 1848 when the United States took over the country from Mexico; and that their boundaries then included an area more than twice the size of the 1882 Reservation.

Nevertheless, a vote on the offered settlement was pushed through, according to traditionalists, by Boyden, the tribal attorney, in order to collect a ten-percent commission of $500,000, after having obtained a $1 million commission for arranging the lease of Black Mesa for stripmining. The referendum took place in October 1976. On that day nearly 2,500 Hopis were attending a ceremonial dance at Shongopovi and did not show up at the polls. Nor did many others. All manifested their opposition by their abstention, in accordance with Hopi tradition. Only 229 votes approving the settlement, and 21 votes against it, were cast from among 7,500 Hopis.

The traditionalists immediately drew up a petition to the Commission signed by 1,000 Hopis, protesting the relinquishment of all rights and claims to the aboriginal lands. The Commission disregarded their appeal, and the Attorney General approved acceptance of the vote.

The issue involved many legal ramifications, and also personalities. Former Secretary of the Interior Stewart Udall, who had granted Peabody Coal Company the Black Mesa lease, was a Mormon. The Hopi tribal attorney, John S. Boyden of Salt Lake City who had formerly run for governor of Utah and had been a candidate for the Commissioner of Indian Affairs, was a Mormon. The Chairman of the Hopi Tribal Council, Abbott Sekaquaptewa, was a member of a staunch Mormon family. His brother Wayne was a Mormon Church leader, publisher of the weekly newspaper *Qua' Toqti*, head of a construction firm, and operator of the craft guild, motel, and restaurant in the Tribal Council's Hopi Cultural Center.

The Tribal Council then granted the Church of Jesus Christ of Latter Day Saints a long lease on 200 acres just north of Old Oraibi for the establishment of a Mormon church.

By now, old Oraibi was a crumbling archaeological ruin occupied by only a handful of traditionalists. The new center of life was Kiakochomovi, New Oraibi, site of the tribal offices promoting modern developments. A White town in effect, it was not a true Hopi village following ritual cycle under the direction of a *kikmongwi*, or village chief. Its affairs were managed, White-fashion, by a governor and a board of directors.

Construction of a large modern Civic Center was begun with a $1.3 million government grant. Its site was claimed to belong to the Sand Clan by a member of the clan with priesthood rights who immediately instituted suit against the Tribal Council. His claim was disputed on the grounds that his priesthood was no longer functional, and that no clan lands remained. Hence Kiakochomovi had annexed the land and deeded the construction site to the Tribal Council.

The cumulative effects of the tragic course of events briefly outlined here were now evident. Few Hopis depended solely upon the earth for a simple existence. They had government and commercial jobs. Children were not taught the meanings of the ceremonials. More and more Hopis were adopting Christianity, especially the Mormon faith, and were entering the mainstream of modern American life.

Yet this change of orientation had brought forth problems never before encountered. Dissension and quarrels between the two factions rent all villages. Murders were not uncommon. Alcoholism was a serious problem. An intangible feeling of spiritual bankruptcy permeated all three mesas, despite modern innovations.

The traditionalist minority still stood firm against what they considered this moral and social disintegration. They opposed every issue with mass meetings, appeals to both Hopis and Navajos, letters to the President and Congress. Members gave talks throughout the country. Delegations vainly sought hearings at the United Nations. And one member attended a special U.N. Committee on Human Rights Conference in Geneva, Switzerland, in September 1977 to hear documentation on "Discrimination Against the Indigenous Peoples of the Americas"— which was not reported by the American press. This was followed in October by a letter to President Jimmy Carter, imploring him to stop the violation of their religious, land, and basic human rights. According to a White support group, "Friends of the Hopis," more than 30,000 telegrams and letters supporting the Hopi statement were sent to President Carter. There was no response.

The leader of this stubborn resistance was small, aging and ill Mina Lansa, the adopted daughter of Chief Tewaquaptewa of Old Oraibi, and custodian of the ancient Bear Clan tablets. When the old chief died in 1960, leaving no Bear Clan successor, his position of *kikmongwi* normally reverted to the Parrot Clan by right of clan succession. The first man in line was his eldest son, Myron, who opposed his father. Next in line was his adopted son, Stanley Bahnimtewa, who was living in Los

Angeles, California, and who agreed to let Mina, his sister, act for him. So, in 1964, Mina became the *kikmongwi* of Old Oraibi, the leader of all traditionalists, and the symbolic mother of the Hopis. She was aided by her husband, John, head of the Badger Clan and chief of the important Powamu Society. Both of them had been friends of mine for twenty years, and I sympathized with their indomitable fight against overwhelming odds. Mina's illness was more serious than we thought when Dan Budnik brought her and John here to Taos in November 1977, hoping that a rest and a healing ceremony by Joe Sun Hawk of Taos Pueblo would be beneficial. Taken then to a hospital in Phoenix, Arizona, she died on January 8, 1978, at the age of 75. She was a great spirit, embodying the ancient traditions and religious beliefs of her people.

Her death deprived the Hopis of their symbolic mother, as Tewaquaptewa's passing had removed their symbolic father. The weekly newspaper *Qua' Toqti*, "The Eagle's Cry," always had ridiculed Mina as the "self-appointed Chieftess of Old Oraibi"; and cautioned in its editorials that her outmoded religious beliefs only reinforced superstition. In Hotevilla, after the death of old Dan Katchongva, there remained a hard core of traditionalists—a "quarrelsome, dissident faction" called by *Qua' Toqti* "Grandfather David and his Gang." Aging "Grandfather" David Monongva was not the recognized *kikmongwi* of Hotevilla, being of a minor clan which had no traditional standing. Nevertheless, he was accepted as a nominal, though ineffectual leader without authority or influence.

Backing them was the white organization characterized by the progressives as the "shoeless and long-haired radical left of the blue-eyed so-called 'Friends of the Hopis.' "

Ostensibly, the progressive Tribal Council faction, which looked to the technological future rather than to the traditions of the past, had affairs well in hand.

Economically oriented, the Tribal Council administration was concerned with managing the complex business of the tribe through an imposing number of departments and committees. There were more than 400 permanently employed members of the staff. This meant that of the total population of 8,000 Hopis, one out of twenty was employed by the tribal administration. The total wages paid all employees, including construction workers, had trebled from less than $1 million in 1973 to $3 million in 1977.

The total assets of the tribe amounted to more than $13 million. The yearly income from Hopi resources, excluding government grants, ranged from $1.5 to $2 million, most of it coming from Peabody Coal royalty payments.

More new construction projects were under way, including another $1 million tribal administration building and the huge $1.3 million Civic Center. Projected for the future were a new high school, a new hospital, and a new highway bisecting the reservation which would increase tourist travel. Moreover, the Tribal Council, politically subservient to the Bureau of Indian Affairs, was attempting to convert the Hopi social structure into the pattern of White communities. Following the lease of Sand Clan land for a new Mormon church, it proposed the establishment of a New Village Community within the ancestral clan holdings of the Badger Clan.

Despite this bright economic future, the Indian Law Resource Center in Washington, D.C., a leading law firm in asserting the rights of Native Americans, undertook legal support of the Hopi traditionalists in 1977. In a lengthy report, it documented the fraudulent means by which the federal government deliberately sabotaged the traditional leadership of the Hopi *kikmongwis* by establishing the B.I.A.-controlled Tribal Council. A second issue concerned the B.I.A. lease of Hopi land for coal strip-mining, and the $5 million settlement for Hopi relinquishment of all Hopi lands. A third primary issue involved John S. Boyden, the B.I.A.-approved legal counsel for the Hopi Tribal Council. The report alleged that Boyden was working for the Peabody Coal Company interests during the time it was strip-mining Black Mesa, and hence revealed a conflict of interest calling for immediate governmental investigation.

Meanwhile, there were growing misgivings even among the progressives. The Peabody Coal Company was pumping water from mile-deep wells at the rate of 3,000 gallons a minute or 40,000 acre feet a year. The water pressure head already had been decreased 10 feet and was being decreased 1.5 feet a year. Moreover, Peabody Coal was not adhering to the rules for pumping water prescribed by the U.S. Geological Survey.

It now appeared that, when the Peabody lease expired, the coal deposits would be exhausted, the land irretrievably ruined, and the water resources depleted. What then would happen to the Hopi bureaucracy, to the people themselves who had forsaken the sacred path and succumbed to materialism?

There remains the Hopi Prophecy.

Copies of it have been distributed throughout the United States and foreign countries; newspapers, magazines, and books have published accounts of it. The accounts vary greatly, and some White commentators have not been reluctant to add their own interpretations. Among them has developed a syndrome of "Prophecy Worship" which insists that the Prophecy be taken literally; that Pahána is an actual person, a coming Messiah; and that the world will be destroyed, save for those people who still adhere to the divine plan.

Our phenomenal interest in this dire Prophecy demands a close look. Why does it coincide so closely with our unconscious fears today? What are its hidden meanings?

Profoundly religious, the Prophecy is a mythic structure of our collective unconscious, the deep substratum of our psyche attuned to all the invisible forces of the living universe. It is differentiated from the conscious pattern of our pragmatic White intellect, built on the rationally limited premise that man is the supreme achievement of Creation, destined to control all the forces of nature.

The ancient Prophecy contains many variations and a multitude of symbols and archetypal images. The clearest exposition was given me in great detail in 1970 by the late Chief Dan Katchongva of Hotevilla, the son of the historic Yukioma. Briefly, Pahána will wear a Red Cap or Red Cloak when he returns. Bringing the sacred stone tablet (or the missing corner) he will be "not one, but many, large in population." With him will be two powerful helpers. One of them will bear the symbol of the swastika, representing the male and purity. The other will bear the symbol of the sun, representing the female and purity. They will shake the earth in warning. Then all three, as one, will bring on the Day of Purification. If they fail in their mission, One from the West will come like a storm. He too will be many people and unmerciful, covering the land like ants. If he, in turn, is not successful in arousing the people to awareness of their misdeeds, the Great Spirit will bring destruction to the earth. But if only a few Hopis remain faithful to their ancient teachings, Pahána and his two helpers will lay out a new life plan leading to everlasting life, in which all people will have one religion, one tongue, and share everything equally.

The swastika and the sun are the two prime symbols in Hopi ceremonialism, still painted on the gourd rattles carried by kachinas during ceremonies. Each carries a profound, esoteric meaning.

The swastika is a form of the universal symbol of the cross. The symbolic meaning is clear. For if the extensions of the four arms of the cross in opposite directions represent division and conflict, their point of intersection signifies reconciliation and unification, the meeting point of the conscious and unconscious.

Looked at another way, mindful of the Hopi concept of time, the horizontal arms of the cross represent our linear concept of time divided into past, present, and future. The vertical arms represent the durational time of the Hopis. And here at their intersection, they merge into one unbroken timeless line.

The swastika form of the cross is equally fecundant in symbolic meaning.

The earliest Hopis, as we remember, made ordered migrations to the four directions. Upon reaching their extremities where the land meets the sea, the leading clans turned right, forming a swastika rotating counter-clockwise to symbolize the earth which they were claiming for their people. The other clans turned left, describing a swastika rotating clockwise with the sun, which symbolized their faithfulness to this supreme creative force.

Having completed their migrations, all clans returned to the center point of intersection. That is to say, after they had made psychological journeys to the limits of consciousness at the vast ocean of the collective unconscious—where the land meets the sea, they found their sacred homeland, the spiritual center of their own inner universe.

Geographically represented by Túwanasavi, The Center of the World, it bears out today both literal and mythical truths. It is a focal point of conflict between two ways of life, the Indian and the White, between the immeasurable past and the impending future. And in their conflict, it may also be a focus of reconciliation.

The symbolic meaning of Pahána, the Lost White Brother, does not carry the literal interpretation so often given it. As related in Katchongva's account of the Prophecy, he is "not one but many." Personifying the original, undefiled, pure spiritual nature of man, he is within us all. He is indeed both one and many, the divine, universal Self embodying all our lesser worldly selves. Slowly but surely, it will manifest itself as our consciousness expands toward a perception of our inherent unity.

This Self, the one universal, eternal Beingness, is known to Tibetan Buddhists as Dharma-Kāya, the essence of Buddhahood. It is curious that when a group of them visited the Hopi mesa they wore the red hats and yellow-red cloaks of their order, similar to the garb of the predicted Pahána, and found many Hopi parallels to their own beliefs.

To place the Hopi Prophecy in larger perspective, we must remember that the ancient Mayas also predicted with astrological and mathematical precision that this present fifth world would end with a cataclysmic destruction in A.D. 2011. How closely this prediction coincides with the Hopi Prophecy and our own growing fears of widespread earthquakes and a shift of the world's axis!

My own interpretations of this ancient Maya prediction, in my book *Mexico Mystique*, may apply to the Hopi Prophecy. The mythical previous worlds of the Mayas, Navajos, Hopis, and Buddhists may not have been actual geographic land masses, although changing configurations in the global landscape have periodically taken place. More important, they were dramatic allegories for the successive stages in the evolution of consciousness in enduring mankind. Hence I have termed the predicted sixth world of the Mayas as the "Coming Sixth World of Consciousness."

The present materialistic phase of Hopi life may appear negative indeed. But if we accept the ancient Nahuatl and Chinese concepts of cyclic changes from one polarity to its opposite, we may view the Hopis as conforming also to the universal law of movement and change, experiencing a painful transition to a new evolutionary stage.

We all stand today on the threshold of a new era, a new cyclical change in world history. Yet this glimpse into the future from the immeasurable past of a people who may be the oldest inhabitants of America also carries a warning. If we are to avert a cataclysmic rupture between the spiritual and material, between our own hearts and minds, we must reestablish our relationship with all the forms of living nature.

THE SACRED MOUNTAINS OF THE WORLD

My own home *tierra*, small and unique as it may seem, nevertheless reflects the indivisible life of the entire universe. Aware of this relation of the part to the whole, the ancient Chinese called it Tao, the undivided One, the Meaning of the World, the Way of Heaven and Earth; and from this rose their earliest religion, Taoism. Other peoples of the far distant past in India, Egypt, Tibet, Mexico, and Britain must have observed the same intimate relationship between the forces of nature around them, the forests and streams, the mountains and stars. From this transcendental unity of heaven, earth, and man, they evolved their own philosophical and religious systems; they built their great civilizations. Over and over again, we encounter in the records they have left us the same motif of sacred mountains, the universal theme of duality, the symbols of the circle and the square, which we find expressed in our own Indian America.

The scope and significance of sacred mountains throughout the world, I began to learn through the friendship of W.Y. Evans-Wentz. A great scholar, his lifelong devotion to psychic and spiritual matters spanned three continents.

Dr. Evans-Wentz was born in Trenton, New Jersey, in 1878, and spent his early years in La Mesa, California, near San Diego. Attending Stanford University, he then studied at Oxford University in England, and at the University of Rennes in Brittany, receiving high degrees from all three.

For four years, he did psychic research among the Celtic peoples of Ireland, Wales, Cornwall, Scotland, and Brittany. This resulted in his first book, *The Fairy Faith in Celtic Countries*, published in 1911. He then spent three years of research in Egypt on the ancient funeral rites described in the *Egyptian Book of the Dead*. Following this work, he traveled throughout Ceylon, India, and Tibet, which led him into an intensive study of Tibetan Buddhism. On this, he became a world authority with the eventual publication of those now well-known, ancient treatises which he edited and annotated: *The Tibetan Book of the Dead, Tibet's Great Yogi Milarepa, Tibetan Yoga and Secret Doctrines,* and *The Tibetan Book of the Great Liberation.*

Dr. Evans-Wentz himself embraced the faith of Mahayāmna Buddhism and settled in India, buying property in Almora, Kumaon Province. Here he lived in an *ashram* at Kasar Devi, hoping to develop it into a research center for Eastern religious philosophies. The outbreak of World War II put an end to his efforts. He returned to the United States, settling in San Diego.

Our correspondence began in 1947, when I was studying the esoteric meanings of Southwest Indian ceremonialism. In Dr. Evans-Wentz' Tibetan Series, I discovered many Tibetan and Hindu parallels to the beliefs and rituals of the Navajos and Pueblos. He too found in my books *The Man Who Killed the Deer* and *Masked Gods: Navajo and Pueblo Ceremonialism* an astonishing fundamental similarity between the esoteric beliefs of the two religious systems.

He was then preparing the fourth and last volume of his Tibetan Series, after which he planned to return to India. Publication of the book was delayed, and his advancing age prevented him from leaving America. Meanwhile a new interest in the Red Man was engrossing him.

He had inherited a great ranch of some five thousand acres about twenty-five miles southeast of San Diego. Lying astride the international border of California and Baja California it embraced Mount Tecate, known to the Cochimas, Yumas, and other Indian tribes as the sacred mountain of Cuchama, the "exalted high place" on whose summit young men had undergone initiation into the sacred rites of their people. From surviving members of the tribes, he began to collect the traditions concerning it.

As his research progressed, he wrote me in 1953 that he was undertaking a book on Cuchama, incorporating accounts of other sacred mountains throughout the world such as Kailas in Tibet, Omei in China, and Arunachala in India. He was not familiar with others in

America, and asked for any information I could give him. Our correspondence increased as I sent him material, and I visited him in San Diego.

He was living in a cheap, downtown hotel as befitting a Pilgrim on the Noble Eight-Fold Path. He was then in his seventies, but looked twenty years younger—a tall, slimly built man with a reticence of manner, and warmth of character. Although I was not a Buddhist, he often addressed me in his letters as "Fellow Pilgrim," "Friend on the Path," and "Brother Waters," and now shared with me his vast experience and mystical insights.

Through him, I met in Los Angeles a close friend, George W. Bass, who had served in a British army detachment in India, and later studied pre-Columbian ruins in Yucatan. He was now preparing illustrations for Dr. Evans-Wentz' book.

Shortly thereafter, Dr. Evans-Wentz conducted a trip to Cuchama for Mr. Bass and his wife; Eddie, his young nephew, who was a psychic; and myself. I had seen Cuchama years before, when as a young engineer stationed in Imperial Valley, I rode the old San Diego and Arizona Railway line periodically to report to my boss in San Diego. The train passed through the Mexican village of Tecate. Above it loomed the chaparral-covered mountain whose Indian name and significance I did not then know. Now, by international agreement, a fire-lookout station had been built on the summit, and the road was opened for us.

On the summit, we stayed several hours looking at unusual rock formations. Young Eddie received the psychic impression that a certain flat area had been the rocky floor of a great cave long before a catastrophe of some kind had lowered the summit of Cuchama to its present height. He picked up two small stones which he believed had been part of the ancient floor. Dr. Evans-Wentz also found a small artifact, from which he received the sensation of fire and smoke, which he drew in with his *prana*. We then offered prayers dedicating this "exalted high place" to the good of all mankind in the centuries to come.

When the Bass family and I returned to Los Angeles, Mr. Bass took the two small stones and an artifact to Charles F. Smith, a psychometrist, for a reading. He too believed one of the stones had once been part of a floor of an immense cave. The other stone showed ancient water marks. From them both, the psychometrist received impressions of smells, heat, and dripping water. Cuchama, he said, had been occupied during three culture periods. The first human beings were remnants of a migrating race already extinct in their original homeland. They were of gigantic size, with short legs and arms, but with enormous torsos developed from drawing in the vital forces of nature. Where they came from, and how long ago, he did not venture to say, save that when they arrived, Cuchama was a lofty beacon peak visible from far out in the Pacific. From the artifact found by Dr. Evans-Wentz, he received the picture of a tall woman wearing a tight headband. The larger piece it had broken from evidently had been a cooking tool or utensil used in comparatively recent times. This confirmed Dr. Evans-Wentz' sensation of fire and smoke.

It is interesting now, years later, to read the account of a recent overnight pilgrimage to Cuchama made by Philip S. Staniford, professor of anthropology at San Diego State University, and five companions. Their psychic impressions, together with drawings of the shape of the peak and its unusual rock formations, he records in an article published in the Summer 1977 issue of *Phoenix* magazine. His experience attests Dr. Evans-Wentz' belief that Cuchama was a sacred mountain of great spiritual power.

During the years that Dr. Evans-Wentz' book took shape, he sent Mr. Bass and me portions and drafts of the complete manuscript for review and whatever help we could give him. Unfortunately, neither of them lived to see it published. Mr. Bass died in Prescott, Arizona, in 1961, writing me a note on the day of his death. Four years later, in 1965, Dr. Evans-Wentz died in Encinitas, near San Diego.

At his death, he left his property in India to the Maha Bodhi Society to establish a Buddhist educational and religious center. The net income from most of his property in California was left to Stanford University for the purpose of providing a professorship and scholarships in Oriental philosophies and religions. Some 2,261 acres of his large ranch, including Cuchama, were deeded to the State of California, with the request that Cuchama itself be made a public property to be "maintained forever as a mighty monument to symbolize goodwill and fraternity between the races and faiths of the Occident and the Orient across the wide ocean of peace over which it looms."

Stanford University, at his bequest, also received a large collection of his Oriental manuscripts and private papers, including his manuscript of *Cuchama and Sacred Mountains*. It is a great pleasure to me now, so many years later, that it will finally be published; and that I have helped to edit and annotate this last work of such a devout and eminent scholar.

Buddhists always have deeply venerated mountains. Their metaphysical Mount Meru, they conceived as the axis of the cosmos, its material image being the great Mount Kailas of the lofty Himalayas. It was natural that Dr. Evans-Wentz' absorbing interest in sacred mountains was based on his own Buddhist faith and his long residence among and below the mighty Himalayas. His book, accordingly, is primarily devoted

to the many mountains and their sacred traditions with which he w
most familiar. There were innumerable others throughout the world I
did not mention, but their functions and traditions were so similar that
a few of them should be mentioned here.

When the Buddhists entered China in the first century, they designated four sacred mountains oriented to the cardinal directions. *Wu-
t'ai-shan*, the North Mountain of Five Peaks, in Shansi Province.
P-u-t'o-shan, the East Mountain, off the coast of Chekiang. *Chiu-hua-
shan*, the South Mountain of Nine Flowers, in Anhwei. And *Omei-
shan*, the West Mountain, in Szechuan.

Long before the introduction of Buddhism, the Taoists held five other
preeminent mountains as sacred. *T'ai-shan* in Shantung Province, the
Mountain of the East. *Heng-shan* in Shansi, the Mountain of the North.
Nan-yueh, or *Heng-shan* in Hunan, the Mountain of the South. *Hua-
shan*, or Flower Mountain of the West in Shensi. And *Sung-shan* at the
center, in Honan Province.

There is a curious ancient belief that a gigantic divine man called
P'an Ku, who existed before the world was created, gave shape to these
five holy mountains. When he died, his head became the T'ai mountain
in the east, his trunk the Sung mountain in the center, his right arm the
Heng mountain of the north, his left arm the Nan mountain in the
south, and his feet the Hua mountain of the west. Hence, this cosmic
man appears in Chinese mythology as the creator of the land which
bears his shape.

To these nine sacred mountains, pilgrims came for centuries to climb
their steep, dangerous trails, praying and depositing offerings at their
many temples, shrines, pagodas, and monasteries. Two resolute
women, Mary Augusta Mulliken and Anna M. Hotchkis, made arduous
pilgrimages to each of them in 1935 and 1936, just a year before the Japanese invasion of China. Their account, including a detailed description
with sketches and paintings, was finally published as a remarkable book
in Hong Kong in 1973.

In Japan, veneration of mountains since antiquity has been carefully
documented in a recent study by H. Byron Earhart of Sophia University, Tokyo, provided me by my friend Bob Kostka. Early as the seventh
century, it relates, there developed *Shugendō*—the "way" by which human beings could gain the religious powers inherent within sacred
mountains by pilgrimages and rituals or by mountain retreats. The
meaning and purpose of *Shugendō* are evident from the derivation of its
name: *Shu*—beginning enlightenment of a pilgrim's inherent divine
nature; *gen*—his innate realization; and *do*—his attainment of what
Buddhists call *nirvāna* and the Japanese *nehan*.

Of the 134 sacred mountains of the *Shugendō* sect, Mount Haguro with 33 main temples was the most important. On it formalities were observed in each of the four seasons, or "four peaks," during which adepts or pilgrims were considered to be "entering the mountain," leaving this world for the "other world." The procession up the mountain and the many rituals symbolized the union of the mythical pair which created the human race; the five stages of gestation within the womb; and spiritual rebirth from the mountain. This also reflected the ancient Japanese belief that the spirits of the dead return to the mountains and are reborn from them.

Shugendō became infused with ritual elements of Buddhism, Taoism, and Shintoism, and new sites were later established. It was officially proscribed in 1872, but after 1945 new sects were formed on the long-rooted tradition.

A striking parallel to *Shugendō* existed in ancient Mexico where the Aztecs observed *Tepeilhuitl*, "The Feast of the Mountains," on the 29th of October. The two great peaks Popocatepetl, the "Smoking Mountain," and Iztaccihuatl, the "White Woman" (now popularly called "Sleeping Woman"), were specially honored. The sixteenth century Dominican friar Diego Durán describes the ceremonies in his *Book of the Gods and Rites and the Ancient Calendar*, now published in English translation.

In homes and sanctuaries, small images of amaranth seed and maize kernels were made to represent the principal mountains in the land. In the center was placed the dough image of Popocatepetl, with eyes and mouth, and dressed in native paper. Close to him was placed the image of Iztaccihuatl, regarded as his wife. Rich offerings were made to them, and many rites were observed. The little images were then decapitated as if they were alive, and the dough was eaten during a ceremony called *Nicteocua*, which means "I Eat God." Following this, children and slaves were sacrificed, and the people climbed to the tops of the hills to light fires and perform ceremonies.

An elaborate ceremony was also held to honor Iztaccihuatl. Two small boys and two small girls in Tenochtitlan (now Mexico City), were richly dressed and carried in decorated litters up the mountain, accompanied by lords and nobles. Here the four children were sacrificed in a large cave where the image of the goddess was kept.

The astute Fray Durán adds a significant comment: "The principal aim in honoring these hills, in praying and pleading, was [not to honor] the hill itself. Nor should it be considered that [hills] were held to be gods or worshipped as such. The aim was another: to pray from that high place to the Almighty, the Lord of Created Things, the Lord by Whom They Lived. These are the three epithets used by the Indians on pleading and crying out for peace in their time. . . ."

From this, it seems that beyond the exoteric rites honoring the mountains as living images, there lay the esoteric meaning of mountains as places of access to the divine power of all Creation, or as openings to higher consciousness.

There are still many ancient shrines on both Popocatepetl and Iztaccihuatl, at one of which a nocturnal ceremony is currently held on May 3rd. Reverence for mountains is common throughout all Mexico. It was not unusual for me, when traveling through the sierras by horseback years ago, to find sacrificed turkey cocks and fresh flowers deposited on mountains remote from any village.

The custom is most noticeable among the Chamulas and Zinacantecos of southern Mexico and Guatemala, descendants of the ancient Mayas. Wooden crosses are found everywhere throughout these highlands—at the foot and on the summit of sacred mountains, and at the opening of springs and caves on their sides. The most imposing I've seen was an array of twenty-one huge crosses, some twenty feet high, standing on top of a bare hill near the remote and primitive village of Romerillo, high in the mountains of Chiapas. At all these *Kalvarios* everywhere, the people come in procession to deposit offerings of pine boughs and flowers, rum and black chickens, and to light candles and burn incense. The cross, explains the anthropologist Evon Z. Vogt, has no Christian meaning to the Zinacantecos. It marks the meeting places of their ancestral Mayan gods, being the "doorway" of communication between them and man. So again, as in the *Shugendō* rites of Japan and the Aztec ceremony of *Tepeilhuitl* in ancient Mexico, we find sacred mountains serving as places of communication between the soul of man and the divine power of Creation, or as openings to higher consciousness.

When in 1935 Dr. Evans-Wentz visited the great sage of India, Sri Ramana Maharshi, he asked him if he had ever had a Guru, a teacher. The sage replied, as reported in *Talks with Sri Ramana Maharshi*, that a Guru is God or the Self, which appears to a seeker in some form, human or non-human, and his own Guru took the form of the sacred hill of Arunachala nearby. Dr. Evans-Wentz, commenting that there were certain major psychic centers in the human body and corresponding centers in the world, then asked if there were any psychic effects in visiting such sacred places. Sri Maharshi affirmed this, replying what is in the world is in the body, and what is in the body is in the world also.

The beliefs of Indian America seem to confirm this Eastern teaching. A pyramid is a sacred mountain. So is the sweat lodge or vision lodge, whose frame is constructed of ten bent willows (the number given to endless time and space). So also is the body of man a pyramid, or sacred mountain. Hence, the processions up sacred mountains, observed in In-

dia, Tibet, China, Japan, Mexico, and in Indian America, were vision
quests, as were the sweat lodge rituals. All adepts were seeking a holy
vision, an opening to higher consciousness, either on the summit of a sacred mountain, at the apex of a man-made stone pyramid, or in the
mind-center of the human pyramid. This belief is still held throughout
the vast Andes in South America, where some thirty or more high peaks
carry shrines on their summits.

In her study of spatial archetypes, Mimi Lobell equates the emergence of the mountain out of the sea of chaos with the rise of the ego and
self-consciousness from the womb-cavern of the unconscious. There began in world history the era of mountain-worshipping and pyramid-
building civilizations in which reverence for the Earth Mother gave
way to that for the Sky Father, and patriarchal replaced matriarchal
patterns. The movement was reflected in the social stratification of different castes, with a divine ruler at the apex of the social pyramid. Yet,
eventually, the ego in turn experienced a spiritual enlightenment, which
again related it to the mother of all creation, the unconscious. Hence
the religious function of the sacred mountain was to enable man to sur-
mount his earthly existence at its summit and achieve unity with the
transcendental universe.

In the religious cosmology of the Navajos in our own Southwest, five
directional holy mountains marked their traditional homeland. *Tsoll-
tsilth*, the Holy Mountain of the South with the directional color of
blue, now identified as Mount Taylor in the San Mateo range in New
Mexico. *Dogo-shee-ed*, the Holy Mountain of the West with the color
yellow, now known as the San Francisco peaks in Arizona. *Debeh-ent-
sah*, the Holy Mountain of the North with the color black, believed to
be Hesperus Peak of the La Plata range in Colorado. And *Siss-na-jini*,
the Holy Mountain of the East with the color white. Its location in modern times has never been accurately determined. Various authorities believe it to be Blanca Peak in Colorado, or Pelado Peak, Abiquiu or
Pedernal Peak in New Mexico. The consensus identifies it as Wheeler
Peak above Taos, the highest peak in New Mexico, and with this I agree
for various reasons. Within these four directional, physical mountains
there loomed at the time of the Navajos' Emergence the great axial core
of the cosmos, *Tsilth-nah-ot-zithly*. This central Encircled Mountain, or
Mountain Around Which Moving Was Done, was similar to the metaphysical axis of the Buddhist cosmos, Mt. Meru, and is invisible to human eyes. It has been identified as the present Huerfano Mountain
above Chaco Canyon in New Mexico—a low hill which is merely the
material image of its metaphysical reality.

There were countless other mountains once held sacred throughout the United States. Too few of them are known to us today for the simple reason that the indigenous Indian tribes have been decimated or uprooted, and the mountains themselves have been desecrated or destroyed.

Pike's Peak in Colorado, at whose foot I was born, was one of the most notable. The Ute Creation Myth centered upon it, and its mythical origin parallels stories of the Flood. Its psychic forces, like a great magnet, drew people to it for centuries. It was a mecca for Utes coming down from the Rockies, and for Arapahoes, Kiowas, and Cheyennes from the Great Plains to the east, who dropped votive offerings in the medicinal springs at its foot. When the White Men came, it was a beacon peak for the "Pike's Peak or Bust" wagon caravans of the gold-seekers. Years later, when I was a boy, it still exerted its spell, drawing trainloads of visitors from all over the world to jog up its canyons by burro, drink from its iron and soda springs, and gather wildflowers at every turn of the trail. But neither its majestic snow-covered summit, nor the virginal beauty of its canyons, could alone account for the serenity and energy it exerted as a spiritual font. If there does exist for each of us a psychological archetype, or a Guru, manifested as a physical mountain, Pike's Peak is mine. I grew up with it, nurtured by its constant living presence.

Today its life-giving energy has been destroyed. There are both a cog-road train and a race-course highway to its summit. The front wall of the range has been stripped bare for gravel. Cheyenne Mountain, just south of the Peak, has been hollowed out to house the combat operations center of the North American Air Defense Command. The Air Force Academy has appropriated the slope of the Peak to the north, while an immense Army base covers the land to the south.

Mount Taylor, the Navajos' holy Mountain of the South, is the focus of the United States' uranium mining industry. Into its side is drilled the world's deepest uranium mine shaft. And on its eastern side, on land belonging to Laguna Pueblo, the largest open pit uranium mine is now in operation.

The San Francisco peaks comprise the Navajos' sacred Mountain of the West. It is also sacred to the Hopis, who carry prayer-feathers to deposit in its shrines and to bring back bunches of spruce for their ceremonies. Today both tribes are protesting through the courts plans to industrialize the mountain as a ski and recreation area.

These are but a few examples, here in the West, of the continuing military, industrial, and commercial onslaughts against the sacred mountains in America. Our destruction and desecration of the living land has made us the richest and most materialistic nation in history. But under our national ethic of economic progress at any price, we have been buying the physical energy derived from nature at the expense of the psychical energy so necessary for our survival as a spiritually healthy commonwealth. Today we are belatedly recognizing the role of physical ecology in our lives, but not that of psychical ecology. For all the living entities of the mineral, plant, animal, and human kingdoms possess an inherent psychical life, as well as a physical life, and all constitute our integrated life-system. Each helps to maintain the life of the whole; and when we do violence to any part, we injure ourselves.

If we accept this concept, we might still endorse the premise that the sacred mountains of the world are repositories of psychic energy upon which mankind draws for its life and development. We may, I suppose, loosely regard them as psychic power plants analogous to our physical power plants. They might better be compared to *chakras*, the psychic centers in the human body that Dr. Evans-Wentz referred to during his talks with the Maharshi, for they serve as focal points or distribution centers located on all continents throughout the planet.

There is a growing belief that sacred mountains and other revered sites were located on a global grid of lines of force. Can we infer then that previous civilizations, and even so-called primitive societies, were aware of such psycho-physical centers positioned in the living earth so that their fields of energy could influence not only the life in their immediate areas, but that of the planet as a living whole? If so, we must belatedly recognize that the physical and psychic realms are but two complementary aspects of one transcendental whole.

XVI

Cuchama and Sacred Mountains

Also in 1981, Waters and this author completed the editing of Dr. Evans-Wentz' Cuchama and Sacred Mountains. In that volume, Dr. Evans-Wentz' work is framed between an Introduction and Addendum by Waters. The Addendum, which follows, constitutes Waters' most recent commentary on current relations between Whites and Indians.

THE INDIAN RENAISSANCE

One can't deny the fundamental truth in Dr. Evans-Wentz' belief that an Indian or "American Renaissance" is under way. Yet it seems too open to general disbelief and rejection when it is not supported by literal fact. Hence these comments are being added to help explain the basis for his belief, and for the factual reality as we view it today.

Perhaps no other portion of his book gave Dr. Evans-Wentz so much trouble. He was wholly in accord with the high aspiration and political achievement of John Collier, Commissioner of the United States Bureau of Indian Affairs, who directed the First Inter-American Indian Conference convened at Patzcuaro, Michoacan, Mexico, in 1940. The Conference resulted in the establishment of an Inter-American Indian Institute to promote the cause of all Indian peoples. The Institute was to be ratified by all governments through treaty, under which they were to establish their own national institutes and to support, through quota payments, the parent Institute. These provisions were carried out by most of the nineteen member nations. The United States, however, as Collier reported later, breached the treaty by refusing to vote the funds. Eventually the Institute broke down as an effective organization, and the plight of Indians throughout the Americas became grievously worse, as will be recounted.

John Collier retired from federal service in 1945, serving for a short time as Advisor on Trusteeship to the American Delegation at the first session of the General Assembly of the United Nations. He then established in Washington, D.C., the Institute of Ethnic Affairs to ameliorate the condition of all dependent peoples throughout the world. It was not a success. Long a personal friend of mine, he retired from public life quietly in Taos, New Mexico, until his death in 1968.

During these years, he wrote two books, *The Indians of the Americas*, 1947 and *On the Gleaming Way*, 1949. Both reaffirmed his belief that the Western Hemisphere would turn to Indian societies for guidance in the future, "even if the nations regress in their Indian programs." Dr. Evans-Wentz subscribed completely to Collier's belief; and, as we have noted, quoted voluminously from Collier's books in his own present volume. It is a pity these two men never met; they were both great idealists, great humanitarians, and great Indianists.

By 1957 it was apparent that the Patzcuaro Conference of 1940 had not achieved the Pan-American Indian Renaissance blue-printed by Collier. I so wrote Dr. Evans-Wentz, after reviewing a draft of his manuscript, saying there was no factual basis for his belief in it.

About the same time, however, he sent me, through George Bass, a booklet entitled *The Coming of the Great White Chief*. It described a secret, ancient city in the mountains of southern Mexico inhabited by white-skinned Chigarau Indians ruled by a Great White Chief, who prophesied the amalgamation of all Indians under his teachings. The amalgamation purportedly had begun at the First Inter-American Indian Conference in Patzcuaro where the Great White Chief had informed the delegates that the time had come to build a magnificent Indian capitol. Five quarries in Central America had been selected to provide white marble for the temple. Soon the transportation of the marble and the migration of tribes toward the north would begin. The tribes would cross the Rio Grande River and journey west toward a range of mountains on which only the morning sun would shine. There they would build the Great White City with its white marble temple.

The booklet, as I wrote Dr. Evans-Wentz and Mr. Bass, seemed to me too spurious to be taken seriously. The Great White Chief had not appeared at the Patzcuaro Conference, which I had attended at the invitation of Mr. Collier. There was no record of an ancient city inhabited by white-skinned Chigarau Indians in the mountains of southern Mexico, which I had visited. The proposed migration north to a site in the

United States, together with the transportation of tons of marble, I could not envision in view of immigration restrictions, customs duties, unavailable land, and other mundane problems.

Mr. Bass answered my letter fully on January 20, 1958.

In spite of crude inaccuracies and phony names [he wrote] I believe the main theme of the booklet contains a revelation of tremendous spiritual significance as it affects the future of the American continent. Otherwise I would not have sent it to you or the Doctor....The whole implies a higher plane of consciousness...The elevation of the "city," its size, its walls, the white or light color of its buildings, and its gates, are but symbols of spiritual conditions....The mighty migration northward and the building of the Temple indicates a flow of spiritual force in the desired direction and the establishment of a New Spiritual Center from the Old American Mystery Center in southern Mexico. And this is the essence of the whole booklet.

White Marble is the symbol of Purity and Truth. The cutting of separate and distinct sizes from the five great quarries indicates the garnered Spiritual Truths from each age of civilization, ours being the fifth and nearing its end in degenerative chaos....The building of the Temple of Truth and Justice denotes the ushering in of the sixth age of civilization centered on the North American continent....

Reference is made to the finding of a range of mountains where *only the morning sun shall shine.* The "morning sun" is the Spiritual Sun which is *always* shining in the "East" as perceived by the Spiritual Eye in man. And the "range of mountains" refers to the Spiritual Heights, progressive levels of consciousness....

The migration indicates the preparation made on higher planes ahead of time, viz: the Spiritual Impulse projected by the Supreme Chiefs, and the reincarnation of souls of a highly evolved class who have had important experiences in American Indian civilization either remote or more recent. Reincarnation takes place as the facilities and needs of the new race are developed on the material plane....

The moral and spiritual regeneration of the Whites seems to be the most necessary thing at the present time....

Mr. Bass sent a copy of his letter to Dr. Evans-Wentz, enclosing a note which read in part, "I can assure you that in sending you the booklet, I had no other thought than a spiritual interpretation....There is no question of the present Indian remnants north of the Rio Grande rejuvenating sufficiently for the work. The Masters and the helpers will use White bodies to a large extent for their work. Many of the helpers are already here, some consciously and others unconsciously preparing the way. As the Solar System progresses into Aquarius, conditions and vibrations will be suitable for their manifestation in the flesh or at least on a much lower plane where their overshadowing influence may be felt. . . ."

Dr. Evans-Wentz agreed with this occult interpretation. At the same time he regarded my literal readings as "trustworthy." He accordingly revised his section of the manuscript, sending it to Mr. Bass saying, "I shall be glad to have you send a copy to Frank Waters, to adjust to his own liking, and to add as much as he wishes, explaining that my free editing is, for him, tentative. If there is no objection on your part and his part, I intend to incorporate the matter as an Appendix in the book. The subject is of vast importance, and is more or less an outgrowth of the booklet discussion. . . . I anticipate that Frank Waters will greatly improve the presentation. No one other than himself is better fitted to add to it."

Hence I rewrote his revised draft, which he in turn rewrote. It included my statement, which he has quoted, that the Indians of the Americas would indeed build a city, but that it would be spiritual, not physical; and that the Renaissance would take place on a rising level of consciousness.

This subject has been developed in my recent book *Mexico Mystique*, whose sub-title *The Coming Sixth Age of Consciousness* parallels Mr. Bass' "sixth age of civilization." The book recounts the ancient Mayas' myth that there had existed four previous worlds successively destroyed by catastrophes. Their present Fifth World, according to their precise mathematical and astronomical computations, had begun in 3113 B.C. and would be destroyed in 2011 A.D., being succeeded by a new Sixth World. These successive worlds seem to me dramatic allegories for the great stages in the evolution of man's expanding consciousness. If so, they warrant a close look at the fantastic prediction made by the Mayas a thousand years ago.

The Mayan date of 2011 A.D. corresponds approximately to the date of 2160 A.D. given in the footnote on page 181 of the present book as the approximate ending of our present Piscean Age and the beginning of the Aquarian Age. It has still greater significance. For as the 2160-year Age of Pisces is the twelfth and last age of the zodiacal cycle, it marks also the end of the present great Precessional cycle of 25,160 years.

The approaching first age in the new Precessional cycle is that of Aquarius. Its astrological sign is the Water Bearer. As water is believed to be a symbol of the unconscious, this betokens another stage in man's continuous psychological development, in which he will add to his conscious, rational knowledge the truths hidden in the unconscious. Its advent seems to be already reflected in our recent interest in modern depth psychology, in ancient myths, and in the religious philosophies of the East and Indian America.

So we can't sell short too hastily the booklet of *The Coming of the Great White Chief*. For all its errors of fact, it reasserted a common myth born from the unconscious of all Indian America: the return of the Great White God to his people; the rebirth of their ancient culture after centuries of submergence; and the beginning of a new era of brotherhood with all mankind. How dear the belief, and how stubbornly it has persisted! From the Aztecs of Mexico, who believed the arrival of the Spanish conqueror Cortés was the return of the Great White God, Quetzalcoatl, to the present Hopis in Arizona who still nurture the prophecy that soon their Lost White Brother, Pahána, will return from the land of the rising sun to initiate an era when men of all races will be united.

The myth, for all its tribal variations, is the same. It is the unconscious projection of Indian America's longing for fulfillment and brotherhood with all races. It is the unfulfilled dream of all humanity. And it is the essence of Dr. Evans-Wentz' present book.

So much for mytho-religious tradition which wells from man's deep unconscious. Attuned to this pole of our dual nature, Dr. Evans-Wentz and Mr. Bass readily discerned the esoteric meaning below the literal surface of the disputed booklet. Most of us are attuned to the other pole, our rational consciousness, which relates us to the daily aspects of worldly life. The reconciliation of these two opposite polarities is, as Jung states, mankind's task for the future.

The difficulty is illustrated by the grievous problems confronting the Indians throughout the Americas. The picture has changed considerably since the regenerative reforms blueprinted by John Collier. The Pan-Indian movement is still a nebulous ideal. Throughout almost all countries the plight of the Indian populations has reached a new low.

In Brazil, the Amazon River basin of 1.5 million square miles had been the homeland of indigenous tribes numbering about one million Indians when Europeans arrived in 1500. There are now scarcely 140,000, and eighty-seven tribes have been obliterated. Their decimation is continuing.

In 1978 an eight-nation multilateral accord, the Amazon Pact, was reached to coordinate economic development of the immense Amazon basin. The network of 14,000 kilometers of highways being constructed includes the 5,000 kilometer Trans-Amazonian Highway bisecting more than half of the 171 tribal areas; the 4,000 kilometer Northern Perimeter Highway cutting through the homeland of the Yamomano tribe in Brazil and Venezuela; and the Santarem-Cuiaba Highway. These highways are opening up the area to multinational corporations like Westinghouse, General Motors, and the World Bank, exploiting the vast ore deposits of iron, aluminum, manganese, tin, and copper, and clearing millions of hectares of rain forest for grazing cattle to supply cheap beef to the United States. In the wake of the highways have come epidemics of measles, influenza, and venereal diseases brought by construction workers, decimating villages of the Yamomanto and the Xingu in Mato Grosso. They have been accompanied by documented methods of genocide including massacre by armed forces, poison, germ warfare, and aerial dropping of napalm bombs. The National Indian Foundation of Brazil, FUNAI, asserting that "The Indian cannot be allowed to impede development," exercises the right to lease Indian lands for development.

Similarly in the Amazon basin in Colombia, the lands of its 70,000 Indians are being taken over by non-Indians.

In Paraguay, the preponderant population of Ache and Guarani Indians is denied the right to speak their own language, to sing their own songs, and to observe their religious rites.

Uruguay has been called the "torture chamber of South America" because of the military forces' persecution of the Indian population.

Half of the Andean population of 13.5 million people are Indians. In Peru the Agrarian Reform Law of 1969 prohibits their calling themselves "Indios." They must identify themselves as "Campesinos" or farmers.

Of Bolivia's population of five million, about four million are Indians suffering genocide and ethnocide under military dictatorship.

In Guatemala, it is estimated that only one percent of its six million population owns eighty percent of the land. The majority of the people are Indians, virtually slaves of the Ladino landholders, and whose average pay is about eighty cents a day.

In Chile the rights of its Mapucha Indians have suffered continuous repression and violation since the coup of the Military Junta in 1973.

And the continuing revolution in El Salvador is too well known for comment here.

There is no need to document these and other anti-Indian measures perpetuated by national governments backed by military aid from the United States and economic support from multinational corporations. They were presented by 125 Indian delegates during a Human Rights Conference in Geneva, Switzerland, in September 1977, held by Non-Governmental Organizations to hear documentation on "Discrimination Against the Indigenous Peoples of the Americas."

The Indian situation in the United States presents a confused picture of contrasts. On the negative side are the Indian substandard levels of life compared to other groups in the country. Indians have the highest infant-mortality rate, the highest school dropout rate, and the highest unemployment; and the lowest percapita income, and lowest life expectancy. Some steps have been taken to raise the levels of Indian housing, health, and education. Yet Congress has cut appropriations for recent Indian programs in health, education, social welfare, and economic development. Bills have been introduced in the House of Representatives to abrogate all Indian treaties, to abrogate all general Indian jurisdiction, and to limit water rights on Indian land. Industrialization of some reservations is being accomplished by the federal government's leasing of lands for coal strip-mining, a highly publicized example being the "Rape of Black Mesa," sacred to the Navajos and Hopis. Lease of this Indian-owned land to private power interests was made by the Department of the Interior through the legal consent of the Tribal Councils of both tribes, but without the general knowledge of their people.

Most tribes consider these Tribal Councils as puppet local governing bodies under the strict control of the Bureau of Indian Affairs. The system is a major bone of contention. Resentment against it has risen to the formation of the militant American Indian Movement, resulting in the occupation of Alcatraz in 1968, followed in 1972 by the AIM's "Trail of Broken Treaties" caravan to Washington, D.C. The latter began as a peaceful presentation of Indian rights to the federal government and ended in the demonstrators' forceful occupation of the BIA headquarters building. In 1973 occurred the bloody, tragic, and second confrontation at historic Wounded Knee, South Dakota. And this was followed in 1978 by the "Longest Walk" of Indian representatives from California to Washington, D.C., to present again their grievances to the Congress. These events, with many others, clearly indicate the still grievous imbalance between Indians and Whites.

On the positive side of the ledger, Congress in 1946 established the Indian Claims Commission, and millions of dollars have been awarded to many Indian tribes in reparation for lands unjustly taken from them. The Alaska Native Claims Settlement Act of 1971 provided for a cash settlement of $962.5 million to be paid over a period of years, plus forty million acres of federally owned land, to the Native Americans of Alaska. Another promising step was the establishment of an American Indian Policy Review Commission, which recommended among other things a complete restructuring of the controversial Bureau of Indian Affairs. Such legislative measures reflect the growing pride of Indians in their natural heritage, and their insistence on their sovereign rights. They also are accompanied by our own recent interest in Indian culture and religion after a century or more of neglect.

All these contradictions and contrasts indicate the still grievous imbalance between Indians and Whites throughout the Americas. Their conflict is rooted in their inherently different views of nature and man. It has resulted in the tragic dominance of materialistic Western civilization over naturalistic Indian society, to the detriment of both. The political, social, and economic balance between them cannot be fully restored until their ideological differences are reconciled on a deeper level.

This reconciliation will take a long time, but it will inexorably take place in compliance with the spiritual laws governing the evolution of all life throughout the universe. Then will be achieved not only the American Renaissance envisioned in the present book, but also the unity of the East and the West—that goal toward which Dr. Evans-Wentz devoted his life and his work.

XVII

America: A Footnote

Weaving his many themes around the continuing focal point of the inter-relatedness of all reality, Waters concludes Mountain Dialogues, *and summarizes much of eighty-three years of thought, with the following hopeful view of America's future.*

Whatever can be said about Western civilization is no more than a footnote in the countless volumes expounding, pro and con, its confusing nature and unpredictable future. By Western civilization we mean, of course, its full flower and greatest power, our America, the United States.

The nature of the world and man as perceived by the great civilizations of the past in Egypt, India, Tibet, China, and Mexico have already been briefly outlined. What impresses us is the similarity of their views. All assert the inherent wholeness of man and his oneness with the universe. Their religious-philosophical systems, primary as some of them might appear or as developed into a comprehensive "sacred science" far beyond the purely mechanistic sciences of today, were based upon universal laws. They were concerned with the development of man's inner being rather than his outer daily life.

Modern spokesmen adhere to the same belief—Schwaller de Lubicz, Jung, Wilhelm, Evans-Wentz, Wachsmuth, Gurdjieff, Ouspensky, and Collin, all the many others I have quoted. They are a small minority, indeed, whose quiet voices are generally ignored. As is their conviction that man replicates the structure and functions of the universe, is susceptible to the cosmic laws that govern the rhythms of nature and the movements of the heavenly bodies, and so inherently reflects the harmonic unity of the universal whole.

In direct opposition is the dogmatic view predominant throughout our materialistic and rationalistic Western civilization whose tentacles are enwrapping the entire globe. It asserts the obsessive belief in economic progress, whose sole objective is to continually increase the Gross National Product. This reflects the assumption that man alone is the arbiter of his destiny, and that modern Western society is the culmination of all his past achievements.

We cannot indict this ruling assumption and its outmoded values without acknowledging the remarkable accomplishments of our highly developed rational consciousness and the technological achievements of modern science. They have served the real purpose of enabling us to comprehend more fully the intuitive truths gained in the past and to envision those areas to be explored in the future.

Modern Western physics is investigating the interrelationships between all constituents of matter. It has abandoned the mechanistic view that matter is comprised of independent "building blocks" of nature—molecules, atoms, electrons, protons, and other sub-atomic particles too infinitesimally small to be observed. As material entities, they do not exist; they are forms of energy. The great physicist Niels Bohr is often quoted as saying, "Isolated particles are abstractions, their properties being definable only through their interaction with other systems." All that is known about them is achieved by projecting them at extremely high speeds in a high-energy particle accelerator to a target area or "bubble chamber." Here they collide with other particles, leaving tracks which are photographed. The properties of the particles are then deduced from a mathematical analysis with the help of computers.

These invisible sub-atomic particles have been said to be only products of theoretical reasoning; and that the physicist's view of nature is not that of nature itself, but merely constructed from his own human postulations. The physicist conducting the experiment is not detached from the "objects" he observes; his own consciousness is involved as a participant rather than as an objective observer. All barriers between the observer and the observed, subject and object, are extinguished. The known and unknown, and the very process of knowing, are fused into one undifferentiated whole. This calls to mind the *I Ching's* oracular readings which result when one throws coins to obtain a hexagram. For in the very act of throwing the coins, there is interjected the psychical state of the questioner which coincides with the physical events outlined by the text.

In light of the scientific concept of our participation in all the phenomena of the world of matter, the complete universe appears to be formed not of separate entities, but is a web of relationships between interconnected parts of a unified whole. Such a concept coincides with the premise of Eastern metaphysics that all things perceived by the senses are but different manifestations of the one universal and eternal Absolute, the Irreducible Real. And this seems to be the one great pattern of the universe—the inter-connectedness of all living systems from the world of man to those of the planets and stars in outer space.

Psychology as an applied science is the product of Western civilization. It is revealing the relationship between matter and the human psyche. Jung, as we recall, had first defined as "archetypes," his own term, the primordial images that have existed in man's collective unconscious since earliest times. Later he defined them as "psychoid archetypes," being both psychic and non-psychic, imprinting not only human and organic life but that of the physical and inorganic world—a bridge connecting spirit and matter. From this he developed his theory of synchronicity: that archetypal energy was manifested in the causally unconnected coincidence of a psychic state and a physical event. Here again we see the energy of the archetype stamping its imprint of wholeness on the spirit of man and on the world of matter. The human psyche and the world of nature appear to be one.

Yet psychology has its limits. It regards gods, spirits, ghosts, and other materializations as mental phenomena projected by the unconscious. The metaphysical East, on the contrary, accepts them as real phenomena appearing to the *sangsaric*, or limited, mind perceiving them.

Another bone of contention between the metaphysical East and the pragmatic West is the stubborn problem of reincarnation. Orthodox Christianity rejects the idea, and Jung himself could not accept it. The Maharshi, already quoted, stated that he had been able to achieve Self-Realization here and now because of his efforts during previous incarnations. He subscribed to the doctrine of reincarnation to the extent that karma, the influence of past lives, is engendered by the Doer. That Doer, however, is the Ego which belongs to the lower plane. Its reincarnations are merely superimpositions which may be transcended by Self-Realization. Hence his characteristic and seemingly contradictory assertion that there is no reincarnation because there is no Ego; there is only the Self. So realize the Self and be done.

Yet today there is an ever-increasing number of people in all walks of life becoming convinced of the existence of a vast Other-World beyond that perceived by our physical senses; and another-dimensional Time in which we coincidentally exist. Psychics and mediums are giving accounts of this realm. Living persons present testimony of their previous incarnations. There are authenticated instances of hypnotic regressions to the prenatal state, a hundred other aspects of the paranormal life we lead beyond our sensory existence.

All these phenomena are no longer ridiculed as belonging to the domain of the occult. Investigations of extrasensory perception, psychokinesis, life after death, and out-of-body experiences are being conducted by governmental agencies, universities, institutions, and individuals which include scientists in many fields. Parapsychology now appears to be at the same stage where Freudian psychology was soon after its inception, and there seems little doubt it is emerging as the new pioneering field of the future. The common denominator of all its categories is the premise of the extended interrelationship between spirit and matter, the living and the dead, and chronological and eternal time.

All these modern scientific advances confirm the belief of ancient civilizations in the inherent wholeness of man and his harmonic relationship with the entire universe. Comprehension of them is largely confined to scientific and academic fields. They exert no influence at all upon the arbitrary and all-powerful forces of federal government, multi-national, military, political, and public media agencies that dictate the course of present Western civilization and the daily life of the general public. Their destructive system of rule seems to be guided by a linear view of time and history, and the assumption that the world is wholly material.

Let us take a close look at these two notions.

Time itself, as we have learned, is not a linear progression of past, present, and future. It is a rounded whole embracing at every moment all the subdivisions of our rationally conceived linear time. The ancient symbol of the Uroboros—a snake biting its own tail—represents the complete circle embracing all time and space, linking the Beginning and the End. All life reflects Time's circular nature and cyclic periodicity: the stars wheeling in their orbits, the succession of seasons and zodiacal ages, the birth, death, and transformation of the earth and all living entities; even civlizations are subject to this organic cycle.

So it is with human history. It does not comprise a straight-line evolution from prehistoric societies up through primitive cultures to the proud apogee of twentieth-century Western civilization. As we have observed, previous civilizations achieved heights of conception and purpose we have not attained. Our Empire State Building cannot be compared to the divinely inspired Great Pyramid of Egypt and the Pyramid of the Sun in Mexico. Our colossal Rose Bowl stadium and others are but commercial sports arenas that bear no relation to the great ball courts of Mesoamerica whose games carried out a religious function. Nor have we achieved a religious philosophy to match those of ancient Egypt, India, Tibet, and China.

Our narrow secular view of history is upheld by orthodox Christianity which measures mankind's life on a linear time-scale from the advent of Christ to an eventual apocalypse, the Second Coming. Ignoring the cosmic cycles of birth, death, and transformation of all living entities in nature, and negating the belief in reincarnation for man himself, it limits him to one, short, worldly life span, and to an eternity in an imagined heaven or hell.

Yet throughout the centuries has run an underground stream of consciousness transcending this linear view. Nourished by Hindu and Tibetan yogis, Chinese Taoists, Gnostics, Cabalists, Sufis, Rosicrucians, and a handful of Christian mystics, it has kept alive the ancient hermetic teachings.

It is useless for idealists to entertain the illusion that we can replace the concepts governing our present life by the teachings of the past. Our all-devouring Western society cannot, willy-nilly, do an about-face. It has gone too far down its linear-historical, one-way road to turn back.

The other main reason for our inability to change horses in midstream, as I see it, is our prevailing stage of consciousness which regards the world as only materially real. Man's consciousness always determines the way he sees it. Alter this and the world changes. Its very planetary shape has changed with man's evolving consciousness; it has been seen as flat, four-square, round, elliptical; as the hub of a circular universe, and lately as an infinitesimal speck in one of numberless galaxies.

Whatever it is, the world as we see it is materially real as the earth underfoot. Its actual weight in tons has been calculated to twenty-two figures, and photographs have been taken of a sub-atomic particle with a diameter of about four-billionths of an inch. Interplanetary space is measured in millions of miles and light-years; time is broken down into millionths of a second, into "shakes." These macro and micro units of measurement have reached the absurdity of the "googol," the number 1 followed by 100 zeros.

But the world as seen by Eastern metaphysics may also be insubstantial and unreal, the construct of our limited consciousness. If this is true, how then will the world appear when our consciousness expands to reveal another view? Will it seem to us that, like children, we were but trying to measure and explore an evanescent soap bubble? The landing on the moon of an astronaut carrying his golf clubs only increased our technological knowledge and evinced our intention to extend our domination to such celestial bodies at the expense of millions of starving people on our own planet. It did nothing to expand our own limited consciousness, and this function seems to be the only valid measure of all human accomplishments. Of what use the probing of still farther interstellar space by cumbersome mechanical hardware for months or years on end, when even the greatest, immeasurable distances can be spanned instantaneously by a thought?

So it is with time. By a dream, a vision, a paranormal experience, we can supersede the linear limits of our presently conceived past, present, and future. How is this possible if time and space are dimensional fields as we now believe them to be? What if they are but manifestations of one universal Consciousness? It would be easier to bridge them within ourselves rather than projecting them outside.

Granting equal validity to both the materialistic and metaphysical views, how then can the world exist as materially real and insubstantially unreal at the same time? Only consciousness determines the way we see it. And there is a great difference between the Eastern and Western concepts of consciousness.

The Tantric teachings of India and Tibet assert there is but one unlimited, universal Consciousness, dissociated from mind and matter. Human consciousness, on the contrary, is associated with the psycho-physical body, being the thinking faculty of the limited mind. What it observes constitutes only the objects we perceive through the physical senses and their extensions as microscopes and telescopes—a small fact-section of the whole spectrum of life. The mind is not an objective observer at all. Because what we call consciousness is really unconscious, for it in turn is the object of the one ultimate observer, the cosmic Consciousness.

Now to this infinite, eternal, and only objective Consciousness is ascribed the power to *Be* and to *Become*. It finitizes itself in the world of shape, name, and form while remaining itself unchanged. This power to evolve in the material world and to involve it again, seems alogical to our pragmatic Western mind. Yet it explains the Eastern belief that a finite stone is also infinite Consciousness limiting and defining itself in matter, just as it limits and defines itself in our pragmatic consciousness. The smallest particle of organic and inorganic matter also embodies infinite Consciousness and its power to *Become*, as shown by the potency of the living germ and cell to expand and multiply, and by the immense power of the material atom when released.

This Tantric explanation of our limited human consciousness seems too philosophically obtuse to be swallowed by our technological, progress-oriented Western leaders, so allergic to Eastern metaphysics. Moreover, modern analytical psychology positively denies the existence of any such Cosmic Consciousness or Universal Mind beyond our limited human mind.

Robert Ornstein, however, recently has offered a more acceptable neuro-physiological explanation of why we think the way we do. He postulates two different functions of the human brain. The left cerebral hemisphere controls the right side of the physical body and our rational thought, which is geared to linear time. The right cerebral hemisphere is connected with the left side of the body and controls the intuitive process, reflecting our holistic orientation in space and time.

What has taken place during Western civilization's rise to world supremacy, he believes, is that we have increasingly relied upon the rational thinking function of the brain's left hemisphere to the extent that we are dominated by its concern with the material aspects of the world. Ours is an intellectual, right-handed culture almost totally repressing the modes of consciousness reflecting intuitive and spiritual perceptions.

This physiological split-brain theory seems paralleled by the psychological postulation that man's duality is caused by the split between the unconscious and the conscious. Both of them are based upon the premise that consciousness is associated with the psycho-physical body, in contrast to the Tantric belief that the mind and its limited consciousness interposes a veil between our innate perception and universal consciousness.

The duality is illustrated on a universal scale by the ancient Chinese symbol, the *t'ai-chi*. Its two halves enclosed within a circle, the Yin and Yang, represent the opposite polarities of all life, male and female, light and dark, winter and summer, etc. That these opposites are complementary and reconcilable is indicated by a Yang spot in the Yin half of the symbol, and a Yin spot within the Yang half. For as the ancient *I Ching* asserts, each polarity eventually changes into its opposite. The enclosing circle is the Uroboros, embracing all time and space, linking the Beginning and the End. And this affirms the circular, cyclical nature of time itself.

The evolutionary expansion of human consciousness thus appears to follow the organic pattern of all Creation. It does not take place gradually, but in cycles of birth, death, and transformation. And our periodic enlargements of consciousness coincide with the cyclic changes dictated by the one cosmic power that governs the indivisible life of all mankind, all nature, the universe itself.

This transcendent power is beyond our comprehension, and beyond our control. Under it, former, secular, linear civilizations have flowered and died. Others have bequeathed to us through their enduring monuments and hermetic records their greater degree of spiritual awareness. Today, in turn, our Western society is suffering the end of its materialistic world dominance at the close of both the present zodiacal age and precessional period. But the future is not as dark as the Maya and Hopi Prophecy predict; despite catastrophes, mankind endures. For this most pivotal hour of change since the beginning of the Christian era marks not only the death, but the transformative rebirth of our current limited beliefs. It will not come overnight nor even in a tragic century. Yet the change is already under way. We can sense its underground movements breaking surface in paranormal experiences of every kind, the receptivity of formal sciences to ancient doctrines, in the political and social revolutions throughout the world. Something of deep import is happening which heralds, if we heed the transformative changes now taking place, a new stage of our ever-expanding consciousness.

NOTES

1. Dates hereafter reflect the time when Waters was first working on a manuscript. A major consideration in Waters scholarship is the fact that he has no compunctions about completing a manuscript and then putting it away for ten, or even twenty or more, years before re-working it for publication. (I am aware of one very beautiful novel "in cold storage" at the time of this writing.) Actual publication dates may be found in the bibliography.

2. Conversation with the author, August 31, 1976.

3. Horace Liveright, who accepted this novel for publication, wrote Waters about "...your very fine novel to which you have given the ghastly and I think cheap title, *The Lizard Woman*." He goes on to suggest the possibility of "Blood Heat" or "Painted Waves." It is quite possible that Liveright, while appreciating the value of the manuscript, did not perceive the significance of the title as a place name. (Letter of June 20, 1929.) This novel has now been re-issued under its original title by Thorp Springs Press, Austin, Texas.

4. Thomas J. Lyon, *Frank Waters* (New York, 1973), p. 69. Lyon also quite rightly notes, "...*Fever Pitch* is not...a bad book."

5. Conversation with Frank Waters, January 27, 1974.

6. *North American Review*, April 1931, pp. 300–309.

7. Lyon, p. 133.

8. Frank Waters, *People of The Valley* (New York, 1941), p. 177.

9. *People*, p. 282.

10. *People*, p. 134.

11. See also Frank Waters, "Fifth World, Ninth Planet" in *Voices from the Southwest: A Gathering in Honor of Lawrence Clark Powell* (Flagstaff, Arizona, 1976), pp. 55–62.

12. Lyon, p. 107.

13. Thomas J. Lyon, "The Works of Frank Waters," a taped lecture for *Cassette Curriculum*, Everett/Edwards, Inc., 1974.

14. It is significant that Waters wrote most of this work during World War II when he held a government job in Washington, D.C.

15. Frank Waters, *The Woman at Otowi Crossing* (Chicago, 1971), p. 240.

16. *Otowi*, p. 240.

17. Lyon, p. 131.

18. Frank Waters, *Pumpkin Seed Point* (Chicago, 1969), p. xi.

19. Frank Waters, *Book of the Hopi* (New York, 1963), p. x.

20. Lyon, p. 53.

21. *Book of the Hopi*, p. x.

22. *Pumpkin Seed Point*, p. xii.

23. Lyon, p. 62.

24. Frank Waters, "The Western Novel: A Symposium," *The South Dakota Review*, Autumn 1964, p. 14.

25. Frank Waters, *Mexico Mystique: The Coming Sixth World of Consciousness*, Chicago 1975, p. vii.

26. *Mexico Mystique*, p. ix.

27. José Arguelles, "Sacred Calendar and World Order," *Shambhala Review*, Vol. 4, No. 5 (March/April, 1976), 13.

SELECTED BIBLIOGRAPHY

A. PRIMARY SOURCES

Novels

Fever Pitch. New York: Liveright Publishing Corp., 1930.
—New York: Berkley Books, 1954.
—Austin, Texas: Thorp Springs Press, 1984 (titled *The Lizard Woman.*)
The Wild Earth's Nobility. New York: Liveright Publishing Corp., 1935.
Below Grass Roots. New York: Liveright Publishing Corp., 1937.
The Dust Within the Rock. New York: Farrar and Rinehart, 1940.
People of the Valley. New York: Farrar and Rinehart, 1941.
—Denver: Alan Swallow, Publisher, 1962.
—Braille edition, New Mexico State Library, 1967.
—Transcription for the Blind, Library of Congress, 1970.
—Chicago: The Swallow Press, 1969.
—Athens, Ohio: Ohio University Press/Swallow Press, 1984.
The Man Who Killed the Deer. New York: Farrar and Rinehart, 1942. (Commonwealth Club Silver Medal Award, 1942.)
—Denver: University of Denver Press, 1950.
—Denver: Alan Swallow, Publisher, 1958, 1962, 1963, 1965.
—Hamburg: Christian Wegner Verlag, 1960. (Translated as *Martiniano und der Hirsch.*)
—Denver: Alan Swallow, Publisher, 1962, 1964, 1965. (Paperback.)
—London: Neville Spearman, Ltd., 1962.
—Paris: Albin Michelle Editions, 1964. (Translated as *L'Homme Qui A Tue Le Cerf.*)
—Flagstaff: Northland Press, 1965. (Illustrated, limited, signed edition.)
—Braille edition, New Mexico State Library, 1967.
—Chicago: The Swallow Press, 1968–1974.
—Baarn, The Netherlands: Hollandia, 1974. (Translated as *De Man Die Het Hert Doodde.*)

211

—New York: Pocket Books, 1971–1981.

River Lady (with Houston Branch). New York: Farrar and Rinehart, 1942.

—London: Cassell and Company, 1948.

—Motion picture, Universal-International, 1949.

The Yogi of Cockroach Court. New York: Rinehart and Company, 1947.

—Chicago: The Swallow Press, 1972.

Diamond Head (with Houston Branch). New York: Farrar and Rinehart, 1948.

—Reader's Choice Library Edition, *Secret Affair,* 1949.

—London: Boardman and Company, 1950.

—Paris: Libraire Hachette, 1951. (Translated as *Pointe de Diamant.*)

—New York: Dell Paper Books, D 127, 1954, 1955.

The Woman at Otowi Crossing. Denver: Alan Swallow, Publisher, 1966.

—Chicago: The Swallow Press, 1970, 1971.

—Athens, Ohio: Ohio University Press/Swallow Press, 1981.

Pike's Peak. Chicago: The Swallow Press, 1971.

—New York: Ballantine Books, 1972.

Non-Fiction

The Colorado, Rivers of America Series. New York: Farrar and Rinehart, 1946.

—New York: Rinehart and Company, 1959.

—New York, Chicago, San Francisco: Holt, Rinehart, and Winston, 1974-1979.

—Athens, Ohio: Ohio University Press/Swallow Press, 1984.

Masked Gods: Navaho and Pueblo Ceremonialism. Albuquerque: The University of New Mexico Press, 1950.

—Denver: Alan Swallow, Publisher, 1962.

—Chicago: The Swallow Press, 1969-1979.

—New York: Ballantine Books, 1970.

—Tokyo: Kagaku Joho Sha, 1974, 1975.

—Athens, Ohio: Ohio University Press/Swallow Press, 1984.

Book of the Hopi. New York: The Viking Press, 1963-1979.

—New York: Ballantine Books, 1969.

—Paris: Payot, 1978. (Translated as *La Livre du Hopi.*)

—Stockholm: Almquist & Wiksell, 1977. (Translated as *En Bok om Hopi-Indianerna.*)

—Dusseldorf: Eugen Diederichs Verlag, 1980. (Translated as *Das Buch der Hopi*; appended is *The Hopi Model of the Universe* by Benjamin Lee Whorf.)

Leon Gaspard. Flagstaff: Northland Press, 1964. (Illustrated, limited, signed edition; standard edition.)

Pumpkin Seed Point. Chicago: The Swallow Press, 1969, 1973.

Mexico Mystique: The Coming Sixth World of Consciousness. Chicago: The Swallow Press, 1975.

Mountain Dialogues. Athens, Ohio: Ohio University Press/Swallow Press, 1981.

Edited, with Charles L. Adams. *Cuchama and Sacred Mountains* by W. Y. Evans-Wentz. Chicago: Swallow Press/Ohio University Press, 1981.

Biography

Midas of the Rockies. New York: Convici-Friede, 1937.

—Denver: University of Denver Press, 1949.

—Denver: Alan Swallow, Publisher, 1954.

—Chicago: The Swallow Press, 1972.

—Athens Ohio: Ohio University Press/Swallow Press, 1981.

The Earp Brothers of Tombstone. New York: Clarkson N. Potter, 1960.

—London: Neville Spearman, Ltd., 1962.

—London: Transworld Publications, 1963.

—New York: Bramhall House, 1966.

Engineering Space Exploration: Robert Gilruth. Chicago: Encyclopedia Britannica Press, 1963.

To Possess the Land. Chicago: The Swallow Press, 1973.

Short Story

"Easy Meat." *North American Review*, April, 1931, pp. 300–309.
Included on page 10 of this volume.

Articles

"Relationships and the Novel." *The Writer*, LVI (April 1943): 105–107.
In one of his few statements on the craft of writing, Waters emphasizes the distinction in fiction between details being "connected with a dead fact" and "related by an emotional tie."

"Crucible of Conflict." *The New Mexico Quarterly Review*, Autumn, 1948, pp. 273–281.
Included on page 82 of this volume.

"The Western Novel: A Symposium." *The South Dakota Review*, Autumn, 1964.
In his contribution to this symposium, Waters discusses such topics as the term "regionalist" and the art of writing in general as well as his own work.

Mysticism and Witchcraft. Fine Arts Series. Fort Collins: Colorado State University, 1966. Reprinted in *South Dakota Review*, XV (1977), 59–70.

Originally a lecture delivered at Colorado State University while Waters was Writer in Residence, this brilliant essay examines the legitimate mysticism and the perverted witchcraft of the Hopi and then relates these considerations to Anglo-European history, down to the present time.

"Quetzalcoatl Versus D. H. Lawrence's *Plumed Serpent.*" *Western American Literature*, Summer, 1968, pp. 103–113.

In this paper originally delivered before the Rocky Mountain American Studies Association, Waters criticizes Lawrence for fictionally restoring the "Aztec vulgarization of Quetzalcoatl" to Mexico in *The Plumed Serpent*, and concludes, "In the intuitive recognition of spiritual unity, rather than that of racial disunity, lies the future of the world."

"Words." *Western American Literature*, Fall, 1968, pp. 227–234.

This paper was originally delivered before the Western Literature Association when Waters was awarded Honorary Life Membership. He discusses the writer's responsibility to respect the integrity of words, drawing upon such diverse sources as the Bible, and the writings of Levi Strauss, Benjamin Lee Whorf, and Clyde Kluckhohn.

"*The Man Who Killed the Deer*—Thirty Years Later." *New Mexico Magazine*, January-February, 1972, pp. 16–23, 49–50.

This invaluable follow-up details the history not only of the writing and publication of the novel but of the eventual return of Blue Lake to the Indians of the Taos Pueblo.

"Crossroads: Indians and Whites." *The South Dakota Review*, XI, No. 3 (Autumn, 1973), 28–38.

Originally a talk made at the Western Writers' Conference in 1973, this article sums up, and provides background for, current White-Indian conflicts.

B. SECONDARY SOURCES

This list is highly selective. Additional sources are listed in Terence A. Tanner's *Frank Waters; A Bibliography* (see page 218). The University of New Mexico Special Collections has completed the initial cataloguing of the Frank Waters papers.

Adams, Charles L., ed. *Studies in Frank Waters; V. Frank Waters: Western Mystic.* Las Vegas: The Frank Waters Society, 1982.

This volume contains seven essays presented at the Special Session on Waters held at the Modern Language Association of America's 1982 meeting. Each essay examines an aspect of Waters' mysticism.

————, ed. *Studies in Frank Waters; VI. "Dialogues."* Las Vegas: The Frank Waters Society, 1984.

This volume contains seven essays presented at the conjoint meeting of The Frank Waters Society and the Rocky Mountain Modern Language Association in 1984. The essays include a discussion of Platonic elements in *Mountain Dialogues;* a discussion of sacred mountains and mountain worship; one of Martiniano's search for faith in *The Man Who Killed the Deer;* a comparison of *Pike's Peak* and *The City of Trembling Leaves;* an in-depth analysis of *The Woman at Otowi Crossing;* excerpts from Waters' own journals; and an appreciative examination of *Mountain Dialogues.*

——————. "Teaching *Yogi* in Las Vegas, or Cockroach Court Revisted." *South Dakota Review*, XV (1977), 37–42.

Originally presented at the 1975 Modern Language Association meeting, this article assesses the novel's recent success in terms of its popularity with students at the University of Nevada, Las Vegas, and attempts to explain the novel's so-long-overlooked meaning.

Arguelles, José. "Sacred Calendar and World Order." *The Shambhala Review*, IV (1976), 12–14. Review of *Mexico Mystique.*

This excellent review of *Mexico Mystique* relates Waters' book to Fray Diego Duran's *Book of the Gods and Rites and the Ancient Calendar* and Tony Shearer's *Beneath the Moon and Under the Sun: A Poetic Re-Appraisal of the Sacred Calendar and the Prophecies of Ancient Mexico.*

Bucco, Martin. *Frank Waters.* Southwest Writers Series, No. 22. Austin: Steck-Vaughn Company, 1969.

This first extended study of Waters' work is limited by the very fact of its date, but shows critical insight—and foresight.

Davis, June H., and Jack L. Davis. "Frank Waters and the Native American Consciousness." *Western American Literature*, IX (1974), 33–34.

Originally presented at the 1973 Rocky Mountain Modern Language Association meeting, this article examines Waters' attempts "to bridge the psychic gap between two vastly disparate cultures" (Indian and White) through a detailed analysis of *The Man Who Killed the Deer, Masked Gods, Book of the Hopi,* and *The Woman at Otowi Crossing.*

——————. "The Whorf Hypothesis and Native American Literature." *South Dakota Review*, XIV (1976), 59–72.

Originally presented at the 1975 meeting of the Rocky Mountain Modern Language Association, this article relates Whorf's theory that one's perception of reality is fundamentally shaped by his linguistic system to *The Man Who Killed the Deer* and to M. Scott Momaday's *House Made of Dawn.*

——————. "Frank Waters' *Mexico Mystique:* The Ontology of the Occult." *South Dakota Review*, XV (1977), 17–24.

Originally presented at the 1975 Modern Language Association meeting, this excellent analysis of *Mexico Mystique* relates Waters' concern with dualities to Robert E. Ornstein's left-brain, right-brain studies.

Grigg, Quay. "The Kachina Characters of Frank Waters' Novels." *South*

Dakota Review, XI (Spring, 1973), 6–16. This issue is dedicated to Frank Waters.

This sensitive interpretation of Waters' fiction, against the background of his non-fiction, explains the central characters of the novels in terms of the Hopi concept of *kachina*.

—————————. "Frank Waters and the Mountain Spirit." *South Dakota Review*, XV (1977), 45–49.

Originally presented at the 1975 Modern Language Association meeting, this article is a lucid and concise interpretation of the Mountain as image and symbol in Frank Waters' work.

Hoy, Christopher E. "A Study of *The Man Who Killed the Deer*." Unpublished M.A. thesis, Colorado State University, 1970.

By far the best M.A. thesis written on Waters (and one that deserves to be published in its entirety), this study consists of an analytical application of the concepts of Jung and Neumann to *The Man Who Killed the Deer*. Two excerpts from it which have been published are listed below.

—————————. "The Archetypal Transformation of Martiniano in *The Man Who Killed the Deer*." *South Dakota Review*, XIII (1975), 43–56.

—————————. "The Conflict in *The Man Who Killed the Deer*." *South Dakota Review*, XV (1977), 51–57.

Kostka, Robert. "Frank Waters and the Visual Sense." *South Dakota Review*, XV (1977), 27–30.

Originally presented at the 1975 Modern Language Association meeting, this unusual article is an appreciative commentary upon, and explanation of, Waters' visual sense, by a highly talented artist.

Lyon, Thomas J. *Frank Waters*. New York: Twayne Publishers, Inc., 1973.

Students of Frank Waters' work will find this informative guide invaluable. It is analytical, carefully reasoned, and (with the acceptable omission of some of the commercial writing) quite thorough.

—————————. "An Ignored Meaning of the West." *Western American Literature*, Spring, 1968, 51–59.

Originally presented at the 1967 meeting of the Western Literature Association, this is an excellent study of Waters as a writer who fits himself *into* the patterns of western nature rather than observing from the outside.

—————————. "Frank Waters and the Concept of 'Nothing Special.' " *South Dakota Review*, XV (1977), 31–35.

Originally presented at the 1975 meeting of the Modern Language Association, this study of *The Woman at Otowi Crossing*, *The Man Who Killed the Deer*, and *The Yogi of Cockroach Court* suggests that "a key to Waters' metaphysics and to his psychology of characterization" can be found in his advice to tune ourselves to "the authentic, wild reality."

_____. "Frank Waters." In *Fifty Western Writers: A Bio-Bibliographical Sourcebook*, ed. Fred Erisman and Richard W. Etulain. Westport, Conn.: Greenwood Press, 1982.
This excellent chapter on Waters, organized under the headings "Biography," "Major Themes," and "Survey of Criticism," examines concisely Waters' intellectual concerns primarily in the light of *The Woman at Otowi Crossing*.

Malpezzi, Frances M. "The Emergence of Helen Chalmers." In *Women and Western American Literature*, ed. Helen Winter Staufer and Susan J. Rosowski. Troy, N. Y.: The Whitson Publishing Co., 1982.
This excellent article traces the development of the central character in *The Woman at Otowi Crossing* from Edith Warner (Waters' real-life model) through the novel, concluding "Edith Warner fictionally transformed becomes Helen Chalmers transfigured. . . ."

Manchester, John. "Frank Waters." *South Dakota Review*, XV (1977), 73–80.
The author, a close friend of Waters and for many years his neighbor in Taos, New Mexico, has written an intimate, personal view of Waters and his work. An earlier and longer version of this article may be found in *Encanto*, July/August, 1970, pp. 4–7.

Milton, J., ed. *Conversations with Frank Waters*. Chicago: The Swallow Press, 1971.
In this transcription of seven taped television interviews, Waters discusses a variety of topics, including autobiographical anecdotes, his own writing, and his personal theories and values.

_____. "The American West: A Challenge to the Literary Imagination." *Western American Literature*, Winter, 1967, pp. 267–284.
This first-rate discussion of the unique problem faced by western writers in utilizing the West's vast and varied landscapes points out Waters' success in dealing with land in mystical terms.

_____. "The Land as Form in Frank Waters and William Eastlake." *Kansas Quarterly*, Spring, 1970, pp. 104–109.
The discussion of the landscape problem is extended and applied to Waters' Colorado trilogy and William Eastlake's *Portrait of An Artist with 26 Horses* and *The Bronc People* to illustrate that western writers are able to use land as "symbol, metaphor, and the source of metaphysics" and hence that "the expansive land becomes the expansive form."

_____. "The Sound of Space." *South Dakota Review*, XV (1977), 11–15.

Originally presented at the 1975 meeting of the Modern Language Association, this article contrasts Waters' work with that of Walter Van Tilburg Clark and Harvey Fergusson to show that "...it is the differences that allow Waters to stand apart, to have special significance, and to be relatively ignored or misunderstood outside the area in which he lives."

Peterson, James. "A Conversation with Frank Waters: Lessons from the Indian Soul." *Psychology Today*, May, 1973, pp. 63ff.
_____. "A Reverent Connection with the Earth." *Psychology Today*, May, 1973, pp. 66–67.
The first of these two excellent articles is perhaps the best published interview with Waters. The second is Peterson's revealing account of the interview.

Pilkington, William T. "Character and Landscape: Frank Waters' Colorado Trilogy." *Western American Literature*, Fall, 1967, pp. 183–193.
This perceptive analysis (and early appreciation) of the out-of-print trilogy suggests that it ought to be reprinted. The author comments effectively on Waters' use of land as character.

Tanner, Terence A. *Frank Waters: A Bibliography With Relevant Selections From His Correspondence.* Glenwood, Illinois: Meyerbooks, 1983.
By far the best piece of scholarship done on Waters to date, this bibliography gives the complete publication history of Waters' writing from 1916–1981. Most of Waters' major works are introduced by invaluable correspondence detailing each work's genesis and development.

Tarbet, Tom. "The Hopi Prophecy and the Chinese Dream." *East West*, May, 1977, pp. 52–64.
This interview was done shortly after Waters' return from The People's Republic of China and examines some similarities between Native Americans and the Chinese.

7   11/08